DATE DUE			
Apr 3 7 8			
Apr 20 78			
Dec 10 '82			

Bernard Shaw's Marxian Romance

Bernard Shaw's
Marxian Romance

Paul A. Hummert

UNIVERSITY OF NEBRASKA PRESS · LINCOLN

Copyright © 1973 by the University of Nebraska Press

All rights reserved

International Standard Book Number 0–8032–0774–3

Library of Congress Catalog Card Number 75–144815

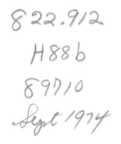
Manufactured in the United States of America

To my mother and father

Contents

Preface	ix
1. Before the Romance	1
2. The Beginning of the Romance	13
3. Marx Shavianized	27
4. The Influence of Ibsen	41
5. The Appearance of the Realist as Hero	79
6. Shaw's Indictment of Capitalism	91
7. Creative Evolution	131
8. From the Lands of Despair to the Land of Hope	149
9. Fabianism and Marxism Reconciled	197
Selected Bibliography	219
Acknowledgments	223
Index	225

Preface

Since 1950, the year of Bernard Shaw's death at the age of ninety-four, numerous articles and books have appeared lauding the work of one of the greatest writers of the two centuries that his long life bridged. Many revivals of his plays on stages all over the world, as well as in films and on television, attest to his continuing popularity. All of this is quite fitting and proper. But there is a danger, which Shaw himself would be the first to point out, that some aspects of his thought—his caustic criticism of his own society and his mission as a builder of a better one; his great admiration for Marx, Lenin, and Stalin; his cynical views on religion, marriage, property, and all the other foundation stones of capitalism—may be ignored or ameliorated in sentimental epitaphs of well-meaning admirers whom he would derisively call Shawdolaters. This study aims at bringing into clearer focus some of the views representing these aspects of his thought; specifically the importance of one particular influence, that of Karl Marx. Though Marxian philosophy played a most significant role in both Shaw's thinking and his art, it has been sorely neglected in Shaw scholarship.

The title, *Bernard Shaw's Marxian Romance,* may seem paradoxical, for throughout his life he not only made light of personal romances, but ridiculed the romances so popular in the theater of his day. The great heroes of his own plays were realists who had outgrown romantic illusions. Yet to maintain that Shaw was devoid of emotions and was never deeply moved by the ideas of his predecessors or contemporaries would be ridiculous. Whenever he discovered a philosophy he thought aimed at the improve-

ix

ment of his fellow man, he responded not only intellectually but with his entire being. Archibald Henderson in his monumental biography, *George Bernard Shaw: His Life and Works* (1911), points out that "the decisive and revolutionary changes in Shaw's truly 'checquered' career were due, in almost all cases, to the adventitious or deliberate influence of some dominant personality in literature or in life." [1]

Such a revolutionary change, or what I call romance, began that day in the British Museum when he opened a French translation of Karl Marx's *Das Kapital*. Shaw's biographers and critics all allude to the momentousness of this occasion in his life. Henderson goes so far as to say that not a single book "has influenced Shaw so much as the 'bible of the working classes.'" He adds significantly that Shaw "found in *Das Kapital* the concrete expression of all those social convictions, grievances and wrongs which seethed in the crater of his being. He became that most determined, most resistless, and often most dangerous of men to deal with, a man with a mission." [2]

In his 1942 biography of Shaw, Hesketh Pearson surely demonstrates the need for a study like the present one when he exclaims:

> As one who has not read Karl Marx, who has no intention of reading Karl Marx, and who would far rather die than read Karl Marx, it is a little difficult for me to trace the precise nature of his influence on Shaw; but that *Das Kapital* had a tremendous effect on him there is not the smallest doubt; it converted him to Socialism, turned him into a revolutionary writer, made him a political agitator, changed his outlook, directed his energy, influenced his art, gave him a religion, and, as he claimed, made a man of him. [3]

Seven years later William Irvine, in perhaps one of the most perceptive critical studies of Shaw, not only isolates Marxism

1. Archibald Henderson, *George Bernard Shaw: His Life and Works* (Cincinnati: Stewart & Kidd Co., 1911), p. 90.

2. Ibid., p. 98.

3. Hesketh Pearson, *G.B.S.: A Full-Length Portrait* (Garden City, N.Y.: Garden City Publishing Co., 1942), pp. 51–52.

from Fabianism in the Shavian synthesis but stresses the permanence of the romance:

> For Shaw the religion of Marx, in the strict sense of drastic and violent revolution, was a brief fanaticism, which, having blazed fiercely for a few weeks, died down and then smoldered malevolently for a lifetime. His sense of humor, his sense of legality, his aversion to violence, fatalism, and mechanism were against it. His hatred of Philistinism, his puritan predilection for the honesty of root-and-branch reform, his growing distrust of democracy and gradualism were for it. The result was a periodic and un-Fabian tendency to revolution. In fact, the story of his nostalgic flirtations with Marxism is but the tale of his Fabian defections told positively.[4]

But one need not go to the scholars of Shaw to realize the profound and lasting impression the father of communism made on him. Probably no one name appears so frequently throughout his works as does that of Karl Marx. Moreover, consider the praise that Shaw lavishes on the author of *Das Kapital*—praise that Henderson calls "for him, the rarest of panegyrics":

> He [Marx] never condescends to cast a glance of useless longing at the past: his cry to the present is always, "Pass by: we are waiting for the future." Nor is the future at all mysterious, uncertain, or dreadful to him. There is not a word of hope or fear, nor appeal to chance or providence, nor vain remonstrance with Nature, nor optimism, nor enthusiasm, nor pessimism, nor cynicism, nor any other familiar sign of the giddiness which seizes men when they climb to heights which command a view of the past, present and future of human society. Marx keeps his head like a god. He has discovered the law of social development, and knows what must come. The thread of history is in his hand.[5]

Shaw's "nostalgic flirtations" with Marxism assumed a more serious character as he gradually became aware of the successful

4. William Irvine, *The Universe of G.B.S.* (New York: Whittlesey House, 1949), p. 84.

5. Quoted in Henderson, *George Bernard Shaw*, p. 161.

results of the Russian Revolution. In typical Shavian fashion
he began to consider himself the teacher of Lenin and Stalin and
thus proceeded to equate Fabianism with Marxism. Especially
after his 1931 visit to Moscow Shaw no longer referred to himself
as a Shavian socialist but a Fabian communist (as in the preface
to *Farfetched Fables*) or simply a communist, as in this 1944
letter to the *Irish Times.*

> Again I am called eccentric in Eire because I am a Com-
> unist, converted to that faith by Karl Marx fourteen years
> before the same thing happened to Lenin. How anyone now,
> faced with the miracles of civilization achieved by the U.S.S.R.,
> in twenty-five years on Communist principles, can describe
> Communism as an eccentricity, is a view I must leave its vision-
> aries to justify.

He concedes that in the first years after the revolution the
Russian Communists committed many blunders, but adds: "Now
they have learned by hard experience what they would not learn
from me, they have become sound Fabians and are on their way
to become complete Shavians." [6]
It is my intention in this study to point out the importance of
Marxist elements wherever they occur in Shaw's works, to indicate, wherever possible, events in Shaw's life that caused him
at times to criticize certain tenets of *Das Kapital* and yet adhere to its basic philosophy until his death. Most importantly I
intend to analyze the role Marx played in shaping Shaw's art as
a dramatist: how his influence contributed to the type of themes,
characters, plots, and dialogue that develop from *Widowers,
Houses* to *Why She Would Not.*
In the first four chapters I have dealt with several of Shaw's
earliest major works. His predisposition to Marxism is already
evident in the first four novels (written between 1879 and 1882)
before he read *Das Kapital.* By his fifth and last novel, *An Unsocial Socialist* (completed in 1883, immediately after he read

6. Shaw, letter to the *Irish Times,* "Not without Honor," 2 August
1944, British Museum Add. MS 50699, fols. 30–31.

Das Kapital), his wholehearted acceptance of practically all of Marx's theories is apparent. This was followed, however, by a rapid change in his attitude toward such theories as surplus value and the proletarian revolution, especially after he joined the Fabian Society in 1884. These changes are reflected in such non-dramatic works as *Essays in Fabian Socialism* (completed in 1889), *The Quintessence of Ibsenism* (completed in 1890), and his first six plays written between 1892 and 1896.

In the next three chapters I have concentrated on the works completed during the period of years (from 1897 through the 1920s) when Shaw was maturing as a dramatist. Despite the many differences in subject matter and variations in treatment, all the plays considered here present as the true hero the realist character who is strong enough to face the truths the idealist character ignores. The realist-hero makes his first embryonic appearance in such works as *Caesar and Cleopatra* (1898) and *John Bull's Other Island* (1904), but not until Shaw turns to the systematic indictment of capitalism does the realist-hero appear fully drawn. His indictment focuses on the foundation stones of capitalism which Marx had singled out in *The Communist Manifesto:* religion in such plays as *The Devil's Disciple* (1897) and *Major Barbara* (1905), law in *Captain Brasshound's Conversion* (1899), medicine in *The Doctor's Dilemma* (1906), and marriage in *Getting Married* (1908). Whereas Shaw's destruction of capitalism is central to chapter 6, his formation of a new religion, Creative Evolution, based on his condemnation of conventional religion from a Marxist viewpoint, is the topic of chapter 7. His synthesizing of Creative Evolution begins with *Man and Superman* (1901–3), and he fully develops the bible for this new creed in *Back to Methuselah* (1921).

Those works written after 1930 which demonstrate Shaw's changing feelings and attitudes toward Marxism-in-action after the Russian Revolution are analyzed in the final two chapters. Two plays, *The Apple Cart* and *Too True to Be Good,* written immediately before his visit to Moscow in 1931, reflect his hopes and fears for the future of socialism in the one country that had adopted it as a system of government, while such plays as *On the*

Rocks (1933), *The Simpleton of the Unexpected Isles* (1934), and *Geneva* (1938), written after the journey, point to the Soviet system as a model. Shaw's final philsosophic compromise—his reconciliation of Fabianism with Marxism—as reflected in his essay in the Webbs' *Truth about Soviet Russia* (1942), *Everybody's Political What's What?* (1944), and the preface to his last complete play, *Farfetched Fables* (1948), concludes my study.

This definitive analysis of an area that has been only partially surveyed previously fills a gap in Shaw scholarship and will contribute to a better understanding of the complex mind of Bernard Shaw and his art.

Bernard Shaw's Marxian Romance

CHAPTER ONE

Before the Romance

Admirers of Bernard Shaw, who came to be so supremely sure of himself in and out of the theater, may not always appreciate that he had to go through a difficult period searching along devious paths for an ideal before emerging as a great prophet of the twentieth century. Yet his first four novels, written between 1879 and 1882, before his Marxian romance began, bear witness to Shaw's early gropings. When these pre-Marxist novels are compared to his fifth and last novel, *An Unsocial Socialist* (completed in 1883 and published in 1884), the impact of *Das Kapital* becomes immediately apparent. Yet even in the first four novels Shaw's predisposition to Marxian principles is so evident that we begin to wonder whether there was any affinity between the early life and environment of the Irish playwright and the German philosopher.

A brief examination of the early lives of the two men reveals both differences and similarities in their backgrounds and education, especially in the way each became interested in socialism. Marx was already in his thirties when Shaw was born in Dublin in 1856. Because the Shaw family, though no longer well off, still retained the pretensions of wealth, his mind was directed to the whole meaning of wealth in society. In the 1921 preface to his first novel, *Immaturity,* Shaw writes:

> Impecuniosity was necessarily chronic in the household. And here let me distinguish between this sort of poverty and that which furnishes an element of romance in the early lives of many famous men. . . . We all know the man whose mother brought him up with nineteen brothers and sisters on an in-

1

come of eighteen shillings a week earned by her own labor. The road from the log cabin to the White House . . . always has a few well fed figures at the end of it to tell us all about it. I always assure these gentlemen that they do not know what poverty and failure is.[1]

Marx was born in Trier in 1818, a Jew in a community of Christians. Napoleon had removed many of the barriers facing Jews in the Rhineland; however, following his defeat in 1815, the Congress of Vienna assigned Trier to the expanding Prussian kingdom and anti-Semitism returned with a certain amount of violence.[2] But Marx's father, Heinrich, who hoped to spare the young Karl religious persecution, became a convert to Christianity. Although biographers disagree on whether his conversion was sincere or dictated by opportunism, it did facilitate Karl Marx's entrance into society. In contrast, Shaw's father, who was a teetotaler in theory but in practice a drunkard, was an important factor in his son's early ostracism from society. Shaw says of him in the preface to *Immaturity*: "Now a convivial drunkard may be exhilarating in convivial company. Even a quarrelsome or boastful drunkard may be found entertaining by people who are not particular. But a miserable drunkard . . . is unbearable. We were finally dropped socially" (1:xv).

Marx's father tried in every way to restrain the cynicism and revolutionary tendencies of his son. Writing to Karl during his student days, Heinrich upbraids him for his disorderly life; by the fifth page of his letter, no longer able to control his anger he bursts forth: " 'Complete disorder, silly wandering through all the branches of science, silly brooding at the burning oil lamp; turned wild in your coat of learning and unkempt hair; and in your wildness you see with four eyes—a horrible setback and

1. *The Works of Bernard Shaw*, 33 vols. (London: Constable & Co., 1930–38), 1:viii. Further quotations from Shaw's novels in this chapter are from the same edition; volume and page numbers will be given in parentheses after the quotation when necessary.

2. John Spargo, *Karl Marx: His Life and Work* (New York: B. W. Heubsch, 1910), pp. 17–18.

disregard for everything decent.' " [3] Shaw's father, on the other hand, encouraged his son's early cynicism. "Thus, when I scoffed at the Bible," Shaw notes, "he would instantly and quite sincerely rebuke me. . . . But when he had reached the point of feeling really impressive, a convulsion of internal chuckling would wrinkle up his eyes; and . . . [he] would cap his eulogy by assuring me . . . that even the worst enemy of religion could say no worse of the Bible than it was the damdest parcel of lies ever written" (1:xxiii).

The restraining and sobering influence of his father is evident in Karl Marx's early schooling. Isaiah Berlin points out that at the local high school Marx "obtained equal praise for his industry and the high-minded and earnest tone of his essays on moral and religious topics." [4] Shaw, reflecting his father's cynicism, found school boring; as a consequence, he wrote in 1921, "I learnt nothing in school, not even what I could and would have learned if any attempt had been made to interest me" (1:xxxii).

Karl Marx studied at Bonn and Berlin and Jena, but not without entertaining notions similar to those of his future pupil. He hated much of the machinery of higher education: "For Marx it was not an easy matter to obtain the coveted degree, so necessary to an academic career. The irregularity of his studies, and the uncompromising independence of his judgment were formidable obstacles. Above all, there was his impatience and his scorn for many of the petty details involved in the examinations." [5] Shaw could not learn anything that did not interest him. "My memory is not indiscriminate: it rejects and selects; and its selections are not academic. I have no competitive instinct; nor do I crave for prizes and distinctions: consequently I have no interest in competitive examinations" (1:xxxii). Marx went through with the examinations and his thesis only as a result of the prodding of his close friend Bruno Bauer, who at one time wrote to him, "Only see that (I know that all reminder of it is unpleasant to

3. Ibid., p. 47.

4. Isaiah Berlin, *Karl Marx: His Life and Environment* (New York: Oxford University Press, 1948), p. 31.

5. Spargo, *Karl Marx*, p. 58.

you, but it cannot be helped) you get through with those nasty examinations, so that you may devote yourself entirely to your logical work." [6] Shaw, by his own admission, would not have entered a university even had his father possessed fifty thousand pounds a year (1:xxxii).

Sharing Shaw's disdain for formal schooling, Marx endangered his position as a student by his interest in tangential studies, but he did complete his doctorate (at Jena, where he could secure the degree with less difficulty than at Berlin). He had intended to join Bauer, who held a professorship at the University of Bonn, but in the meantime Bauer was dismissed because of his radical work, *Kritik der evangelischen Geschichte der Synoptiker.* Another friend, a former member of the young Hegelians, Arnold Ruge, published a radical political journal, *Deutsche Jahrbucher,* to which Marx and Bauer contributed until it was suppressed by the Saxon government in 1843. Marx wrote for and helped edit a series of radical journals, but they too were eventually suppressed. These ventures, although failures, enabled him to clarify his thoughts and channel them into his life's work;[7] they also embittered him and perhaps lighted the revolutionary flame.

In Paris Marx edited another radical journal, *Rhenische Zeitung;* after it was suppressed he prevailed upon Ruge to revive the *Deutsche Jahrbucher* in France where Saint-Simon, Fourier, and Proudhon had been conducting advanced radical studies in socialism and economics. In studying the works of these men, Marx, who had become interested in the "poor dumb millions" while editor of the *Rhenische Zeitung,* began to center his attention on the working classes.[8] Basically, as we shall see, his philosophy was to be a synthesis of Hegel, Feuerbach, Saint-Simon, Fourier, Proudhon, and later—after his meeting with Engels, also a former young Hegelian—of the English Ricardians. The point here is that Marx discovered his life's work through

6. Ibid., p. 59.
7. Ibid., pp. 62–68.
8. Ibid., p. 67.

personal association with advanced political thinkers and through a study of their writings in much the same manner that Shaw was to discover his life's work. It is my contention that Hegel played the same role for Marx that Marx did for Shaw. Just as Marx rejected much of Hegel in arriving at his philosophical synthesis, so Shaw rejected and altered much of Marx in forming his views of society. And just as Marx continued to revere Hegel, though he criticized him, so Shaw continued to respect Marx to the end of his life, even though he, too, severely criticized his master.

Shaw's road was far rougher than Marx's path through university training. As Archibald Henderson observes, "Of political economy he knew absolutely nothing," although he had read "Mill on Liberty, on Representative Government, on the Irish Land Question" and was familiar with the "evolutionary ideas and theories of Darwin, Tyndall, Huxley, Spencer, George Eliot, and their school." [9] Shaw himself said that three great utopian socialists emerged in the nineteenth century—Saint-Simon, Fourier, and Robert Owens—but "not one of these men came forward as champions of the proletariat," and he characterized them as dreamers filled with "fads and guesses which are impartially strung together on a thread of logic and the further they are elaborated in theory the more absurd they become in practice." [10] Shaw's mind, like Marx's, demanded a scientific explanation; he had to find his Hegel. But Shaw left a record of his search in his first four novels, while Marx at an early age "burned all his poems and plots for novels." [11]

In 1876, Shaw left Dublin to join his mother in London. He served briefly as a ghost reviewer on the musical periodical *Hornet,* but when he praised the musical revolutionary Wagner, he was promptly discharged. So, in true nineteenth-century fashion, he recorded his intellectual gropings in five partially autobiographical novels.

9. Henderson, *George Bernard Shaw*, p. 94.

10. George Bernard Shaw, "Socialism, Utopian and Scientific," British Museum Add. MS 50677A, fol. 7.

11. Spargo, *Karl Marx*, p. 51.

The first of these, *Immaturity* (completed in 1879 but not published until 1930), as William Irvine aptly states, "seems to have come out of the void, without much relation either to England or to the year 1878." [12] It is the story of a young man of Shavian temperament testing the world about him but finding no satisfactory answers to his questions. Even though Shaw had not yet heard of Karl Marx, we have hints of how ready he was for the conversion to the principles of that revolutionary. Robert Smith, a youth of eighteen, is the chief character of the novel and has found work in a counting house owned by Messrs. Figgis and Weaver. Shaw describes Smith's work as sheer drudgery which gained him a salary of one pound a week. "In return, he spent nearly two-thirds of his waking existence recording their transactions in large canvas-covered ledgers . . . which numbed his faculties and wasted his time" (1:11). Shaw is unconsciously documenting Marx, who had said, "The average price of wage labor is the minimum wage, i.e. that quantum of the means of subsistence which is absolutely requisite to keep the laborer in bare existence as a laborer. . . . the laborer lives merely to increase capital." [13]

Unaware of any Marxian implications, Smith comes to a revolutionary conclusion after musing on the structure of modern society: "Being clerks, we're all gentlemen. . . . I would rather be the meanest handicraftsman than a clerk, except that I would be under the thumb of a trades union. If that abominable office . . . were consumed to ashes tonight, I would contemplate the ruins tomorrow morning with the liveliest satisfaction" (1:51–52). But these are merely the meditations of a disgruntled adolescent, not yet the smolderings of a Marxist; Shaw adds significantly that "Smith smiled at his own folly."

Toward the end of the novel, however, the whole subject of class society appears in a fairly ripened stage. After accepting a position as private secretary to an Irish member of Parliament,

---

12. Irvine, *The Universe of G.B.S.,* p. 22.

13. Karl Marx, *The Communist Manifesto,* in *Capital, the Communist Manifesto, and Other Writings,* ed. Max Eastman (New York: Random House, The Modern Library, 1932), p. 336.

Smith is introduced to the so-called upper classes. When his old friend, a seamstress, captures the love of an artist, Cyril Scott, who is a pet of the upper crust, the discussion of the impossibility of Scott's marrying a seamstress raises the issue of class society. Isabella, the daughter of Smith's employer, does not think that the seamstress will ever be accepted by the best society; and Lady Geraldine, an enlightened, liberal aristocrat, presents Shaw's views when she retorts: " 'That opens the question of which society is the best. . . . There is—so they all say, at least—an inaccessible circle of awful people, the true cream of humanity, expensive, impervious to light, indigestible, stagnant, and uppermost, just as cream ought to be. But it is as impossible to live amongst such people as it would be for the Queen to have her crown continually on her head' " (1:269). Later, when Isabella remarks that Smith at least was never a shopman, Lady Geraldine replies, "Nonsense! I cannot understand how you Irish people are so far behind your time in that respect. If I were an Irishman, I would be an ardent republican. I would wear red caps, and keep a stand of pikes in my pantry. You are worse than the Hindus in your devotion to caste" (1:271–72).

The comments of Smith and Lady Geraldine are only glances at a problem that Shaw was considering but that had not yet been defined for him and hence had not yet become a principal theme. In the preface to *Immaturity* written four years after the Russian Revolution, Shaw reflects on Smith's thoughts about a class society:

> The born Communist, before he knows what he is, and understands why, is always awkward and unhappy in plutocratic society and in the poorer societies which ape it to the extent of their little means: in short, wherever spiritual values are assessed like Income Tax. . . . He is ashamed of his poverty, in continual dread of doing the wrong things, resentfully insubordinate . . . . Your born Communist . . . worries himself and everybody else until . . . [he] is led by some propagandist pamphlet, or by his own intellectual impulses . . . to investigate the economic structure of society. . . .

As it happens, I was a born Communist and Iconoclast (or Quaker) without knowing it; and I never got on easy terms with plutocracy and snobbery until I took to the study of economics, beginning with Henry George and Karl Marx. [1: xviii–xix]

Shaw's second novel, *The Irrational Knot* (completed in 1880 and published in 1885), shows that his quest for a social philosophy became more intense as some of John Stuart Mill's posthumous works and his own experiences during musical evenings in the West End took effect on his thinking.[14] The chief character, Conolly, is a working man, a fine electrician, whose musical talent allows him entrée into society's upper strata. Shaw created here a character and a situation which would permit him to contrast the bourgeoisie with the proletariat.

Shaw unknowingly expresses Marx's views on the bourgeois family in the scene following the revelation by Marmaduke, an aristocrat, of his offer to marry Conolly's sister, Susanna, an actress. Nellie McQuinch, a forerunner of the emancipated Shavian "new woman," speaks for Shaw:

Can you wonder at his preference? When we went to see that woman [on the stage] last June I envied her. There she was, clever, . . . earning her living, fascinating a crowd of people, whilst we poor respectable nonentities sat pretending to despise her—as if we were not waiting until some man in want of a female slave should offer us our board and lodging and the privilege of his lordly name with "Missis" before it for our life long services. . . . It is all very well for us fortunate good-for-nothings to resort to prostitution . . . to secure ourselves a home and income. Somebody said openly in Parliament the other day that marriage was the true profession of women. So it is a profession; except that it is a harder bargain for both parties, and that society countenances it, I dont see how it differs from what we—bless our virtuous indignation—stigmatizes prostitution. [2:97–98]

Three years later Shaw read in *The Communist Manifesto:*

14. Irvine, *The Universe of G.B.S.,* p. 25.

Abolition of the family! Even the most radical flare up at this infamous proposal of the Communists.

On what foundation is the present family, the bourgeois family, based? On capital, on private gain. . . .

The bourgeois sees in his wife a mere instrument of production. . . .

Bourgeois marriage is in reality a system of wives in common, and thus, at the most, what the Communists might possibly be reproached with, is that they desire to introduce, in substitution for a hypocritically concealed, an openly legalized community of women. For the rest, it is self-evident that the abolition of the present system of production must bring with it the abolition of the community of women springing from that system, i.e., of prostitution both public and private.[15]

Comparing these two passages, we see that Shaw was already a more radical thinker than those whom Marx had considered "most radical."

The theme of class society recurs throughout *The Irrational Knot*. When the Reverend George Lind attempts to persuade Conolly to abandon the idea of marrying his sister, Marian, because she is of a "higher rank," Conolly proceeds to show the ridiculousness of class distinctions with a Marxist proof for the superiority of the proletariat. His argument is a simple one, that the working classes are superior "by actual measurement round the head and round the chest, and round our manners and characters" (2:168). But this argument reaches a climax when later on Miss McQuinch and Conolly discuss why his marriage to Marian later became a failure. He claims that he made a *mésalliance* for Marian's sake and then realized how infinitely beneath him and his class was the one he married into. A three-page sermon follows, and its theme and tone could have come right out of *The Communist Manifesto*. He proudly exclaims that he is a worker belonging "to the class that keeps up the world by its millions of serviceable hands and serviceable brains." He scorns the aristocrats as loafers and would never condescend to admit

15. Marx, *The Communist Manifesto*, in *Capital, the Communist Manifesto, and Other Writings*, 338–40.

them as his equals. "The man who is working at the bench is my equal," he shouts, "whether he can do my day's work or not, provided he is doing the best he can. But the man who does not work anyhow, and the class that does not work, is a class below mine" (2:282).

In a 1905 preface to *The Irrational Knot* Shaw explains that he did not recognize the importance of money in a capitalistic society at the time he wrote the book, but now he did, for he had read *Das Kapital*. Of course he Shavianized the stark, humorless Marxian statements, but nevertheless the following excerpt from the preface provides the lately acquired scientific basis for Conolly's sentiments:

> It is the secret of all our governing classes, which consist finally of people who, though perfectly prepared to be generous, humane, cultured, philanthropic, public spirited and personally charming . . . are unalterably resolved . . . to have money enough for a handsome and delicate life, and will, in pursuit of that money, batter in the doors of their fellow-men, sell them up, sweat them in fetid dens, shoot, stab, hang, imprison, sink, burn and destroy them in the name of law and order. And this shows their fundamental sanity and rightmindedness; for a sufficient income is indispensable to the practice of virtue. . . . If I could convince our impecunious mobs of this, the world would be reformed before the end of the week; for the sluggards who are content to be wealthy without working and the dastards who are content to work without being wealthy, together with all the pseudo-moralists and ethicists and cowardice mongers generally, would be exterminated without shrift to the unutterable enlargement of life and ennoblement of humanity. We might even make some beginnings of civilization under such happy circumstances. [2:xvi–xvii]

Money is all-important; convince the proletariat of this fact, and it will become the governing class. Surely this reasoning supports Marx's first step of the revolution, that "the working class is to raise the proletariat to the position of the ruling class, to win the battle of democracy." [16]

16. Ibid., p. 342.

Shaw's next two novels demonstrate that the young artist was collecting the ideas that were to become dominant themes in his later works. In *Love among the Artists* (completed in 1881 and published in 1908), he abandons socialism for the time and treats a theme that was to appear in several of his later plays—the artist and love. But in *Cashel Byron's Profession* (completed in 1882 and published in 1886), although Shaw's pre-Marxist views on socialism occur only incidentally and are not as organic as they had been in *The Irrational Knot,* the author still focuses attention on capitalist society. In a rather incidental episode of this novel it seems that Britain had conquered an African kingdom but, finding the conquest too troublesome and expensive, had decided to restore the unprofitable booty to its king. However, before the king resumed his authority it was thought advisable that he should go to London where he could be impressed by the marvels of English civilization "especially in the matter of cannon and high explosives." Shaw then describes the king's reactions:

But when the African king arrived, his freedom from English prepossessions made it difficult to amuse, or even to impress him. A stranger to the idea that a handful of private persons could own a country and make others pay them for permission to live and work there, he was unable to understand why such a prodigiously rich nation should be composed chiefly of poor and uncomfortable persons toiling incessantly to create riches, and partly of a class that confiscated and dissipated the riches thus produced without seeming in the least happier than the unfortunate laborers at whose expense they existed. [4:107–108]

Like the African king, Shaw at this stage was a stranger to the idea of a society of haves and have-nots. No answer is given to the character in the novel, but Shaw was to find one soon. Karl Marx, with scientific graphs and formulas, would answer all the doubts and queries expressed by the characters of the four pre-Marxist novels. And an examination of his fifth and final novel, his first post-Marxist work, reveals a totally different Shaw, a familiar Shaw, a Shaw with complete self-assurance. As Archibald

Henderson observes, "he found in *Das Kapital* the concrete expression of all those social convictions, grievances and wrongs which seethed in the crater of his being. He became that most determined, most resistless, and often most dangerous of men to deal with, a man with a mission. 'From that hour,' I once heard Mr. Shaw say, 'I became a man with some business in the world' " [17]

17. Henderson, *George Bernard Shaw*, p. 98.

CHAPTER TWO

The Beginning of the Romance

Shaw's first four novels traced his intellectual gropings; his fifth, *An Unsocial Socialist* (completed in 1883 and published in 1884), recorded the solutions he found in *Das Kapital*. His first acquaintance with Marx's work came indirectly through his association with other intellectuals. Between 1879 and 1883, Shaw had joined various debating societies, among them the Zetetical, whose members debated current political philosophies, evolution, and atheism and discussed the works of John Stuart Mill, Charles Darwin, Herbert Spencer, T. H. Huxley, Thomas Malthus, and Charles Ingersoll.[1] On the night of September 5, 1882, Shaw as usual was searching for a lecture or debate on social topics similar to those discussed in the Zetetical Society, and while walking past Memorial Hall, he noticed a placard announcing a lecture sponsored by the Land Nationalization Society. The speaker was Henry George, an American economist whose book on the subject, *Progress and Poverty* (1880), had aroused attention in England. Shaw's incipient socialistic feelings were stirred by George's speech. He read the book with great enthusiasm and became further imbued with Georgite principles through the Land Reform Union, a new organization which had been formed to study land nationalization.

During a discussion of *Progress and Poverty* at a meeting of the Social Democratic Federation, a Marxist organization, the casual fashion in which the members dismissed Henry George's ideas moved Shaw to protest. But when he attempted to defend the one book that, he thought, had solved his problems, he was

1. Henderson, *George Bernard Shaw*, pp. 91–92.

told that no one could discuss land nationalization intelligently until he had read Karl Marx's *Das Kapital*.[2] Since this work had not yet been translated into English, he had to read a French edition available only at the British Museum. It was there, in the library, that the drama critic William Archer caught his first glimpse of Shaw: "a young man of tawny complexion and attire studying alternately—if not simultaneously—*Das Kapital,* and an orchestral score of *Tristan and Isolde*." [3] Though Shaw later discovered that the abstract economics of Marx left something to be desired, *Das Kapital*'s denunciation of capitalism left a permanent mark. It suggested the themes of many of his greatest plays and awakened in him un-Fabian revolutionary tendencies which persisted to the end of his life.

Marx found the basis of his thinking in the philosophy of Hegel, who, like Kant and Fichte before him, believed that reason is supreme and therefore that the laws of thought are the laws of the universe. For Hegel, however, the idea of *Geist* (the spirit of the times and the spirit of the people) is supreme; a solitary individual is not a whole in himself; he is only a fragment of a greater whole, a ripple in the *Geist*. But the *Geist* is not unchangeable; it is subject to change according to a logical pattern known as the Hegelian dialectic, which is composed of a thesis (an idea), an antithesis (an opposing idea), and a synthesis of the thesis and antithesis, which forms a new thesis. Hegel said that pure thought or Universal Abstract Mind can be considered a thesis; pure thought, however, negates itself and thereby reveals itself as the world of matter which becomes an antithesis. Universal Mind then returns to itself and thereby reveals itself as the world of spirit, embodied in mankind as a synthesis. This combination is the state, the most perfect embodiment of *Geist*.[4] Therefore, true freedom is obedience to the will of the state.

In Marx's rearrangement of the Hegelian dialectic, he was influenced by Ludwig Feuerbach, who already had inverted the

2. Irvine, *The Universe of G.B.S.*, p. 43.

3. Henderson, *George Bernard Shaw*, p. 97.

4. Summarized from William H. McGovern, *From Luther to Hitler* (New York: Houghton Mifflin, 1941), pp. 239–335.

Hegelian system by putting man in place of the absolute idea. Marx carried Feuerbach's materialism to its logical conclusion. The Hegelian dialectic, he later wrote, "stands on its head." Marx "turned it right way up" [5] by rejecting reason and idea as the supreme governing factors and substituting economic systems of production. The dialectic underlying all of Marx's history of mankind, which prepares for the first part of *Das Kapital,* is composed of a thesis (feudalism), and antithesis (bourgeois society or capitalism), and a synthesis (classless society or communism). His belief that economic conditions produce religions and philosophies was clarified by Friedrich Engels:

> Marx discovered the simple fact (heretofore hidden beneath ideological outgrowths) that human beings must have food, drink, clothing, and shelter first of all, before they can interest themselves in politics, science, art, religion and the like. This implies that the production of the immediately requisite material means of subsistence, and therewith the existing phase of development of a nation or an epoch, constitute the foundation upon which the state institutions, the legal outlooks, the artistic and even the religious ideas are built up. It implies that these latter must be explained out of the former, whereas the former have usually been explained as issuing from the latter.[6]

Taking the dialectic for granted as a working hypothesis, Marx devoted most of his time to studying the economic structure of capitalist society. In his preface to *Das Kapital,* he describes the scope of the work. The first volume is an analysis of "the capitalist's method of production, and the relations of production and exchange appropriate to that method." The second volume examines "the processes of the circulation of capital in three sections, respectively entitled: 'The Metamorphoses of Capital and Their Cycles,' 'The Turnover of Capital,' and 'The Reproduction and Circulation of the Aggregate Social Capital.'" The

5. Quoted in George H. Sabine, *A History of Political Theory* (New York: Henry Holt & Co., 1949), p. 691.

6. Quoted by Max Eastman, Introduction to Marx, *Capital, the Communist Manifesto, and Other Writings,* p. xii.

third volume "unravels the mystery of the fact that the capitals invested in different branches of production, although they 'work' under the most widely varying conditions; nevertheless, at any particular country, they secure much the same gains and produce an average rate of profit. . . . The world of commodities regulates . . . the course of the processes and the balancing of the profits in a way that is independent of individual intelligence and with a certainty which is far beyond the power of human functioning." [7] It was after reading the first volume of this complex study that Shaw completed his last novel, *An Unsocial Socialist* (1883), reflecting his wholehearted acceptance of Marxist principles even though later he was to modify them considerably. William Irvine justly criticizes the book because "the author cheerfully sacrifices art to economics," but adds the significant appraisal that the novel is, "in a peculiar sense, a complete Shaw, an epitome not only of all his literary vices and virtues but of nearly all his ideas and poses." [8]

Even more significant is Shaw's own appraisal in a forword added in 1930, where he states that the ideas "of the ficticious Trefusis anticipated those of the real Lenin." [9] One year after he wrote this statement—in 1931—Shaw spent an hour in Lenin's tomb and later exclaimed, "I do not know whether there will ever be a man to whom so much significance will be given as the future will give to Lenin." [10]

The chief character of *An Unsocial Socialist,* Trefusis, enthusiastically preaches his author's newly found faith as he stumbles about in a plot whose incidents are clumsily arranged solely to give him that opportunity. To weave his sermons into the plot, Shaw creates a character with a double identity. The young Trefusis is a born aristocrat who has abjured his class by becom-

7. Quoted in Otto Ruhle, *Karl Marx: His Life and Works* (New York: The New Home Library, 1943), pp. 323, 353, 356–57.

8. Irvine, *The Universe of G.B.S.,* pp. 32–33.

9. *The Works of Bernard Shaw,* 5:vii. Further quotations from *An Unsocial Socialist* in this chapter are taken from this volume; page numbers are given in parentheses after the quotations when necessary.

10. H. W. L. Dana, "Shaw in Moscow," *American Mercury* 25 (1932): 349.

ing a laborer and assuming a new name, Jeff Smilash. Thus, as Trefusis, he can preach Marxism effectively to his own class, and, as Jeff Smilash, can enlighten the laboring classes in language they can understand. We see here an anticipatory John Tanner–'Enry Straker of *Man and Superman* fame rolled into one.

As the novel opens, Trefusis has already assumed the role of Jeff Smilash, abandoned his aristocratic wife, and moved to a dilapidated Swiss-style cottage situated two miles from Alton College. The college housed in a converted country house near Lyvern was actually a finishing school for young ladies whose head mistress was a Miss Wilson. Shaw makes it clear that Marxist principles could never find a place in the school's curriculum. After all, the young ladies were taught that abandoning arable land to cattle, "which made more money for the landlord than the men whom they had displaced," is a sound economic practice. Shaw continues: "Miss Wilson's young ladies, being instructed in economics, knew that this proved that the land was being used to produce what was most wanted from it; and if all the advantage went to the landlord that was but natural, as he was the chief gentleman of the neighborhood" (27).

Young Smilash, after meeting Miss Wilson, persuades the schoolmistress to let him do odd jobs around the place. In this way he is able to offset false economic principles with the ideas of Marx. One day, his abandoned wife, Henrietta, accompanied by her parents, comes to the school to visit a "poor" cousin whose education they are paying for and who is about to be expelled for her insubordination and unruly ways. The young wife chances to see Jeff Smilash whom she immediately recognizes as Trefusis. In true Victorian fashion she promptly faints; and after carrying her across the fields, Trefusis finally puts her down on the bank of a soft, mossy hollow. At this unlikely moment, with her parents in hot pursuit, Trefusis decides to explain his reason for deserting her by giving her a condensed version of *Das Kapital* and *The Communist Manifesto* in some ten to eleven pages.

Shaw makes the sermon more pointed by choosing appropriate occupations for Trefusis's ancestors. After revealing that his mother's father was a capitalist landowner and his own father a capitalist cotton manufacturer, Trefusis relates his father's success story. Like Marx's typical capitalist, Old Jesse Trefusis began by offering the starving proletariat of Manchester the "use of his factory, his machines, and his raw cotton on the following conditions: They were to work long and hard, early and late, to add fresh value to his raw cotton by manufacturing it. Out of the value thus created by them, they were to recoup him for what he supplied them with: rent, shelter, gas, water, machinery, raw cotton—everything, and to pay him for his own services as superintendent, manager, and salesman" (73). Echoing Marx, Trefusis adds, "So far he asked nothing but just remuneration." These opening words of Trefusis sum up, without any alterations whatsoever, the economic tenets found in volume 1, chapter 6 of *Das Kapital:*

> In order to purchase the commodities necessary to maintain human life, human labor power offers itself for sale in the market as a commodity. The buyer of the labor power pays a price which corresponds more or less to its value. This value is determined by the average cost of production at the time and place where the commodity is sold. The average cost of the production of labor power depends on the expenditure for food, clothing, and other necessities that keep the commodity (labor power) in fit condition—this cost determines the price of labor power, which is called wages.[11]

Trefusis then shows how his father, like Marx's typical capitalist, achieved a value over and above the amount he had originally invested in his laborers. After they had paid him in full for his investment, they were to keep just enough to save them from starving and hand over the balance to reward his virtue in saving money. This balance is the surplus explained by Marx's surplus value theory:

> The labourer . . . finds in the workshop not only the means of production necessary for working six hours, but also those necessary for working twelve hours. If 10 lbs. of cotton absorbed

11. Summarized from *Capital,* in *Capital, the Communist Manifesto, and Other Writings,* pp. 34–38.

6 working hours and be transformed into 10 lbs. of yarn, then 20 lbs. of cotton will absorb 12 working hours and be transformed into 20 lbs. of yarn. Let us consider the problem of this prolonged labour process. Five working days are now materialised in the 20 lbs. of yarn, i.e. four in the cotton and the lost steel of the spindle, and one absorbed by the cotton during the process of spinning. Expressed in gold, the value of five working days is $7.50. That is therefore the price of the 20 lbs. of yarn. The latter still costs $37\frac{1}{2}$ cents per lb. But the total value of the commodities entering into the process [$5.00 for cotton, $1.00 for the consumed instruments of labor, and 75 cents for labor power] was $6.75, whereas the value of the yarn is $7.50. The value of the product has increased to the extent of one ninth over and above the value advanced for its production. $6.75 have been transformed into $7.50. A surplus value of 75 cents has been obtained. The trick has succeeded at last.[12]

In a Marxist postscript,[13] Trefusis explains that the laborers were forced to work out the surplus value for his father or starve because all the other factory owners offered them no better conditions.

Following Marx's economic history to the letter, Trefusis next tells Henrietta that the laborers amassed a large surplus value for Jesse Trefusis. And Jessie, being a shrewd man, used the profit to install machines that could be operated by women and children, since they "were cheaper and more docile, he turned away about seventy out of every hundred of his *hands* (so he called the men), and replaced them by their wives and children, who made more money for him faster than ever" (74). In these few words Trefusis summarizes Marx's treatment of the Industrial Revolution whose inventions afforded cheaper labor for the capitalist:

12. Ibid., pp. 44–45.

13. Marx said that if the proletarian "does not succeed in selling his labour power as a commodity, he has only one option, to starve. He is blessed with the gift of freedom; but, should he try to use that freedom for any other purpose than to sell his labour power, he is condemned to irretrievable starvation" (Otto Ruhle, *Karl Marx*, p. 327).

In so far as machinery does away with the need for any considerable expenditure of muscular power, it becomes a means for the utilization of workers with comparatively little strength, and whose bodily growth is immature but whose limbs are all the more supple. The labour of women and children was, therefore, the first word in the capitalist utilization of machinery. . . . In former days, the worker used to sell his own labour power, being ostensibly, in this respect, a free person. Now he sells his wife and his children. He becomes a slave-trader.[14]

Trefusis ends the lengthy narration of his father's career by summarizing Marx's theory that the accumulation of capital marks the end of private property based on the labor of the owner and the beginning of capitalist private property maintained by the exploitation of others' labor and that when such centralization becomes complete, the world's goods will be owned by a few large monopolies. He tells Henrietta that by this time his father had long ago given the chore of managing his factories to paid clever underlings for a few hundreds a year and bought shares in other concerns operating on the same principle. He then "pocketed dividends made in countries which he had never visited by men whom he had never seen; bought a seat in Parliament from a poor and corrupt constituency, and helped to preserve the laws by which he had thriven" (74). As a result of these investments, his father lived like a gentleman forevermore—nay, not only his father, but he himself, who never did a stroke of work, is now wallowing in wealth "whilst the children of the men who made that wealth are slaving as their fathers slaved, or starving, or in the workhouse, or in the streets, or the deuce knows where" (75).

Henrietta, interested only in getting back her husband, becomes a convenient devil's advocate. She replies with the typical argument used by capitalists: "It cannot be helped now. Besides, if your father saved money, and the others were improvident, he deserved to make a fortune." But Shaw now had the answer; his protagonist, unlike Smith in *Immaturity*, or Conolly in *The*

14. Ibid., p. 338.

Irrational Knot, need not fumble for a reply. Marx's surplus value theory provided Shaw, at this time, an airtight rejoinder. Trefusis answers his wife's argument with firm conviction:

> Granted but he didnt make a fortune. He took a fortune that others made. . . . if he had lived a century earlier, invested his money in a horse and a pair of pistols, and taken to the road, his object—that of wresting from others the fruits of their labor without rendering them an equivalent—would have been exactly the same, and his risk far greater, for it would have included risk of the gallows. . . . Therefore I turn my back on them [the men who imitate his father]. I cannot sit at their feasts knowing how much they cost in human misery, and seeing how little they produce of human happiness [75–76]

There could be no answer to this scientific analysis, and so Henrietta "seemed a little troubled" and "smiled faintly." The capitalist manufacturer was condemned beyond doubt; he is nothing but a highwayman.

But there was still another "respectable" segment of English society to be torn down and another tangential Marxian theory to be exposed; the wife again becomes the convenient devil's advocate. Granted that her husband's father was a robber, still, she urges, "Your mother belonged to one of the oldest families in England." Trefusis's reply becomes another Marxist sermon of some four or five pages in which he reviews the life of his maternal grandfather:

> When he was a boy, there was a fairly prosperous race of peasants settled here, tilling the soil, paying him rent for permission to do so, and making enough out of it to safisfy his large wants and their own narrow needs without working themselves to death. But my grandfather was a shrewd man. He perceived that cows and sheep produced more money by their meat and wool than peasants by their husbandry. So he cleared the estate. That is, he drove the peasants from their homes as my father did afterwards in his Scotch deer forest. Or, as his tombstone has it, he developed the resources of his country. I dont know what became of the peasants; *he* didnt know, and I presume, didnt care. I suppose the old ones went into

the workhouse, and the young ones crowded the towns, and
worked for men like my father in factories. [77]

Marx goes so far as to blame the displacement of peasants for
the real beginning of capitalism:

> In the history of primary accumulation we must regard as
> epoch-making all revolutions that acted as stepping-stones for
> the capitalist class in course of formation. Above all, this ap-
> plies to those moments when great masses of human beings
> were suddenly and forcibly torn away from the means of sub-
> sistence, and hurled into the labour market as masterless pro-
> letarians. The expropriation of the agricultural producers, the
> peasants, their severance from the soil, was the basis of the
> whole process. In different countries, the history of this expro-
> priation assumed different forms, running through its various
> phases in different orders of succession, and at different his-
> torical periods. Only in England can it be said to have had a
> typical development.[15]

Surely the last sentence bolsters Trefusis's condemnation of his
maternal grandfather.

But Trefusis does not stop here. Marx had provided the solution to the problem both in the final pages of the first volume of
Das Kapital and in far greater detail in *The Communist Manifesto*. Therefore Shaw now gears his plot to personalize Marx's
scientific treatment of the solutions. Trefusis, in answer to his now
exhausted wife's original question (asked some ten pages ago),
why he had deserted her, explains that he is helping to free those
Manchester slaves; and to bring that about,

> their fellow slaves all over the world must unite in a vast
> international association of men pledged to share the world's
> work justly; to share the produce of the work justly; to yield
> not a farthing—charity apart—to any full grown and able
> bodied idler or malingerer, and to treat as vermin in the com-
> monwealth persons attempting to get more than their share
> of wealth or give less than their share of work. . . . Capitalism,
> organized for repressive purposes under pretext of governing

15. Ibid., pp. 346–47.

the nation, would very soon stop the association if it understood our aim. [80]

Trefusis's argument is clearly based upon Marx's assertion that communists "never cease for a single instant to instill into the working class the clearest possible recognition of the hostile antagonism between bourgeoisie and proletariat . . . . Working men of all countries, unite!" [16]

But Trefusis makes another statement that deviates from a chief tenet of Marx's solution. He says that the capitalist thinks his proposed association is engaged in gunpowder plots and conspiracies to chop off crowned heads: "I use heaps of postage stamps, pay the expenses of many indifferent lecturers, defray the cost of printing reams of pamphlets and hand-bills which hail the laborer flatteringly as the salt of the earth, write and edit a little socialist journal, and do what lies in my power generally" (81). In contrast, Marx presented a doctrine of world revolution: "The Communists disdain to conceal their aims and views. They openly declare that their ends can be attained only by the forcible overthrow of existing social conditions. Let the ruling classes tremble at a Communistic revolution." [17] We can see already the incipient Fabian who prefers Sidney Webb's evolutionary methods to revolutionary ones. In the appendix to the novel, written in 1888, after Shaw had joined the Fabian Society, Trefusis, addressing his author, says that his former sweetheart, whom he had practically forced to marry Erskine, his aristocratic friend, had "become an extreme advocate of Socialism." He adds significantly: "[She] being in a great hurry for the new order of things, looks on me as a lukewarm disciple because I do not propose to interfere with the slowly grinding mill of Evolution, and effect the change by one tremendous stroke from the united and awakened people (for such she—vainly, alas!—believes the proletariat already to be)" (266). Yet, in 1930 Shaw hailed Trefusis as a "Bolshevist" who "anticipated the real Lenin" (a discrepancy I shall explain in later chapters).

16. Marx, *The Communist Manifesto,* in *Capital, the Communist Manifesto, and Other Writings,* pp. 354–55.
17. Ibid., p. 355.

In sum, Shaw, through Trefusis, accepts without qualification two central doctrines discovered in *Das Kapital:* Marx's economic dialectic, i.e., the explanation of history through class struggles culminating in the final struggle (whether it be revolution or parliamentary reform) of the proletariat with the bourgeoisie, and Marx's surplus value theory as the basis for all economic ills. Marx and Engels had determined the solution to these problems in 1848, many years before the publication of *Das Kapital* and summarized the chief points in *The Communist Manifesto:*

1. Abolition of property in land and application of all rents of land to public purposes.
2. A heavy progressive or graduated income tax.
3. Abolition of all right of inheritance.
4. Confiscation of the property of all emigrants and rebels.
5. Centralization of credit in the hands of the state, by means of a national bank with state capital and an exclusive monopoly.
6. Centralization of the means of communication and transport in the hands of the state.
7. Extension of factories and instruments of production owned by the state; the bringing into cultivation of waste lands, and the improvement of the soil generally in accordance with a common plan.
8. Equal liability of all to labor. Establishment of industrial armies, especially for agriculture.
9. Combination of agriculture with manufacturing industries; gradual abolition of the distinction between town and country by a more equable distribution of the population over the country.
10. Free education for all children in public schools. Abolition of children's factory labor in its present form. Combination of education with industrial production, etc.[18]

Trefusis includes all of the ten points in explaining his socialist platform during an amusing scene in which he succeeds in getting the signatures of two unsuspecting aristocrats, Erskine and Sir Charles, on his platform. After he plagues them with a seven-page reiteration of the ideas he had earlier presented to his wife,

18. Ibid., pp. 342–43.

Sir Charles, a little dazed, asks what is going to be the culmination of it all. Trefusis barks, "Socialism or Smash" (213). He later explains: "When England is made the property of its inhabitants collectively, England becomes socialistic. Artificial inequality will vanish then before real freedom of contract; freedom of competition, or unhampered emulation, will keep us moving ahead; and Free Trade will fulfil its promises at last" (216). Or as Marx had said, "In place of the old bourgeois society, with its classes and class antagonisms, we shall have an association in which the free development of each is the condition for the free development of all." [19] But now Erskine intervenes and asks Trefusis,

"And the idlers and loafers, . . . What of them?"
"You and I, in fact," said Trefusis, "die of starvation, I suppose, unless we choose to work, or unless they give us a little out-door relief in consideration of our bad bringing-up."
"Do you mean they will plunder us?" said Sir Charles.
[Trefusis replies:] "I mean they will make us stop plundering them. If they hesitate to strip us naked, or to cut our throats if we offer them the smallest resistance, they will show us more mercy than we ever showed them . . . . Eh, Erskine?" (216–17).

Thus Trefusis, the protagonist of *An Unsocial Socialist*, expresses Marxist opinions that we will find basic to themes in plays throughout Shaw's career. Indeed, in the very appendix in which Trefusis champions Shaw's Fabian views, he says to his author: "What Hetty and I said to one another that day when she came upon me in the shrubbery at Alton College was known only to us two. . . . All due honor, therefore, to the ingenuity with which you have filled the hiatus . . . by a discourse on 'surplus value,' cribbed from an imperfect report of one of my public lectures, and from the pages of Karl Marx" (269).

Shaw had discovered an answer to the economic ills of the society in which he lived. But Shaw being Shaw was soon to Shavianize Marx's doctrines.

19. Ibid., p. 343.

CHAPTER THREE

Marx Shavianized

After enthusiastically accepting Marx and expounding his doctrines in *An Unsocial Socialist*, Shaw began almost immediately to work out his own brand of socialism. In a March, 1884, letter to *Justice*, the journal of the Social Democratic Federation, he questions Marx's surplus value theory. Since the first installment of *An Unsocial Socialist* did not appear until April, 1884 (in a socialist monthly, *To-day*), Shaw's first printed words concerning Marx were, ironically, unfavorable. His initial condemnation of Marx would be difficult to understand in view of his future eulogies for the great revolutionary had Shaw himself not shed some light on the subject. Richard W. Ellis, who collected this letter along with others on the subject, explains that "Mr. Shaw has confessed that he was completely carried away by *Das Kapital* .... but that he could not make the two ends of the economic argument meet exactly, which he attributed to his own economic ignorance, and that he pointed out his difficulty in this letter to *Justice* as a joke which a skilled economist could refute easily." [1] In typical Shavian fashion, he boldly condemns so that he can be enlightened, and his facetiousness is reflected in the name signed to the letter—G.B.S. Larking.

In his letter Shaw calls Marx's surplus value theory a "preposterous absurdity." He condemns Marx for hating the civilization "whose culture he inherited, whose society he enjoyed," and he censures *Justice* for promulgating such a man's "preposterous"

---

1. Richard W. Ellis, ed., *Bernard Shaw and Karl Marx: A Symposium 1884–1889* (New York: Random House, 1930), p. vi.

theory. Even more surprising, in view of future Shavian concepts, he ends the letter with a burst of British patriotism:

> You poison our prosperity at its source, and embitter those reflections on our national greatness which were once the pride and solace of Englishmen. I dare avouch that you shall never persuade us that we are either slaves or thieves. Something within us gives you the lie. We have said that, "Britons never will be slaves," we have said that, "an honest man's the noblest work of God," and we mean both.[2]

Shaw never received an answer to the letter.

In the meantime, he took other steps to educate himself in economics and sociology. He was unwilling to join the Social Democratic Federation "not because of snobbery, but because [he] wanted to work with men of [his] own mental training."[3] The members of the federation were obviously not men of Shaw's mental ability; moreover, their aim was to work closely with the working class. Shaw, like Marx, sought the fellowship of the rebelling sons of the bourgeoisie. He had found a kindred spirit in Marx because his "whole life had bred in him a defiance of middle-class respectability"[4] and *Das Kapital* was principally a scientific exposé of the evils of the bourgeoisie.

Shaw was attracted to the Fabian Society when their tract, *Why Are the Many Poor?* fell into his hands; "The moment I saw the words 'Fabian Society' on it, I realized that here was a good title which immediately suggested an educated body, so I found out the Society's address from the tract and turned up at [Edward R.] Pease's rooms for the next meeting."[5] Later he persuaded Sidney Webb, whom he had first met at the Zetetical Society, to attend meetings with him; and he joined the society on September 5, 1884. He, Sidney Webb, Graham Wallas (a Fabian essayist), Sidney Olivier (a noted Millite), and others met

2. Ibid., pp. 7–8.
3. Quoted in R. F. Rattray, *Bernard Shaw: A Chronicle* (Luton: Leagrave Press, 1951), p. 48.
4. Henderson, *George Bernard Shaw*, p. 97.
5. Quoted in Rattray, *Bernard Shaw: A Chronicle*, p. 48.

frequently to discuss *Das Kapital*.[6] At the early Fabian Society meetings, they engaged primarily in heated discussions of Marxian economics and revolutionary measures. Shaw himself admits: "It must not be assumed that anarchism encountered any resistance among us on the ground of association with physical force. The Fabian Society was warlike in its origin." [7]

But Shaw's idolatry of Marx was soon to be severely shaken by a Unitarian minister, the Reverend Philip H. Wicksteed, whose criticism of Marx's surplus value theory appeared in *To-Day* (vol. 2, 1884:388ff.). Following the political economist William Stanley Jevons, Wicksteed claims that abstract utility, not abstract labor, determines the value and hence the price of a commodity. He argues that according to Jevons's laws of indifference and variation of utility, if we assume that hats and coats are equally important and that eight hats can be manufactured during the same time necessary to manufacture one coat, if follows that hats will be made until one hat is worth only one-eighth the value of one coat. Then coats will be made also. In short, he says that the force of demand at the margin of supply determines exchange value.[8]

The members of the Fabian Society prevailed upon Shaw to answer Wicksteed and defend the surplus value theory which he, as G.B.S. Larking, had attacked. Shaw consented only under the conditions that Wicksteed be permitted space for a rejoinder.[9] Shaw's reply which appeared in *To-Day* (vol. 3, 1885: 22ff.) is filled with bombast but fails to deal with the minister's crucial points. He simply says that he has not the slightest intention of defending Karl Marx since it is impossible to suspect Marx "of having lost sight of the supply-and-demand phenomena . . . in the face of the 'Misère de la Philosophie,' and several passages in 'Capital' " and that neither he nor anyone else has "access to

---

6. Thomas Anson Knowlton, *The Economic Theory of George Bernard Shaw*, University of Maine Studies, 2nd ser., no. 39 (Orons, Maine: The University Press, 1936), p. 10.

7. Shaw, "The Early History of the Fabian Society," *Fabian Tracts* (London: The Fabian Society, 1884–1901), Tract 41 (1892) , p. 3.

8. William Irvine, *The Universe of G.B.S.*, p. 76.

9. Henderson, *George Bernard Shaw*, p. 156.

the unpublished volumes of that work to answer for the way in which so subtle a reason may have reconciled these contradictions." Not only does Shaw admit "contradictions" in the socialist bible; he even praises Wicksteed for "being a sworn enemy of dogma" and for "leading the assault which must have been made sooner or later upon the economic citadel of Collectivism." [10]

Wicksteed's answer, which appeared in the same volume of *To-Day,* effectively destroyed Shaw's arguments. Here was a man who obviously knew more economics than Shaw. Shaw, characteristically, sought out Wicksteed; he sat at the minister's feet in a circle called the Hampstead Historical Society. As a result of Wicksteed's teaching, Shaw with qualifications discarded the Marxist value theory. He explained to Henderson: "The Marxian steel was always snapping in my hand. The Jevonian steel held and kept its edge, and fitted itself to every emergency." [11] But in 1948, Shaw had some different remarks to make concerning Marx's value theory. He stated that Marx was sometimes pragmatically right when he was theoretically wrong; he agreed that Marx's value theory works well enough in modern industrial practice, just as Newton's erroneous first law of motion worked well enough in astronomical practice before Einstein upset it, but added that "the truth is that value creates labor." Indirectly he praised the theory when he concluded that Marx "by lumping . . . [rent and interest] together as surplus value . . . took them into account as hard facts and came out pragmatically right."[12]

Even in the three articles (appearing in the *National Reformer,* vol. 1, 1887: 84-86; 106-108; 117-118) in which Shaw, fresh from his mastery of the Jevonian theory, lashes out at the Marxist value theory, there is always a deep respect for Marx and the other features of *Das Kapital.* The first of these articles contains a eulogy to Karl Marx. Shaw builds up to it by stating that among other economists "one catches repeated flashes of something like the Marxian spirit, but never so like as to sustain a

10. Quoted in Ellis, *Bernard Shaw and Karl Marx,* pp. 72–73, 71.

11. Henderson, *George Bernard Shaw,* pp. 159–60.

12. Shaw, "Bernard Shaw on Peace," British Museum Add. MS 50699, fols. 196–97.

close comparison. The remarkable historian sense is wanting."
He continues, referring now to Ruskin in his *Modern Painters,*
especially the chapter "The Moral Landscape":

> There is, perhaps, a feeble reflection of Marx's implacable
> contempt for the external aspect of capitalistic civilization in
> the petulant outcry against railroads and machine-made goods,
> . . . but its usual accompaniment is a proposal to escape by
> "restoring" medievalism on much the same lines as those
> adopted by the architects who "restore" our cathedrals. There
> is none of this futile retrogressiveness in Marx. . . . Marx keeps
> his head like a God. He has discovered the law of social devel-
> opment, and knows what must come. The thread of history is
> in his hands.[13]

To be sure, he criticizes Marx for ignoring labor's variations of
skill, for not referring to variations of the fertility of raw material, and for lumping together the product and wage of labor
power as surplus value without considering subdivisions into
rent, interest, and profits; but he quickly adds, "You can no more
get rid of such a man by a quip or two at his use of the word
value, than you can of Mahomet by explaining that the dove
which whispered to him really came to pick a pea out of his ear,
or of Comte by burlesquing the ritual of the Religion of Humanity."

Again, in the last of three articles, Shaw points out the falla-
cies in *Das Kapital,* but writes:

> I must now leave the subject with a confession that I never
> took up a book that proved better worth the reading than
> "Capital." It is unavoidable that the merits of the book should
> occupy a relatively unsignificant space here; whilst, on the
> contrary, its errors occupy a relatively significant space. In
> pointing out these errors and so implying that Marx was
> fallible, I have incurred the risk of being accused, as I once
> was by an enthusiastic Marxite at a public meeting, of attempt-
> ing to pooh-pooh Marx as an idiot. Undoubtedly I have taken
> a course somewhere between that and worshiping him as a
> God.[14]

13. Quoted in Ellis, *Bernard Shaw and Karl Marx,* pp. 114–15.
14. Ibid., pp. 168–69.

Two years later, after the publication of the second volume of *Das Kapital,* Henry Hyndman, a Marxolator and the founder of the Social Democratic Federation, accused Shaw of believing Marx a fool. In his reply one might expect Shaw in his usual manner of exaggeration to sneer at Marx in order to sneer at Hyndman; instead, he answers: "I do not, with Hyndman's powerful logic, proceed to infer that Marx was an idiot, *Das Kapital* a tissue of nonsense, Socialism an illusion, Jevons immensely Marx's superior . . . I am quite willing to allow in the handsomest manner, that Marx was the Aristotle of the nineteenth century." And he completely exonerates Marx as a cause of all the bitter controversy: "Let me in conclusion explain that I do not accuse Carl Marx of Marxism, and that I think he deserved something worthier from his pupils than idolatry." [15] Indeed, Shaw was too like Marx to be anyone's slave—that is why the romance continued—and an examination of Shaw's writings as a young Fabian discloses many important relationships between his full-blown theory and Marxism.

Two long essays by Shaw epitomize his economic views at this time, and these views remained constant until the Russian Revolution of 1917. The essays were included in *Essays in Fabian Socialism* (completed in 1889 and published over a period of years) which was based on a "course of seven lectures on the 'Basis and Prospects of Socialism' " [16] and edited by Shaw.

In studying these two important essays, we must keep in mind, first, that Shaw wrote them fresh from his discovery of Jevons, and, second, that Shaw and the Fabians at this time were in bitter controversy with Hyndman and his Social Democratic Federation, the down-the-line Marxist organization. Hence when Shaw said that in "1889 we published 'Fabian Essays' without a word in them about the value theory of Marx," [17] we can understand what he meant, even though he expressly did praise Marx's

15. Ibid., pp. 186–87, 200.
16. Rattray, *Bernard Shaw: A Chronicle,* p. 70.
17. Quoted in Henderson, *George Bernard Shaw,* p. 181.

surplus value theory in a footnote to his own first essay of the volume.[18]

But what Marxist elements remain in the full-blown Shavian conception of socialism? Henderson gives us a clue when he quotes Shaw's admonition: "Read Jevons and the rest for your economics, and read Marx for the history of their working in the past, and the conditions of their application in the present. And never mind the metaphysics." [19]

In the essay entitled "Economic"—which opens the first section of *Essays in Fabian Socialism*, "The Basis of Socialism"—Shaw purports to analyze the economic basis of socialism. Following Ricardo, he begins by showing how man appropriated the land. He says that the original occupier of a fertile piece of land, whom he calls Adam, is the ancestor of all the landed gentry (and who "developed by centuries of civilization into an Adam Smith" [4]) and then traces the steps whereby he secures his independence. Adam manages to make a thousand pounds from the produce of his land. When neighbors arrive, they must settle on less fertile ground since Adam appropriated the best plot for himself. But Adam will let his patch of fertile land to the first newcomer at a rent of five hundred pounds a year. Since the yield will be one thousand pounds, the newcomer will have five hundred pounds left for himself and will have the advantage of living in the center of society, rather than on its outskirts. The newcomer himself will initiate such an arrangement, and Adam may retire as the first idle landlord with a continual income of five hundred pounds rent. After Adam does this he becomes, in Shaw's words, a drone. This process is repeated by other workers as newcomers move in, and finally all the land is taken up (5–6).

Thus far Shaw follows Ricardo's principles of rent to the letter. But now a new phenomenon appears in the form of a man who

18. *The Works of Bernard Shaw*, 30: 27: "This excess of the product of labor over its price is treated as a single category with impressive effect by Karl Marx, who called it 'surplus value' (*mehrwerth*)." Further quotations from *Essays in Fabian Socialism* in this chapter are from the same volume; page numbers are given in parentheses after the quotation when necessary.

19. Henderson, *George Bernard Shaw*, p. 161.

cannot appropriate any land for himself either through economic rent or the rent of ability. This man is Marx's proletarian, and Shaw uses Marx's term. The proletarian must eat, but food costs money and he has nothing to sell—except himself. At this point, Shaw supplements the Ricardian theories with pure Marxism: "But now all the disguise falls off: the proletarian renounces not only the fruit of his labor, but also his right to think for himself and to direct the industry as he pleases" (12). Although Shaw does not admit it, he is paraphrasing Marx who said in *The Communist Manifesto:* "These laborers who must sell themselves piecemeal, are a commodity, like every other article of commerce . . . they are daily and hourly enslaved by the machine, by the overlooker, and, above all, by the individual bourgeois manufacturer himself." [20] Of course Marx is referring to a later development pertaining to factories, but Shaw in this same essay indicates how the proletarian who had sold himself to the landlord also becomes the laborer who sells himself to industry: "If a railway is required, all that is necessary is to provide subsistence for a sufficient number of laborers to construct it" (20). But a single landlord could not afford to finance the building of a railroad. He must join a number of possessors of surplus wealth and they will form a financial machinery to distribute the shares in the capital. Shaw says that such a combination merely modifies the terminology and superficial aspect of exploitation, and adds, "But the modification is not an alteration: shareholder and landlord live alike on the produce extracted from their property by the labor of the proletariat" (21).

In explaining exchange value, however, Shaw departs from Marx and, again, reflecting Wicksteed's influence, returns to Jevons's theory of abstract utility. Where Wicksteed used coats and hats to demonstrate his point, Shaw uses umbrellas. If every man were able to purchase two umbrellas, the second would be of less use than the first; therefore the price of the second umbrella would have to be reduced and naturally the public would buy the less expensive umbrella. "This is how the exchange value

20. Karl Marx, *Capital, the Communist Manifesto, and Other Writings,* ed. Eastman, p. 328.

of the least useful part of the supply fixes the exchange value of all the rest" (14).

Yet, all of this intermingling of economic theories is relatively unimportant. What is important at this stage of Shaw's development as a socialist and artist is his strict adherence to Marx's history of the development of economics and his reluctant refusal to accept Marx's revolution as a means of solving the world's problems.

These two elements emerge clearly in "The Transition to Social Democracy," Shaw's final essay in *Essays in Fabian Socialism*. In his historical analysis Shaw covers the following periods: medievalism to capitalism; anarchy to state interference; state interference to state organization. He almost directly paraphrases Marx when he demonstrates how the feudal system became farcical as its communistic basis was transformed into private property:

> The gild [sic] system had no machinery for dealing with division of labor, the factory system, or international trade: it recognized in competitive individualism only something to be repressed as diabolical. But competitive individualism simply took possession of the gilds, and turned them into refectories for aldermen, and notable additions to the grievances and laughing stocks of posterity. . . . Political economy soon declared for industrial anarchy; for private property; for individual recklessness of everything except individual accumulation of riches; and for the abolition of all the functions of the state except those of putting down violent conduct and invasions of private property. [36]

Marx had written in *The Communist Manifesto:*

> The feudal system of industry, under which industrial production was monopolized by closed guilds, now no longer sufficed for the growing wants of the new market. The manufacturing system took its place. The guild-masters were pushed on one side by the manufacturing middle class . . . in one word, the feudal relations of property became no longer compatible with the already developed productive forces; they became so many fetters. They had to burst asunder; they were burst asunder.

Into their places stepped free competition, accompanied by
social and political constitutions adapted to it, and by eco-
nomical and political sway of the bourgeois class.[21]

Continuing the historical analysis, Shaw refers outright to
Karl Marx and his analysis of England's prosperity under capitalism: "Karl Marx . . . convicted private property of wholesale
spoliation, murder and compulsory prostitution; of plague, pestilence, and famine; battle, murder, and sudden death. . . . no one
ventured to pretend that the charges were not true. The facts were
not only admitted; they had been legislated upon" (39). We see,
in this praise of Marx's analysis, embryonic themes for future
dramas: "compulsory prostitution" as a result of the capitalist
system becomes the theme of *Mrs. Warren's Profession;* "plague,
pestilence, and famine" as a result of private property's "wholesale spoliation" becomes the theme of his first play, *Widower's
Houses* and, in a way, the basis for so late a play as *Major
Barbara.*

Shaw returns to his Ricardian definition of rent when he explains how socialism will attempt to do away with the social evils
pointed out by Marx. Socialism will transfer rent from the class
which now appropriates it to the whole people; this rent is defined as that part of the produce which is individually unearned.
Marx, it will be remembered, defined capitalist private property
as that property maintained by the exploitation of others' labor.
It seems to me that Shaw's *rent* and Marx's *capitalist private
property* are pretty much the same. However, Shaw once more
veers away from Marx's labor theory and returns to Jevons when
he says:

So long as the fertility of land varies from acre to acre, and
the number of persons passing by a shop window per hour
varies from street to street, with the result that two farmers or
two shopkeepers of exactly equal intelligence and industry will
reap unequal returns from their year's work [Jevons's utility
value theory based on the law of supply and demand], so long
will it be equitable to take from the richer farmer or shop-

21. Ibid., pp. 322, 326.

keeper the excess over his fellow's gain which he owes to the bounty of Nature or the advantage of situation, and divide that excess or rent equally between the two. [40]

Thus we have, again, a curious blend of Ricardo's rent theory, Marx's value theory, and Jevons's utility theory.

A few years before Shaw wrote his *Essays in Fabian Socialism* he was flirting with revolution. In a lecture entitled "Driving Capital Out of the Country," composed on June 17, 1885, Shaw states that labor will continue to be bought and sold in the open market until the workers take the Land, the Plant, the Skill, and the Brains of the country in their own hands. In short, until the Revolution." Attempting to dispel any fears that people may have concerning the results of such a revolution, he argues that the threat of capitalists' leaving the country and taking with them all its wealth is nonsense. It would be "potable property,"— he adds scoffingly, "Lady Dudly takes her jewels—Well we have done without them for a long time, we can for a time longer." [22] A March, 1886, speech entitled "Points Disputed Among Socialists" presents two methods of instituting socialism in England: "Force as soon as possible or Christian persuasion; but in the other case, a declaration of Revolution." [23]

But the first real break with Marx appears when Shaw in *Essays in Fabian Socialism* begins to explain how socialism is to come about; it is extremely interesting to trace the manner in which Shaw makes the break. He first discounts Marx's theory of revolution and his appeal to the proletariat to effect this change: "I am afraid that in the ordinary middle-class opinion Socialism is flagrantly dishonest, but could be established off-hand tomorrow with the help of a guillotine, if there were no police, and the people were wicked enough. In truth, it is as honest as it is inevitable; but all the mobs and guillotines in the world can no more establish it than police coercion can avert it" (40). But Shaw feels that the problem of dropping the rent arising out of the people's industry into the people's pocket is made difficult

22. British Museum Add. MS 50700, fols. 16–17.
23. Ibid., fol. 93.

by determining where the people's pocket is. "Who is the people?" he asks, "what is the people?" Hegel, not Marx, provided his answers. Shaw returns to Hegel's perfect state as the representative and trustee of the people. He says that the Whigs who followed Jeremy Bentham and John Austin could never dream of a good state. To them it was a necessary evil, as Hobbes had earlier described it. But Shaw concludes that Hegel specifically taught the idea of a perfect state and his followers saw nothing impossible in converting the existing state into one which is at least practically trustworthy, if not absolutely perfect. Such a "practically trustworthy" state can be effected by making "the passing of a sufficient examination an indispensable preliminary to entering the executive" and by making "the executive responsible to the government, and the government responsible to the people" (42). Marx, of course, changed Hegel's dialectic of the perfect state to his dialectic of class warfare, arriving at state ownership through out-and-out revolution of the proletariat. The difference between Marx's and Shaw's methods for effecting socialism is indicated in the table. Thus, Shaw followed Marx up to the second antithesis, whereupon he substituted Fabian evolution for Marxian revolution as the means for achieving a classless

	MARX'S DIALECTIC	SHAW'S DIALECTIC
Thesis	Feudalism	Feudalism
Antithesis	Free trade	Free trade
Synthesis	Capitalism	Capitalism
New Thesis	Capitalism	Capitalism
Antithesis	Proletarian revolution	Social legislation effecting state ownership of rent and private property
Synthesis	Classless society	Classless society

society. At this time (1889) Shaw is committed to cautious or gradual change: "I need not enlarge on the point: the necessity for cautious and gradual change must be obvious to everyone here, and could be made obvious to everyone elsewhere if only

the catastrophists [those preaching Marxian revolution—Hyndman and the Social Democratic Federation], were courageously
and sensibly dealt with in discussion" (44). Nevertheless, in the
concluding paragraph of this essay, Shaw indicates that he still
retains respect for Marxian revolution:

> The Socialists need not be ashamed of beginning as they did by
> proposing militant organization of the working classes and
> general insurrection. The proposal proved impracticable; and
> it has now been abandoned—not without some outspoken
> regrets—by English Socialists. But it still remains as the only
> finally possible alternative to the Social Democratic program
> [Fabian evolutionary method] which I have sketched today.
> [63]

Shaw, then, even though he prefers Fabian evolution, continues
to leave Marx's revolution as a "possible alternative."

Edward R. Pease later discussed Shaw's "Fabian defection" in
The History of the Fabian Society (1916). To his statement that
"the Fabians realized from the first that no such revolution was
likely to take place, and that constant talk about it was the
worst possible way to commend Socialism to the British working
class," Pease appends the following footnote:

> On this passage Shaw has written the following criticism,
> which I have not adopted because on the whole I do not agree
> with it: "I think this is wrong because the Fabians were at
> first as bellicose as the others, and Marx had been under no
> delusion as to the commune and did not bequeath a tradition
> of its repetition. . . . We did not keep ourselves to ourselves;
> we aided the working class organizations in every possible way;
> and they were jolly glad to have us. In fact the main difference
> between us was that we worked for everybody (permeation)
> and they worked for their own societies only. The real reason
> that we segregated for purposes of thought and study was that
> the workers could not go our pace or stand our social habits." [24]

Pease pointed out another of Shaw's aberrations from the typical
Fabian position when he accused him of not possessing "that

24. Edward R. Pease, *The History of the Fabian Society* (New York:
E. P. Dutton & Co., 1916), pp. 61–62.

unquestioning faith in recognized principles which is the stock-in-trade of political leadership" and of admiring, of all the Fabian leaders, only Mrs. Annie Besant because of "her gift of splendid oratory and her long experience of agitation." [25] It is significant that Pease's account of Shaw's un-Fabian leanings was published in 1916, one year before the Russian Revolution. Most of his rejections of and compromises with Karl Marx were resolved after Lenin's successful revolution and especially after Shaw's 1931 visit to Moscow. Several manuscripts bequeathed to the British Museum in 1961 document Shaw's change of attitude after the Russian Revolution. He wrote in 1946 that after trying to rush too quickly into communism Lenin was "forced to announce a New Economic policy which was in fact Fabian, and which had a prodigious civilizing influence, besides carrying its union of socialist republics through a frightfully defensive war against all the military might of Germany and her allies." [26]

Concerning the revolutionary rather than the evolutionary method of introducing socialism into the world, Shaw is far more sympathetic toward revolution by 1936 when he praised William Morris (in a letter to his widow, Mae Morris) for doubting the efficacy of instituting socialism through parliamentary procedures (the Fabian way, which caused Morris to break from that society). He said that Morris did not live to see the Irish question "staved off by thirty years of twaddle in the House of Commons," adding:

> Had Morris lived to be 85, he would have seen a great Communist state founded in Russia (of all places) by a revolution of peasants greedy for bits of land of their own and deserter soldiers bent on peace at any price overthrowing a Liberal revolution and presently finding itself manipulated by a little group of Marxists into a union of Communist Republics.[27]

25. Ibid., p. 62. For the best study of this fascinating woman, see Arthur Nethercot's definitive biography, *The First Five Lives of Annie Besant* (Chicago: University of Chicago Press, 1960).

26. Shaw, "New Fabian Essay, 60 Years After," British Museum Add. MS 50689, fol. 12.

27. Shaw, "Morris as I Knew Him," British Museum Add. MS 50665, fol. 222.

CHAPTER FOUR

The Influence of Ibsen

Karl Marx provided Shaw with a basis for analyzing the evils of a capitalist society; from the work of Henrik Ibsen he learned that social evils could be dramatized and made personal. However, it was William Archer who got Shaw started as a dramatist by asking him to write the dialogue for the plot of a play that Archer had already constructed. Shaw took to his task with great enthusiasm and within six weeks came to Archer announcing that he had "used up all the plot." [1] Archer rejected the first act on the grounds that Shaw had ignored his plot. Undaunted, Shaw soon brought him a second act. While Shaw was reading it, Archer fell sound asleep, a reaction Shaw found so dampening that he put the manuscript away. ("Later," according to R. F. Rattray, "he discovered that it was a habit of Archer's to present the appearance of being asleep and that in fact he had not been asleep on this occasion.") [2] For the time being, Shaw's career as a playwright was checked, but all roads led him to the dramatic stage. "Socialism led him to Ibsen," Irvine remarks, "and musical criticism led him through Wagner and the opera to a renewed interest in Shakespeare, and Shakespeare apparently led him to dramatic criticism and once more to Ibsen and the new drama." [3]

Shaw's introduction to Ibsen's work came through Eleanor Marx-Aveling, who in 1888 published a volume of translations of Ibsen's plays, including *Pillars of Society* and *An Enemy of*

1. Quoted in Irvine, *The Universe of G.B.S.,* p. 156.
2. Rattray, *Bernard Shaw: A Chronicle,* pp. 50–51.
3. Irvine, *The Universe of G.B.S.,* p. 156.

the People. Earlier Shaw had been associated with her in socialist activities, and now they appeared together on the stage. Shaw is quoted as saying that "at the first performance of *A Doll's House* in England, on a first floor in a Bloomsbury lodging house, Karl Marx's daughter played Nora Helmer; and I impersonated Krogstad at her request with a very vague notion of what it was all about." [4] He had seen how abstruse economics could be put into music—it will be recalled that he had read *Das Kapital* together with the score of *Tristan and Isolde*—and now he was confronted by a work which showed that the evils of capitalistic society could be treated effectively in another art form—drama.

At this time, however, Shaw was much more interested in Ibsen's ideas than he was in Ibsen, the dramatist. He was still inflamed by Marx's castigation of a capitalist society, and here was a man who also castigated it but in terms of plots and characters rather than economic graphs and tables. In the first preface to *The Quintessence of Ibsenism* (1891), Shaw reminds the reader that the work "is not a critical essay on the poetic beauties of Ibsen, but simply an exposition of Ibsenism." [5] In fact, in its original form the year before, it was delivered as a paper to the Fabian Society analyzing the socialistic aspect of Ibsen's writings. Before he printed it, Shaw discarded a comment which shows his disdain for the pre-Marxist utopian socialists: "[Ibsen] was born in 1828, and therefore formed his political ideas whilst Socialism was still the most outrageously idealistic of the new 'isms.' " [6]

If we approach *The Quintessence* keeping in mind its original intention, we will be able to see how Shaw attempts to blend Marx's economic and historic treatment of capitalistic society with Ibsen's dramatic treatment of this same subject. Before dis-

4. Rattray, *Bernard Shaw: A Chronicle,* p. 68.

5. *The Works of Bernard Shaw,* 19:14. Further quotations from *The Quintessence of Ibsenism* and *The Sanity of Art* in this chapter are from the same volume; page numbers will be given in parentheses after the quotations when necessary.

6. "Discards from the Fabian Lectures on Ibsen and Darwin When Publishing Them as the Quintessence of Ibsenism and Methuselah Papers," British Museum Add. MS 50661, fol. 27.

cussing the plays, he spends quite a bit of time analyzing the salient ideas that underlie them. First he shows how pioneers of thought from time immemorial were persecuted just as Ibsen was being persecuted at the time that Shaw was writing the essay, and then he points out why Ibsen was a pioneer or a revolutionary. Shaw divides the history of philosophy into three eras: the Age of Faith, which preached "man's duty to God, with the priest as the assessor"; the Age of Reason, which preached "man's duty to his neighbor, with society as the assessor"; and the Age of Will, which Ibsen is preaching, and which is based on "man's duty to himself, assessed by himself" (25). And just as Voltaire, the rationalist, was a pioneer in leading man from the Age of Faith to the Age of Reason and was thus persecuted, so now Ibsen, who is leading man from the Age of Reason to the Age of Will, is a pioneer and is thus being persecuted.

The idea of duty, an important one in Ibsen's dramas, will also play a prominent role in Shaw's plays, especially in relation to women. Shaw divides the role of duty into three historical stages: Man at first develops a sense of duty to God through abstract fear: "He personifies all that he abstractly fears as God, and straightway becomes the slave of his duty to God." [7] In this stage man imposes slavery on his children and threatens them with hell-fire if they neglect their so-called duty to God as they try to be happy. Man emerges from this stage when he ceases to fear anything and dares to love something: "This duty of his to what he fears [then] evolves into a sense of duty to what he loves. . . . the God of Wrath becomes the God of Love [Christianity]." And Shaw admits that as a result of this change of allegiance from fear to love man did become "a humanitarian, an altruist, acknowledging only his duty to his neighbor." But he adds that at this point in the rationalist stage of the evolution of philosophy occurs "the capitalist phase in the evolution of industry," (26) and thus Marx's economic conception of history enters the picture.

7. See also Arthur Nethercot, "The Quintessence of Idealism," *PMLA* 62 (September 1947): 844–59.

Man, now made altruistic, unfortunately "falls under the dominion of Society, which, having just reached a phase in which all the love is ground out of it by the competitive struggle for money, remorselessly crushes him." Then, by implication, Shaw cleverly associates Marx's classless society with Ibsen's Age of Will just as he had associated capitalistic society with the Age of Reason. Capitalistic society will continue to crush man "until, in due course of the further growth of his courage, a sense at last arises in him of his duty to himself. And when this sense is fully grown, the tyranny of duty perishes; for now the man's God is his own humanity; and he, self-satisfied at last, ceases to be selfish" (26). These words almost paraphrase Marx's statement in *The Communist Manifesto:* "In place of the old bourgeois society, with its classes and class antagonisms, we shall have an association in which the free development of each is the condition for the free development of all." [8] Shaw finally arrives at one of Ibsen's salient dramatic themes: "The evangelist of this last step [man's duty to himself] must therefore preach the repudiation of duty" (26). It is only after capitalism is destroyed that man will cease to be selfish. Shaw refers to Marx's teacher, Hegel, in a footnote explaining duty and will:

> The acts which make the murderer and incendiary infamous are exactly similar to those which make the patriotic hero famous. "Original sin" is the will doing mischief. "Divine grace" is the will doing good. Our fathers, unversed in the Hegelian dialectic, could not conceive that these two, each the negation of the other, were the same. [22]

Analyzing Ibsen's treatment of ideals and idealists, Shaw begins by referring (not by name but by implication) to Marx's economic conception of history. Capitalistic society "has to force marriage and family life on the individual, because it can perpetuate itself in no other way" (28–29). In *The Communist Manifesto* Marx

8. Marx, *Capital, the Communist Manifesto, and Other Writings,* ed. Eastman, p. 343. Further quotations from Marx in this chapter are from the same edition; page numbers will be given in parentheses after the quotations when necessary.

had said,"On what foundation is the present family, the bourgeois family, based? On capital, on private gain" (339). Shaw builds upon this Marxian basis. He imagines a capitalist community of a thousand people organized to perpetuate the family. Seven hundred, the philistines, are satisfied with the family arrangement. Two hundred and ninety-nine, the idealists, find it a failure but put up with it because they are in a minority, persuading themselves that "whatever their own particular domestic arrangements may be, the family is a beautiful and holy natural institution." They proclaim the ideal of marriage in "fiction, poetry, pulpit . . . platform oratory, and serious private conversation" (30). One is unaccounted for—the realist, the man strong enough to face the truth the idealists ignore. He knows that "the alleged natural attractions and repulsions upon which the family ideal is based do not exist; and [that] it is historically false that the family was founded for the purpose of satisfying them" (31). In other words, the realist grasps the true historical reason for the founding of the family—the reason that Marx had given— "capital, private gain." The realist also knows that once the social ends which the family subserves are provided otherwise, its compulsory character can be abolished. Although Shaw does not explain *otherwise,* its meaning is implied from his previous argument. *The Communist Manifesto* declares that the abolition of capitalism "must bring with it the abolition of the community of women springing from that system, i.e., of prostitution, both public and private [the family]" (340). Shaw's discussion of ideals as masks leads him to Ibsen's contention that a woman must tear off the mask of family and repudiate this ideal if she wants to be herself. He concludes his general treatment of Ibsenism by returning to his original analysis of duty to an ideal. Shaw presents the Ibsenist doctrine:

For we now see that the pioneer must necessarily provoke such outcry as he repudiates duties, tramples on ideals, profanes what was sacred, sanctifies what was infamous, always driving his plough through gardens of pretty weeds in spite of the laws made against trespassers for the protection of the worms which feed on the roots, always letting in light and air to hasten the

putrefaction of decaying matter, and everywhere proclaiming
that "the old beauty is no longer beautiful, the new truth no
longer true." [45]

Of course the pioneer is the realist, the revolutionary—the Marx
of the mid-nineteenth century, the Ibsen of that century's end.

Having explained the salient ideas underlying Ibsen's plays,
Shaw analyzes the plays. In discussing Ibsen's *Emperor and Galilean* he uses Marx's theory of class warfare to disprove Darwin's
theory of natural selection which he accuses Ibsen of sometimes
accepting. Natural selection, the gloomiest doctrine of the nineteenth century, fortunately was "demolished philosophically by
Butler, and practically by the mere march of the working class"
(56). According to this theory, "progress can take place only
through an increase in the severity of the material conditions of
existence; and as the working classes were quite determined that
progress should consist of just the opposite, they had no difficulty in seeing that it generally does occur in that way" (56–57).
The result was the war between the working classes and the middle classes, who wished "to be convinced that the poverty of the
working classes and the hideous evils attending it were inevitable
conditions of progress, and that every penny in the pound on
the rates spent in social amelioration, and every attempt on the
part of the workers to raise their wages by Trade Unionism or
otherwise, were vain defiances of biologic and economic science."
Marx's dialectic of class warfare, of course, had given the lie to
such a concept: "How far Ibsen was definitely conscious of all
this is doubtful," Shaw writes, "but one of his most famous
utterances pointed to the working class and the women as the
great emancipators." Ibsen's theory of the growth of the will,
the theme of *Emperor and Galilean,* "made him a meliorist without reference to the operation of Natural Selection" (57).

Shaw employs Marx again in his analysis of the motives and
actions of Hedda Gabler. Hedda has no ethical ideals, only romantic ones. While she seeks to gratify her inquisitiveness about
things society has forbidden her, her teacher in the ways of the
world, Lövborg, makes advances to her which she repulses, not

because she believes them wrong, but because she fears social ostracism. But Hedda has not reckoned with the boredom caused by "a life of conformity without faith"; a scourge "unknown among revolutionists [boredom], is the curse which makes the security of respectability as dust in the balance against the unflagging interest of rebellion." (This idea is embodied in many of Shaw's later characters, and it caused his periodic flirtations with Marx's theory of proletarian revolution, which is really a "rebellion" against "conformity without faith" in capitalist society.) Boredom, Shaw continues, "forces society to eke out its harmless resources for killing time by licensing gambling, gluttony, hunting, shooting, coursing, and other vicious distractions for which even Idealism has no disguise" (92–93). Hedda lives in a capitalist society, and since she cannot afford gambling and the other vices which are available only to people who have more than enough money to keep up appearances, she relieves her boredom by dancing. Later, after she marries a man she does not love, she becomes a viciously selfish woman who destroys Lövborg, the man she did love but would not marry because he was below her social station. Suicide is the only answer to "conformity without faith." Shaw adds, "Like all people whose lives are valueless, she has no more sense of the value of Lövborg's or Tesman's or Thea's lives than a railway shareholder has of the value of a shunter's" (95).

Marx's economic conception of history and denunciation of capital as the root of all social evils are better exemplified in Shaw's analysis of *Little Eyolf*. It begins with his statement of a belief, which, it seems to me, impelled him to write plays: "Though the most mischievous ideals are social ideals which have become institutions, laws, and creeds, yet their evil must come to a personal point before they can strike down the individual" (103). Marx had already treated "the most mischievous ideals" as fully as possible in *Das Kapital*. It remained for the artist, the dramatist, to show how the evils of these social ideas "come to a personal point" and "strike down the individual." *Little Eyolf* treats a social ideal become a law—capitalist unearned income. To test the social ideal of marriage, Ibsen had to test it in a family who lived on unearned income, legalized in a capitalist society. As an artist, he could never have shown how the evil from a social ideal such as marriage comes to a personal point in a working-class home, since "to the man who works for his living in modern society home is not the place where he lives, nor his wife the woman he lives with. . . . [They] see less and know less of one another than they do of those who work side by side with them" (104–5). He here echoes Marx's statement in *The Communist Manifesto* that "in its completely developed form this family exists only among the bourgeoisie. But this state of things finds its complement in the practical absence of the family among the proletarians" (339).

Shaw analyzes the horror of the marriage dramatized in *Little Eyolf*. The husband, Allmers, a man of leisure supported by unearned income from investments of his wife's dowry, must live at home and submit to the devouring passion of that wife, Rita, who has forced him to resign as a schoolmaster and imprisons him in their house where he pretends to occupy himself by writing a book. So possessive is Rita that she is jealous not only of the book Allmers is writing but of their son, little Eyolf, because he demands much of Allmers's attention. One day when Allmers and Rita are making love, the child, completely forgotten, has a fall which cripples him for life. As the years wear on, Eyolf becomes more and more odious to his mother; she thinks of him when a Rat Wife asks if she has any "little gnawing things" she wants to get rid of. The Rat Wife's method is to bewitch the rats so that when she rows out to sea they follow her and are drowned. Her description of the rats causes Rita to have qualms of conscience and makes Allmers send her away. But little Eyolf falls under her spell and when the Rat Wife rows out to sea he follows her and is drowned.

The situation between husband and wife becomes more unbearable since Allmers's book, now discarded, and Eyolf, now dead, can no longer distract him from his hated wife. Shaw comments, "If ever two cultivated souls of the propertied middle class were stripped naked and left bankrupt, these two are. They cannot bear to live; and yet they are forced to confess that they dare not kill themselves" (108).

Shaw praises Ibsen's solution to *Little Eyolf* as a communistic one. Ibsen breaks from his "long propaganda of Individualism . . . and explicitly insists for the first time that 'we are members one of another.' " Shaw interprets Christ's statement, "Inasmuch as ye have done it unto one of the least of these my brethren ye have done it unto me" as "an explicit repudiation of the patronizing notion that 'the least of these' is *another* to whom you are invited to be very nice and kind: in short, it accepts entire identification of 'me' with 'the least of these.' " Ibsen, like John Stuart Mill, proved that "the way to Communism lies through the most uncompromising Individualism. . . . When a man is at last brought face to face with himself by a brave Individualism, he finds himself face to face, not with an individual, but with a species, and knows that to save himself, he must save the race" (109–10).

Shaw maintains that Rita becomes that type of person by caring for the wretches with whom she had forbidden little Eyolf to play: "They too are little Eyolfs. Inasmuch as she can do it unto one of the least of these his brethren she can do it unto him." He concludes that after Rita's decision, "the world and the home suddenly take on their natural aspect. Allmers offers to stay and help her. And so they are delivered from their evil dream, and, let us hope, live happily ever after" (111). Although Shaw's review of *Little Eyolf* is another example of sacrificing art to economics, the communistic interpretation of Ibsen's conclusion does indicate his frame of mind at this time.

When *The Quintessence of Ibsenism* was republished in 1913 with a new preface, it included an analysis of several of Ibsen's plays which have had not yet been produced when it was originally written. Among these was *John Gabriel Borkman*. Shaw begins his discussion of this play by distinguishing between the organizer of the business and the man who, like Borkman, has a genuine passion for precious metal. Shaw prefers the latter. Since he regards a disinterested passion for money or precious metal as more or less natural, he poses the problem of why, then, there is so much poverty in the world. His answer is a Marxist one: "Poverty is general, which would seem to indicate a general lack of [disinterested passion for wealth]; but poverty is mainly the result of organized robbery and oppression (politely called Capitalism) starving the passion for gold as it starves all the passions" (112).

In Ibsen, Shaw saw the role that an artist can play in making the world conscious of the evils of a capitalistic society. He knew that the average person would never plough through *Das Kapital,* and that even if he should he would not become aroused over the vast social evils, no matter how powerful the Marxian rhetoric: "Jones is not struck down by an ideal in the abstract, but by Smith making monstrous claims or inflicting monstrous injuries on him in the name of an ideal" (103). Shaw credited Marx with revealing to him the evil of social ideals: "He opened my eyes to the facts of history and civilization, gave me an entirely fresh conception of the universe, provided me with a purpose and a mission in life." [9] Ibsen channeled that purpose and mission in life into an art form just as had Wagner, but Ibsen's art form was more congenial to the Shavian temperament. And so, armed with Marxist facts and inspired by Ibsen's art, Shaw unearthed the drama that he had buried in 1885.

This first play, *Widowers' Houses,* completed in 1892, was written during the years the Fabians were striving to emerge as a society independent of any single influence. For this reason Shaw was perhaps at the height of his reaction against Marxist dogmatism, especially Marx's theory of proletarian revolution. We have already pointed out that Shaw, in 1889, following Hegel's theory of the perfect state, believed socialism could be adopted only through the state itself. At this time (1891) the Fabian Society was divided into two factions. One faction, the anarchists, held that profits and monopoly should be abolished; everybody should receive the fruits of his own labor; and land should be left to its occupiers. Shaw and his faction believed that human nature cannot cooperate spontaneously on large

---

9. Pearson, *G.B.S.: A Full-Length Portrait,* p. 51.

issues. Socially created value can be wisely distributed and invested only by society itself. In other words, the state must appropriate economic rent.

Shaw's earlier experience on Bloody Sunday, 1887, must have also convinced him of the impossibility of anarchism. On that day tens of thousands marched to Trafalgar Square to protest the government's policy in Ireland and to assert the right of assembly. Soon after the parade began, a handful of police dispersed the mob who retreated in confusion. A man rushed up to Shaw crying, "Shaw, give us a lead. What are we to do?" "Nothing," said Shaw. "Let every man get to the Square as best he can." [10]

In "The Impossibilities of Anarchism," which Shaw wrote in 1888 and read to the Fabian Society in 1891, he accepts Hegelian statism and champions state socialism which he calls democracy. He objects to the anarchists who would do away with the state and let the individual's conscience see to equal distribution of the land's wealth. The anarchists, basing their principles on the Marxian tenet that the natural wage of labor is its product, reach the following laissez-faire doctrine: "Enforce then only those land titles which rest on personal occupancy or cultivation; and the social problem of how to secure to each worker the product of his own labor will be solved simply by having everyone minding his own business." [11] Shaw uses the Ricardian-Jevonian theory to refute the anarchists:

> We see also that such a phrase as "the natural wage of labor is its product" is a misleading one, since labor cannot produce subsistence except when exercised upon natural materials and aided by natural forces external to man. And when it is so produced, its value in exchange depends in nowise on the share taken by labor in its production, but solely on the de-

10. Quoted in ibid., p. 22.
11. *The Works of Bernard Shaw*, 30:71. Further quotations from "The Impossibilities of Anarchism," "The Fabian Society, What It Has Done and How It Has Done It," and "Socialism Equipped with All the Culture of the Age" in this chapter are from the same volume; page numbers will be given in parentheses after the quotations when necessary.

mand for it in society. The economic problem of Socialism is
the just distribution of the premium given to certain portions
of the general product by the action of demand. As Individualist Anarchism not only fails to distribute these, but deliberately permits their private appropriation, Individualist
Anarchism is the negation of Socialism. [78–79]

Shaw's demonstration of the impossibility of trusting the individual's conscience betrays his lack of faith in the worker: "Public
opinion has been educated to regard the performance of daily
manual labor as the lot of the despised classes. . . . The man who
works nine hours a day despises the man who works sixteen.
. . . One is almost tempted in this country to declare that the
poorer the man the greater the snob" (84). Nevertheless, he takes
a wistful look at the Marxian revolutionary, whose thoughts he
describes: "Under color of protecting my person and property
you forcibly take my money to support an army of soldiers and
policemen . . . for the subjection of my person to those legal
rights of property which compel me to sell myself for a wage to
a class the maintenance of which I hold to be the greatest evil of
our time. . . . Evolution under such conditions means degeneracy:
therefore I demand the abolition of all these officious compul-
sions, and proclaim myself an Anarchist." But he is convinced
that such action "does not mend the matter in the least, nor
would it if every person were to repeat it with enthusiasm, and
the whole people to fly to arms for Anarchism" (92–93).

"The Impossibilities of Anarchism" ends by admitting all of
the evils of the existing capitalist state, yet his solution, based on
Hegel's perfect state, is the Fabian one of parliamentary reform:

> A House of Commons consisting of 660 gentlemen and 10 work-
> men will order the soldier to take money from the people for
> the landlords. A House of Commons consisting of 660 workmen
> and 10 gentlemen will probably, unless the 660 are fools, order
> the soldier to take money from the landlords for the people.
> With this hint I leave the matter, in the full conviction that
> the State, in spite of the Anarchists, will continue to be used
> against the people by the classes until it is used by the people
> against the classes with equal ability and equal resolution. [103]

Although he opposes the Marxist doctrine of abolition of the state, it must be remembered that Marx himself envisioned a time *in the future* when the state *will* wither away. He did not espouse what his followers, the anarchists, preached, the immediate abolition of the state. Shaw writes, "I do not deny the possibility of the final attainment of that degree of moralization [when a state will be unnecessary]; but I contend that the path to it lies through a transition system" (86).

A lecture delivered in 1931, however, reveals Shaw's later disillusionment with the transition system: "Parliamentary delay may cause and prolong human suffering beyond anything that could be reasonably expected from a civil war, and even the humanitarian objection to a killing match may fall to the ground." [12]

Shaw sums up the accomplishments of the Fabian Society in another brief essay, "The Fabian Society—What It Has Done and How It Has Done It," which appeared early in 1892. He believes that the society leaned too heavily on Marx and Engels in the beginning. Yet he describes tract 4, "What Socialism Is," as containing "nothing that was not already to be found better stated in the famous Communist Manifesto of Marx and Engels" (129). In still another brief note on the Fabian Society entitled "Socialism Equipped with All the Culture of the Age" (1892), he states: "By far our most important work at this period was our renewal of that historic and economic equipment of Social Democracy of which Ferdinand Lassalle boasted, and which had been getting rustier and more obsolete ever since his time and that of his contemporary Karl Marx" (146).

He then shows how the Fabians used Marx but improved upon him: they introduced the Jevonian theory of value, which "was scouted as a blasphemy against Marx, with regard to whom the Social Democratic Federation still maintains a Dogma of Finality and Infallibility which has effectually prevented it from making a single contribution to the economics of Socialism since its

---

12. Shaw, "Lectures 1917–1933: 'What indeed?'" British Museum Add. MS 50688, fol. 219.

foundation" (147). The remainder of the essay adds nothing new to the tenets found in *Essays in Fabian Socialism*.

It is not surprising that in 1892, in the midst of all these Fabian activities, Shaw should emerge as a dramatist. He had learned from Ibsen that social thinking could be dramatized, and *Widowers' Houses*, the first of the *Unpleasant Plays*, does just that. Certain Marxist elements are clearly present in its theme and in the preface. However, the preface was not written until 1898 and it will be discussed with the works of that year. This procedure will be followed for prefaces of later date than the plays when events in Shaw's life may have caused changes in his opinions and hence dichotomies between the ideas expressed in the plays and those in the later prefaces.

Widowers' Houses, like *An Unsocial Socialist*, reflects Shaw's intense interest in socialism; however, Trefusis's enthusiastic acceptance of Marxist theory is clearly tempered by Shaw's newly discovered Fabian theories. The play presents an interesting blend of these two approaches to the solution of social problems.

The opening scene is set at fashionable Remagen on the Rhine, where two Marxian drones are spending their unearned incomes. William de Burgh Cokane, the older of the two, is somewhat displeased with his friend, Dr. Harry Trench, because he does not observe the social amenities proper to his class. Cokane's thumbnail sketch of aristocratic society is mainly for the audience's benefit, and Shaw's Marxian disgust with people who live on unearned incomes is overly apparent in the ridiculous advice that Cokane gives his young friend. Cokane disapproves of the casual clothes they are wearing because they are "négligé, my dear fellow, négligé. On the steamboat a little négligé was quite en règle; but here . . . . How are they to know that you are well connected if you do not shew it by your costume?" [13] This Carlylian "clothes philosophy" comes a bit too crudely from the mouth of a sophisticate, but it is an opportunity

13. Shaw, *Complete Plays with Prefaces*, 6 vols. (New York: Dodd, Mead & Co., 1963), 4:496. Further quotations from *Widowers' Houses* in this chapter are from the same volume; page numbers will be given in parentheses after the quotations when necessary.

to dramatize Marx's "jeremiad against the bourgeoisie." [14] Cokane even chides Trench for calling him "Billy" in public. "My name," he says stiffly, "is Cokane."

Cokane is attempting to introduce Trench to a prosperous-looking young lady, Blanche Sartorius, who is traveling on the Continent with her father, and he refers to Trench's aristocratic family in a tone loud enough to be overheard by Blanche and, more particularly, her father. For their benefit Cokane remarks that Lady Roxdale, Trench's aunt, wants him to marry. And then, in case the audience has not yet realized the worthlessness and superficiality of a drone's life, he lectures Trench on the importance of ceremonials, which are really the foundation of the entire aristocratic system. Only after this "jeremiad" does Shaw allow the two drones to meet Blanche Sartorius and her father. As it happens, Trench already has met Blanche, and when they are left alone he proposes to her and kisses her. The kiss is seen by Cokane, who again lectures Trench on the social amenities, the roots of British society.

This general description of Marx's hated bourgeois class (in which category Shaw placed the British aristocracy) is followed by revelations of specific evils. In the next scene Sartorius spells out the conditions which Trench must meet if he is to marry Blanche. This scene is the play's most effective dramatic expression of a Marxian tenet (in *The Communist Manifesto*), the belief that the bourgeoisie "has reduced the family relation to a mere money relation" (324). Up to this point, the audience might wonder at Shaw's description of the play as unpleasant, for even the exposition of bourgeois decadence has been made comic. But there is nothing funny in his dramatization of a typical bourgeois marriage arrangement with all of its ugly "money relations." Sartorius informs Trench that "there shall be no difficulty about money," but hastens to say that he "must have a guarantee on my side that she will be received on equal terms by your family." Echoing the ugly bourgeois term, Trench exclaims, "Guarantee!" Sartorius, unruffled, replies: "Yes, a reasonable guarantee. I shall

14. Quoted in Henderson, *George Bernard Shaw*, p. 97.

expect you to write to your relatives explaining your intention, and adding what you think proper as to my daughter's fitness for the best society. When you can shew me a few letters from the principle members of your family, congratulating you in a fairly cordial way, I shall be satisfied. Can I say more?" (508).

Later in the scene the commercialism of the arrangement is stressed again when Cokane decides to find out more about Sartorius. After all, he tells Trench, "If you are going to get money with your wife, doesnt it concern your family to know how that money was made?" (510). The ensuing conversation between Cokane and Sartorius suggests two shrewd businessmen haggling over the price of a commodity. Sartorius actually dictates the letter that Cokane was writing to Lady Roxdale, which ends: "The young lady will inherit the bulk of her father's fortune, and will be liberally treated on her marriage. Her education has been of the most expensive and complete kind obtainable; and her surroundings have been characterized by the strictest refinement. She is in every essential particular—" (513). Here Cokane interrupts to suggests that the style is "too much in the style of a prospectus of the young lady." Sartorius grudgingly agrees but insists that he wants Trench's family to be fully aware of his daughter's "breeding." Cokane assures him that he will need only to inform them of his own respectable profession, and Sartorius confesses that he works for his living; he manages a large estate in London. Lady Roxdale is one of the chief landlords and, what is more, Trench's entire income is derived from a mortgage on the property. This disclosure prepares for the later irony of Trench's objecting to Sartorius's source of income.

Lickcheese, Sartorius's employee, is first encountered in act 2. The significance of his Jonsonian name becomes apparent from Shaw's description: "a shabby, needy man, with dirty face and linen . . . [a] pertinacious human terrier, judged by his mouth and eyes, but miserably apprehensive and servile before Sartorius" (517). Lickcheese represents Shaw's conception of the proletariat at this time. He is at the mercy of his employer, yet he wants to be like him, even though Sartorius is only a petty bourgeois. However, Lickcheese is introduced at this point primarily to give the audience a deeper insight into the manner in which the absentee landlord receives his unearned income. Lickcheese, having been charged by Sartorius for spending "one pound four" for repairs to a stairway in one of the tenements, says: "Well, Mr Sartorius, it is hard, so it is. No man alive could have screwed more out of them poor destitute devils for you than I have, or spent less in doing it. I have dirtied my hands at it until theyre not fit for clean work hardly; and now you turn me—" Sartorius "interrupting him menacingly" yells: "What do you mean by dirtying your hands? If I find that you have stepped an inch outside the letter of the law, Mr. Lickcheese, I will prosecute you myself" (519). Shaw wants to make sure that the audience realizes how all social ideals of society become laws—an extremely important Marxist doctrine.

Lickcheese's exposition breaks off with the appearance of Trench and Cokane. Trench gleefully shows Sartorius letters from Lady Roxdale and Sir Harry Trench, his godfather, approving of his marriage to Blanche. To provide contrast with Lickcheese's previous description of the tenement houses, Trench casually remarks that Sir Harry has offered his house at St. Andrews to the newlyweds: "It's the sort of house nobody can live in, you know; but it's a nice thing for him to offer. Dont you think so?" (520). Trench obviously means that the house is too spacious. But Shaw has not yet finished with the evils of absentee landlordism, so the plot must be manipulated to give Lickcheese a further hearing. Shaw certainly shows greater artistry in this maneuver than he did in *An Unsocial Socialist* when Trefusis, while being pursued by hs wife's parents, spouts a ten-page exposition of *Das Kapital*. Here he skillfully blends Lickcheese's exposition into the plot by making his revelations have a direct bearing on Trench's proposed marriage to Blanche Sartorius.

Immediately after Sartorius leaves to inform his daughter of her acceptance by Trench's family, Lickcheese approaches Trench and Cokane "humbly, but in mortal anxiety and haste," and asks them to plead with Sartorius to rehire him. Cokane persuades Trench to permit Lickcheese to state his case. The speech that follows contains two elements dominant in Shaw's mind at this time, the first Marxist, the second Fabian: an intense hatred for the capitalist system which permits the exploitation of the poor, and a conviction that the poor are unable to help themselves since they are ignorant and want to be like the capitalist who exploits them. Lickcheese paints a pitiful picture of the condition of the tenement dwellers: "Why, see here, gentlemen! Look at that bag of money on the table. Hardly a penny of that but there was a hungry child crying for the bread it would have bought. . . . And because I charged him [Sartorius] four-and-twenty shillin to mend a staircase that three women have been hurt on . . . he gives me the sack." Trench is outraged: "You took money that ought to have fed starving children! Serve you right! If I had been the father of one of those children, I'd have given you something worse than the sack. I wouldnt say a word to save your soul, if you have such a thing. Mr Sartorius was quite right" (522). But because Lickcheese himself is a proletarian, the only excuse he gives for carrying out Sartorius's orders is "the thought of my own children depending on me for giving him satisfaction." Sartorius discharged him, he tells Trench, not because he was too hard but because he was not hard enough.

Shaw also makes it clear that Sartorius is not a unique villain but merely one of many produced by the capitalist system. Lickcheese says, "I dont say he's the worst landlord in London: he couldnt be worse than some; but he's no better than the worst I ever had to do with." Again Shaw's distrust of the proletariat comes to the fore as Lickcheese brags about his ability as a collector: "Ive screwed more and spent less on his properties than anyone would believe that knows what such properties are" (523). It's the old idea of the proletariat aping the bourgeois that Shaw held at this time.

Lickcheese's revelations are now woven directly into the plot. Trench tells Blanche that he will not accept her father's money but gives her no reason; she, of course, calls off the marriage. The irony is climaxed by Sartorius's revelation to Trench: "What Lickcheese did for me, I do for you. He and I are alike intermediaries: you are the principal. It is because of the risks I run through the poverty of my tenants that you exact interest from me at the monstrous and exorbitant rate of seven per cent, forcing me to exact the uttermost farthing in my turn from the tenants" (534). Shaw at last gets to the root of the trouble—unearned income. In *The Communist Manifesto* Marx had argued, "It has been objected that upon the abolition of private property all work will cease and universal laziness will overtake us. According to this, bourgeois society ought long ago to have gone to the dogs through sheer idleness; for those of its members who work acquire nothing, and those who acquire anything *do not work*" [italics added] (338). Trench agrees with Sartorius, who says, "Every man who has a heart must wish that a better state of things was practicable. But unhappily it is not" (535). He is thus persuaded to accept his future father-in-law's money, but the strong-minded Blanche still refuses to accept him.

In act 3 Shaw's Marxian hatred for the capitalist system is again mingled with his Fabian mistrust of the proletariat who wants to be bourgeois. Lickcheese, the former proletarian, returns in the dress of the bourgeois. He has made a small fortune and proudly tells Sartorius about it. Shaw's Fabian solution to the evils of society also comes to the fore, the solution based on Hegel's idea of the state. Lickcheese had advised a slum landlord to repair his houses, after which the property was bought by the mint. The landlord made a handsome profit and in turn rewarded Lickcheese. Lickcheese knows that the city wants to build a new street through Sartorius's slum property, which would turn it into frontage worth thirty pounds a foot. All Sartorius has to do is make the property look presentable.

Sartorius sees this suggestion as a cure to all his troubles. Cokane, who has become Lickcheese's secretary, has been urging Trench to follow Lickcheese's advice. At a meeting of the four, both Cokane and Sartorius try to persuade Trench to tear down the slums, but Trench will have no part of it. Lickcheese advises Trench to get in on the deal: "You see, it's like this, Dr Trench. Theres no doubt that the Vestries has legal powers to play old Harry with slum properties, and spoil the houseknacking game

it they please. That didnt matter in the good old times, because
the Vestries used to be us ourselves. . . . Well, that cock wont
fight any longer; and, to put it short, the game is up for men in
the position of you and Mr Sartorius" (552). The Fabians will
educate the public to the ways of the vestries. Five years later
Shaw himself became a vestryman. The Lickcheeses, the proletarians, will never revolt because they want to be bourgeois, and
when they become bourgeois, they will refer to the days of
capitalist exploitation as "the good old times."

Widowers' Houses is ample evidence that in 1892 Shaw still
retained an intense hatred for the capitalist system, but has replaced Marx's faith in proletarian revolution with a strong
belief in the state as the only potential agency for reform. Shaw's
Marxian hatred of the capitalist system cannot be dismissed
lightly, however. Three-fourths of *Widowers' Houses* is devoted to
the Marx-inspired exposition of the evil born of capitalism. The
characters' weaknesses, demonstrated by their compromises, are
a result of the system, which, as Marx in *The Communist Manifesto* had said, "has drowned the most heavenly ecstasies of religious fervor, of chivalrous enthusiasm, of Philistine sentimentalism, in the icy water of egotistical calculation" and "has left no
other nexus between man and man than naked self-interest,
than callous 'cash payment' " (323). Shaw portrays the all-per-
vading evil of capitalism in the "naked self interest" of Lickcheese's and Sartorius's dealings with the poor, the "callous 'cash
payment' " spirit in Sartorius's arrangement for his daughter's
marriage. He demonstrates how Trench's "chivalrous enthusiasm" for the poor is "drowned in the icy water" of his own
egotistical calculation of the loss of his income.

It is ironic that in 1944, six years before his death, Shaw recti-
fied a personal situation like Trench's in the play. In "Mr. G. B.
Shaw's Offer to Carlow," he accused himself of being an absentee
landlord having inherited the property in Carlow from his
great-grandfather, Thomas Gurly. To wipe the slate clean, he
offered the property to the Council on Trust in Carlow with
the stipulation that it be used "for purposes which exclude its
sale to private owners, the use of its revenue to relieve the rates

directly, or for alms giving of any kind confining it to improvements, home modernization, and experimental innovations." He also insisted that "it shall not be a closed trust but the nucleus of a civic improvement fund well advertised and open to all citizens who desire to follow my example." [15] Had Dr. Trench followed Shaw's example, perhaps *Widowers' Houses* would have been classified as a pleasant play.

The Philanderer (1898), second in the volume Shaw later called the *Unpleasant Plays*, was completed in 1893. While it is a brief artistic holiday from socialism, it must not be imagined that Shaw's interest in socialism waned during 1893. Great things were happening to the Fabian Society. The "Election Manifesto of 1892" shows clearly the Fabians' new interest in the formation of a labor party. The Liberals won the election, but when the government refused to raise the wages or improve the working conditions of its employees, Webb and Shaw collaborated on an article, "To Your Tents, O Israel," which appeared in the *Fortnightly Review* (November 1, 1893). They reviewed the promises the government had made to its employees and had failed to keep. Several prominent members of the Fabians resigned from the society in protest of the article.[16] Also at this time William Morris tried to incorporate the three socialist societies—the Fabians, the Social Democratic Federation, and his own group, the Hammersmith Society—but his efforts were in vain, since Shaw and Hyndman could not agree. Morris and Hyndman saw revolution as the only way to end capitalism, and Shaw then believed in the evolutionary course. In 1930, however, Shaw wrote in his elegy to Morris: "We . . . urged [the workers] to save themselves through Parliament, the municipalities, and the franchise. Without, perhaps, quite converting Morris, we convinced him that things would probably go our way. It is not so certain today as it seemed in the eighties that Morris was not right." [17]

15. Shaw, "Mr. G. B. Shaw's Offer to Carlow," British Museum Add. MS 50699, fol. 14.

16. Irvine, *The Universe of G.B.S.*, p. 92.

17. *The Works of Bernard Shaw*, 30:319–20.

The Philanderer only indirectly reflects these socialistic endeavors. True, five years later, Shaw wrote in the preface to the first volume of *Plays: Pleasant and Unpleasant* that in *The Philanderer* he attempted to expose marriage laws "which represent to some of us a political necessity (especially for other people), to some a divine ordinance, to some a romantic ideal, to some a domestic profession for women, and to some that worst of blundering abominations, an institution which society has outgrown but not modified, and which 'advanced' individuals are therefore forced to evade." [18] The exposé is peripheral, however, for Shaw's chief concern in *The Philanderer* is to satirize those who were making Ibsenism their bible.

But Shaw could not long remain away from the subject which had preoccupied him since he had read Marx. Toward the end of his life he said that when Marx "published facts as to the condition to which Capitalism had reduced the masses, it was like lifting the lid off hell." [19] *Widowers' Houses* treated "private prostitution" in the scene in which Sartorius "sells" his daughter to the aristocracy; *Mrs. Warren's Profession* reveals capitalism as the cause and promoter of "public prostitution."

The first act opens at Mrs. Warren's cottage, where we meet her daughter, Vivie, and a visitor, Praed, an architect. From their conversation we learn that Vivie is an Ibsenist "new woman" who has repudiated her duty to society and embraced her duty to herself. Praed at first seems pleased by her unconventionality. "I am a born anarchist," he says. "I hate authority. It spoils the relation between parent and child." [20] But he soon proves

18. *Complete Plays with Prefaces,* 3:xxvii. Further quotations from this preface, the preface to *Mrs. Warren's Profession,* and the preface to the second volume of *Plays: Pleasant & Unpleasant* in this chapter are from the same volume; page numbers will be given in parentheses after the quotation when necessary.

19. Shaw, "The Webbs," Preface to Sidney and Beatrice Webb, *The Truth about Soviet Russia* (New York: Longmans, Green & Co., 1941–42; 2nd ed., 1944), p. 6.

20. *Complete Plays with Prefaces,* 3:35. Further quotations from *Mrs. Warren's Profession* in this chapter are from the same volume; page numbers will be given in parentheses after the quotation when necessary.

to be quite conventional; he becomes markedly ill at ease when he learns that Vivie knows nothing of her mother's "activities."

Also in the first act we meet Frank Gardner, the brash, emancipated young man in love with Vivie; her mother, Mrs. Warren, "decidedly vulgar, but, on the whole, a genial and fairly presentable old blackguard of a woman"; Sir George Crofts, "A gentlemanly combination of the most brutal types of city man, sporting man, and man about town" (40); and the Reverend Samuel Gardner. In the persons of Mrs. Warren, Sir George, the clergyman, and the architect, Shaw presents a cross section of capitalist society which obviously must clash with Vivie and Frank.

As in *Widowers' Houses*, a speech exposing a social evil is put in the mouth of a proletarian when Mrs. Warren reveals her past to Vivie, but the description of the causes of prostitution is far more detailed than that of the evils of tenement housing. Because Mrs. Warren is speaking from personal experience, not as a student of economics, and because her speech is woven into the action of the drama, it is also far more powerful than Trefusis's sermon in *An Unsocial Socialist*.

After the icy words of Vivie, an undaughterly new woman, finally penetrate the sentimental fat of motherhood, Mrs. Warren, "with all her affectations of maternal authority and conventional manners gone, and an overwhelming inspiration of true conviction and scorn in her" (64), spews out a loathing of capitalist society unmatched outside the pages of *The Communist Manifesto*. One of her two "respectable" half sisters, she says, "worked in a whitelead factory twelve hours a day for nine shillings a week until she died of lead poisoning. She only expected to get her hands a little paralyzed; but she died" (66). Surely such a speech has more immediate impact than Marx's observation in *The Communist Manifesto* that "the more modern industry becomes developed, the more is the labor of man superseded by that of women. Differences of age and sex have no longer any distinctive social validity for the working class. All are instruments of labor, more or less expensive to use, according to their age and sex" (329).

The other "respectable" half sister married a "Government

laborer . . . and kept his rooms and three children neat and tidy on eighteen shillings a week—until he took to drink" (66). Their parents pointed with pride to this half sister, says Mrs. Warren, thus personalizing *The Communist Manifesto's* statement that "all family ties among the proletarians are torn asunder and their children transformed into simple articles of commerce and instruments of labor" (339). Mrs. Warren then informs Vivie that her real sister, Liz, left home one night never to return. Mrs. Warren in the meantime worked as a scullery maid, a waitress, and finally became a barmaid at Waterloo Station: "fourteen hours a day serving drinks and washing glasses for four shillings a week and my board." One night her sister Liz entered the bar "in a long fur cloak, elegant and comfortable with a lot of sovereigns in her purse" (66). Liz persuaded Mrs. Warren to join her as part owner of a house of prostitution in Brussels. Mrs. Warren states that none of their girls were ever treated as she was in the scullery or at the Waterloo bar and then asks her daughter if she and Liz were foolish to trade in their good looks and get all the profits rather than permit other people to profit from their good looks by employing them as barmaids or waitresses and pay them starvation wages. Vivie agrees that Mrs. Warren and Liz were quite justified "from the business point of view," and Mrs. Warren responds: "Yes; or any other point of view. What is any respectable girl brought up to do but catch some rich man's fancy and get the benefit of his money by marrying him?—as if a marriage ceremony could make any difference in the right or wrong of the thing!" (67–68). Even the style of this outburst recalls Marx when in *The Communist Manifesto* he explodes, "The bourgeois clap-trap about the family . . . about the hallowed correlation of parent and child . . . disgusting" (339).

Mrs. Warren tells Vivie that she would rather her daughter become a prostitute than try the Waterloo bar, or marry a laborer, or even go into a factory—"How could you keep your self respect in such starvation and slavery?" (69). No, in the capitalist system prostitution is necessary for the very poor, and "If people arrange the world that way for women, theres no good pretending it's arranged the other way" (70).

Perhaps Shaw's bitterest indictment of British society comes in the scene between Vivie and Sir George Crofts. Crofts asserts that he is no worse than any other shareholder in any other business venture. His brother, the donor of the scholarship Vivie had won at Newham College, gets his 20 percent from a factory of six hundred girls who have to turn to prostitution because of the ridiculous salaries they are paid. In consequence, Sir George feels he is justified in taking 35 percent of the profits from Mrs. Warren's brothels. "When I think of the society that tolerates you, and the laws that protect you!" Vivie replies. "When I think of how helpless nine out of ten young girls would be in the hands of you and my mother! The unmentionable woman and her capitalist bully—" (85).

The prefaces written in 1898 and 1902 confirm that Shaw's chief aim in writing these two plays was to expose a corrupt society. Explaining his classification of *Widowers' Houses* as an unpleasant play, he wrote: "I have shewn middle class respectability and younger son gentility fattening on the poverty of the slum as flies fatten on filth" (xxvii). As for *Mrs. Warren's Profession*, it "was written in 1894 to draw attention to the truth that prostitution is caused, not by female depravity and male licentiousness, but simply by underpaying, undervaluing, and overworking women so shamefully that the poorest are forced to prostitution to keep body and soul together" (3). He believed that "nothing would please our sanctimonious British public more than to throw the whole guilt of Mrs Warren's profession on Mrs Warren herself. Now the whole aim of my play is to throw that guilt on the British public itself. . . . Though it is quite natural and *right* for Mrs Warren to choose what is, according to her lights, the least immoral alternative, it is none the less infamous of society to offer such alternatives" (22, 23). The Fabian solution in no way weakens the Marxist conviction which forms the dominant themes of *Widowers' Houses* and *Mrs. Warren's Profession*.

Although the *Unpleasant Plays* reveal Shaw's artistry to a far greater extent than *An Unsocial Socialist,* still, in comparison with the later plays, the Marxian theme is painfully obtrusive.

Only Shaw's messages in *Widowers' Houses* and *Mrs. Warren's Profession* are remembered now; the characters and plots are too closely akin in function to the graphs and formulas of *Das Kapital,* the speeches too similar to the rhetoric of *The Communist Manifesto.* Shaw's Marxian hatred of capitalism and his Fabian enthusiasm for parliamentary reform had to be more thoroughly digested before his themes could be subtly blended into the complex characters acting out his mature dramas.

Arms and the Man (1894) and *Candida* (1898) were both composed in 1894, the same year in which *Mrs. Warren's Profession* was written. Although the skillful blending of theme, character, and plot is already apparent, and socialism plays a less direct part, Marx is by no means forgotten. Marxist elements propel the most hilarious incidents and condition the motives of many characters who may seem far removed from obvious socialistic settings. Whether Shaw's hero is a "chocolate cream soldier" like Bluntschli in a very light comedy or "the devil's disciple" in a much more serious melodrama, he scorns to act on the basis of the social ideals which are the foundations of capitalism. Shaw clarifies this important tenet in a 1929 addendum to the preface for the first edition of *John Bull's Other Island* (called "Preface for Politicians" and written in 1906). Criticizing the Protestants of Ireland for refusing his advice to work for a single parliament ruling an undivided Ireland, he wrote: "It is a pity they did not begin their political education, as I began mine, by reading Karl Marx. It is true that I had occasion to point out that Marx was not infallible; but he left me with a very strong disposition to back the economic situation to control all the other situations, religious, nationalist, or romantic, in the long run." [21] It is the economic situation controlling "all the other situations" that Shaw's realist-heroes oppose; even the mild satire in the *Pleasant Plays* spotlights society's monetary basis.

The *Pleasant Plays,* however, are really too pleasant to be called Shavian; they are primarily Shaw's own reaction against the equally un-Shavian heavy-handed propaganda of the *Un-*

21. Ibid., 2:501–2.

pleasant Plays. Shaw is still seeking the proper dramatic medium for his serious theses, as he admits in the preface to the second volume of *Plays: Pleasant and Unpleasant*. In an obvious critical reference to *Widowers' Houses* and *Mrs. Warren's Profession,* he says that "it is easy to dramatize the prosaic conflict of Christian Socialism with vulgar Unsocialism," but that the dramatist must not be content to portray merely obvious conflicts of unmistable good with unmistakable evil. He adds, however, in characteristic fashion: "Even in my unpleasant propagandist plays I have allowed every person his or her own point of view." [22]

In *Candida,* which I will analyze first because it is the most mature of the *Pleasant Plays,* the theme is no longer propagandist but is merged artfully with the action. Although the play is primarily an Ibsenist treatment of the idealist, realist, and philistine, socialism is not forgotten. Its treatment in this play is similar to Shaw's treatment of Ibsenism in *The Philanderer.* Now, however, the target is not the Ibsen faddists but the Fabian faddists. In 1894 the Fabian Society was making itself felt in London. Members of all classes were beginning to remark on the evils of capitalism pointed out by the Fabians, and even clergymen were beginning to align socialism with Christianity. It is not surprising, then, that Shaw should foresee the danger of unqualified persons taking up socialism as a fad. His target-character is the Reverend James Mavor Morell, a very advanced clergyman whose bookshelves hold such volumes as *"Progress and Poverty, Fabian Essays, A Dream of John Ball,* Marx's *Capital,* and half a dozen other literary landmarks in Socialism." [23] Bursting with the zeal of the socialist agitator, Morell tells his curate, Lexy, "We have no more right to consume happiness without producing it, than to consume wealth without producing it" (204). He condemns Burgess, his father-in-law, and the bourgeois class with the vehemence of Karl Marx: "You paid worse wages

22. Ibid., 3:110, 111.
23. Ibid., 3:200. Further quotations from *Candida* and *Arms and the Man* in this chapter are from the same volume; page numbers will be given in parentheses after the quotation when necessary.

than any other employer—starvation wages—aye, worse than starvation wages— to the women who made the clothing. Your wages would have driven them to the streets to keep body and soul together. [*Getting angrier and angrier*] Those women were my parishioners" (209).

A thoroughgoing socialist, Morell is nonetheless a fool, an idealist fascinated by his own rhetoric, who has made the scientific tenets of socialism into ideals, just as the capitalists transformed the tenets of Adam Smith. Because he acts only with regard for socialistic ideals, never honestly as a realist without regard for ideals, he is ineffectual as a socialist preacher. He fails to convince both Burgess, who considers him an idiot, and Prossy, who is in love with him. His own wife, Candida, sums up his inability to preach socialism:

> Look at your congregation at St Dominic's! Why do they come to hear you talking about Christianity every Sunday? Why, just because theyve been so full of business and money-making for six days that they want to forget all about it and have a rest on the seventh; so that they can go back fresh and make money harder than ever! You positively help them at it instead of hindering them. [240]

The evidence suggests that Shaw was already beginning to doubt the efficacy of the Fabian evolutionary process. In a 1944 article, "Fabian Successes and Failures," he almost echoes Candida's speech to Morell when he wistfully admits, "I preached every Sunday for twelve years; and every Monday my crowded and enthusiastic audiences went back to their Capitalistic routine as if I had merely played the organ to them." [24] Moreover, socialist preachers like Morell could be harmful to the cause. Also in 1944, in a reply to the editor of the *Free Thinker,* Shaw explains that he debated with G. W. Foote, a secularist, "to wake up the National Secularist Society and make its old guard of Individualists aware that Mill's Essay on Liberty was no

24. Shaw, "Fabian Successes and Failures," British Museum Add. MS 50869, fol. 202.

longer the latest word, and that the Christian Socialist Clergyman were leaving them nowhere even as bible wreckers." [25]

Morell, the representative of "Christian Socialist Clergyman," finds his first meeting with Marchbanks a shattering experience. Although Marchbanks is young, nervous, and cowardly, he is a realist in the making; and when he penetrates Morell's rhetoric, Morell immediately becomes unsure of himself. He is given pause when Marchbanks lashes out, "You are very calm and sensible and moderate with me because you can see that I am a fool about your wife; just as no doubt that old man [Burgess] who was here just now is very wise over your Socialism, because he sees that you are a fool about it" (221). Morell becomes wrathful as Marchbanks continues to strip down his socialistic ideals: "Ive seen you do whats called rousing the meeting to enthusiasm: that is, you excited them until they behaved exactly as if they were drunk. And their wives looked on and saw what fools they were" (223). These tongue-lashings lead to the climax of the play, Morell's forcing Candida to choose between him and Marchbanks.

Morell never fully understands the aim of true socialism, the doing away of private property and the repudiation of the entire capitalistic system. Earlier, when Burgess admits that the socialist influence has to be reckoned with, he says to Morell, "You and your crew are gettin hinfluential: I can see that. Theyll ave to give you somethink someday, it it's honly to stop your mouth. You ad the right instinc arter all, James: the line you took is the payin line in the long run for a man o your sort." Morell replies, "Shake hands, Burgess. Now youre talking honestly. I dont think theyll make me a bishop; but if they do, I'll introduce you to the biggest jobbers I can get to come to my dinner parties" (213).

When the climax comes, Candida chooses Morell. She must keep him happy in his dream world: "Ask me what it costs to be James's mother and three sisters and wife and mother to his children all in one. . . . Ask the tradesmen who want to worry James and spoil his beautiful sermons who it is that puts them off. When there is money to give, he gives it: when there is money

25. Shaw, "To the Editor of the Free Thinker," British Museum Add. MS 50689, fol. 112.

to refuse, I refuse it. I build a castle of comfort and indulgence and love for him, and stand sentinel always to keep little vulgar cares out" (266–67). Marchbanks wants none of this protection of ideals; realizing that Candida for all her realism is the philistine mother-woman, he rushes out into the night with this secret in his heart. His disgust is Shaw's disgust. Socialism can never become a reality through the efforts of a Morell. It is the ruthless realist, the Marxian repudiator of all ideals, the superman, who alone can save the world from capitalism.

The theme of the play indicates, then, Shaw's early distrust of the evolutionary method of promulgating socialism, since such a method could easily include Morells, babies, and windbags who would provoke indifferent reactions similar to those of Burgess and Prossy and thus delay the overthrow of capitalism. *Candida* is an early example of what Irvine calls the tale of Shaw's "Fabian defections told positively." Shaw endorsed this description in a reply to Beverly Baxter, drama critic of the *Evening Standard*, who had said Shaw had Ellen Terry in mind when he wrote *Candida*. Replying on November 25, 1944, Shaw gives a succinct analysis of both the play and the character of the Reverend James Morell: "Candida Morell is entirely imagined, and the play is a counterblast to Ibsen's *Doll's House*, shewing that in the real typical doll's house it is the man who is the doll." [26]

Although two of the *Pleasant Plays, Arms and the Man* (1894) and *The Man of Destiny* (1898), are set in foreign lands and early times, the "business in the world" which Marx had bequeathed to Shaw is not wholly neglected. *Arms and the Man* presents evidence of the class struggle within the Petkoff household. Louka, the realist maidservant, scorns Nicola's admiration of his employers. But Nicola is not the fool she thinks he is. The stage directions describe him as a "middle-aged man of cool temperament and low but clear and keen intelligence, with the complacency of the servant who values himself on his rank in servitude, and the imperturbability of the accurate calculator who has no illusions" (145). It is really Nicola who acts as cupid after

26. Shaw, British Museum Add. MS 50699, fols. 86–87.

he discovers that Louka is in love with Major Sergius, who is not only far above her station but is supposedly betrothed to Raina Petkoff, her aristocratic mistress. Nicola tells Louka: "The way to get on as a lady is the same as the way to get on as a servant: youve got to know your place: that's the secret of it. And you may depend on me to know my place if you get promoted." At this point they are interrupted by Sergius, and to indicate to him that Louka has the makings of a lady, Nicola says, "I was only speaking to this foolish girl about her habit of running up here to the library whenever she gets a chance, to look at the books. Thats the worst of her education, sir: it gives her habits above her station" (179). (Louka had not been reading.) Later, when Raina informs her father that Louka is engaged to Nicola, Nicola adroitly explains, "I beg your pardon, sir. There is a mistake. Louka is not engaged to me. . . . She had a soul above her station; and I have been no more than her confidential servant. I intend, as you know, sir, to set up a shop later in Sofia. And I look forward to her custom and recommendation should she marry into the nobility" (190–91). In other words, though both Nicola and Lickcheese in *Widowers' Houses* ape the upper classes, Nicola is a far more complex proletarian. Bluntschli, the realist-hero, recognizes Nicola's cleverness; when Sergius asks him whether Nicola's action is the "finest heroism" or "the most crawling baseness," Bluntschli replies, "Never mind whether it's heroism or baseness. Nicola's the ablest man Ive met in Bulgaria. I'll make him manager of a hotel if he can speak French and German" (191). Lickcheese in Shaw's first play is admittedly a most despicable proletarian—a mere puppet to illustrate Shaw's Fabian distrust of the lower classes. Louka and Nicola exemplify his growing change of attitude toward proletarians and foreshadow such delightful characters as old Doolittle in *Pygmalion*.

It is Louka who brings out the realist side of Sergius's nature and who will therefore make a better man of him. She will convert him to her ways and destroy the idealism nurtured by Raina, a member of his own class. Sergius shows firmness when

Catherine, Raina's mother, tells him that he is bound by his word to marry her daughter. He replies, "Nothing binds me." Shaw's stage directions indicate Bluntschli's feelings:

> BLUNTSCHLI [*Much pleased by this piece of common sense*] Saranoff: your hand. My congratulations. These heroics of yours have their practical side after all. [*To Louka*] Gracious young lady: the best wishes of a good Republican! [192]

Bluntschli is a realist who views the society in which he lives as it is, not as it should be. The hilarious scene in which he categorizes his pieces of property and compares their worth with the Petkoff's property displays the realist's Marxian penetration into the basis of bourgeois marriage. Nicola also accepts society as he finds it and with his pseudo-humble ways will succeed. Bluntschli and Louka explode the idealism of Raina and Sergius, and hence all four are on the road to salvation. Indeed, Sergius will be a better man after marrying Louka just as Raina will be a better woman after marrying Bluntschli, for, according to Shaw, man must know himself before he can know society or do anything to reform society. Morell thought he knew society but failed as a reformer because he did not know himself. Since Marx was a realist, he could effectively repudiate the false ideals of a capitalist society. The realist, the Marxian repudiator of ideals, is the true hero of Shaw's dramas.

The same Marxist-Ibsenite philosophy underlies the playlet *The Man of Destiny*. Napoleon is great because he is a realist. "What is the secret of your power?" the Lady asks, and answers, "Only that you believe in yourself. You can fight and conquer for yourself and for nobody else. You are not afraid of your own destiny. You teach us what we all might be if we had the will and courage; and that [*suddenly sinking on her knees before him*] is why we all begin to worship you. [*She kisses his hands.*]" [27]

---

27. *Complete Plays with Prefaces*, 1:720. Further quotations from *The Man of Destiny* in this chapter are from the same volume; page numbers will be given in parentheses after the quotation when necessary.

Later Napoleon declares that he has no fear of the low or the high people in society. The low will simply make a hero or idol of him; the high are unscrupulous and really have no purpose and knowledge, but he quickly brushes aside his fear because they are "chained hand and foot by their morality and respectability." The Lady answers, "Then you will beat the English; for all shopkeepers are middle people" (742). Napoleon's response combines Marx's condemnation of the bourgeois with Ibsen's condemnation of idealism. The English race includes both these elements, but the English are idealists only after they are bourgeois. They cloak their desire for money in all sorts of ideals. They send missionaries to conquer a land whose goods they want; when the missionaries are killed by the natives, the British navy conquers them in the name of Christianity and of course takes their market of goods as their just reward. At home the English sell their children to work in factories sixteen hours a day, but they never admit that they are wrong. They do everything on principle and duty. Napoleon sees through all their pretenses; he is the realist, therefore the conqueror, therefore the hero of Shaw's play.

The last of the *Pleasant Plays, You Never Can Tell* (1898), was written, Shaw said in the preface to the second volume of *Plays: Pleasant and Unpleasant* "to comply with many requests for a play in which the much paragraphed 'brilliancy' of *Arms and The Man* should be tempered by some consideration for the requirements of managers in search of fashionable comedies for West End theatres." [28] Although the play is in theatrical fashion, with eating and drinking scenes and the duel of the sexes, Shaw begins here his indictment of the capitalist professions which have to debase their skills to cater to an affluent and class conscious public.

The opening scene shows why the chief concern of the young dentist Valentine over money forces him to obey slavishly every convention of English society. He is hungry, but he refuses a luncheon invitation from the charming Clandon twins because they do not know who their father is. His explanation, although

28. Ibid., 3:113.

humorously put, is significant, since it foreshadows future serious treatments of this theme. Twice before, says Valentine, he had set up practice as a man of medicine with conscientious principles. He told his patients the brute truth about their illnesses rather than what they wanted to hear, and was ruined as a result. Since his recognition that monetary reward is the basis of the medical profession, he has become a "five shilling" dentist and he dare not associate with those whom society frowns upon. Because the twins do not know their own father, it would be too great a risk to associate with them, for his "respectable" patients would immediately ostracize him for such unconventional behavior. The problem is solved and Valentine is able to accept the luncheon invitation when he discovers that the twins' grandfather is a canon of Lincoln cathedral. Later, when their older sister, Gloria, and Mrs. Clandon arrive, Valentine is delighted because his landlord will think business is booming.

The same theme is pursued when the waiter surprises Mr. Crampton, the "unknown" father of the three Clandons and Valentine's landlord, with the calm announcement that the waiter's son is a lawyer. (This son, Bohun, will later settle the Clandon-Crampton marriage difficulties.) The waiter, one of Shaw's realists, perceives the Marxian economic basis of most positions in capitalist society. He says that he gets on very well with his son, considering the difference in their stations; and when he analyzes that difference he again points out the pecuniary basis of all positions. Humorously he notes that though he has to wear the uniform of a waiter, his son must wear the wig of the lawyer. He even equates their positions by comparing his waiter's tips to his son's lawyer's fees and wonders therefore why his being a waiter should in any way jeopardize his son's position as a lawyer. He concludes with hilarious logic, "If it's a little against a barrister to have a waiter for his father, sir, it's a little against a waiter to have a barrister for a son." [29]

---

29. *Complete Plays with Prefaces*, 6:666. Further quotations from *You Never Can Tell* in this chapter are from the same volume; page numbers will be given in parentheses after the quotations when necessary.

The Marxist indictment of bourgeois marriage is lightly touched upon when Valentine asks Mrs. Clandon for Gloria's hand. Before she can respond, he adds quickly, "I know what youre going to say: Ive no money."

> MRS CLANDON. I care very little about money, Mr Valentine.
> VALENTINE. Then youre very different to all the other mothers who have interviewed me. [682]

These Marxist indictments are not organic in *You Never Can Tell,* since Shaw meant this play to be a fashionable comedy, but they are important to his development as a dramatist because they will appear in later plays as serious themes.

In 1895, while writing his *Pleasant Plays,* Shaw was made dramatic critic for the *Saturday Review.* He had already had much experience as a critic of other art forms: in 1885 he served briefly as art critic for the *Pall Mall Gazette,* and was music critic first for the *Star* from 1888 to 1890, and then for the *World* from 1890 to 1894. In 1895 Max Nordau, a revered music critic, was being widely discussed because of his new book, *Degeneration* (originally published as *Entartung* in German). When Benjamin Tucker asked Shaw to write a reply to Nordau for his periodical *Liberty,* a journal of philosophical anarchy published in New York, Shaw welcomed the opportunity. The essay, which appeared in *Liberty* under the title "A Degenerate's View of Nordau," [30] was published in England as *The Sanity of Art: An Exposure of the Current Nonsense About Artists Being Degenerate* (1895).

The essay mixes many Marxist elements, including revolution, with Fabian elements, especially in the discussion of Ibsenism. Shaw compares Nordau's contempt for heterodoxy in art with conventional man's contempt for heterodoxy in religion but is pleased that the cocksureness of the conservative is countered by an equal amount of cocksureness in a revolutionary such as Shelley. He states that Tucker's function as a philosophic anarchist in American society "is to combat the attempts that are constantly being made to arrest developments by using the force

30. Henderson, *George Bernard Shaw,* pp. 245–46.

of the State to suppress all departures from those habits of the majority which it pretentiously calls its morals" (314). Of course Shaw is referring to the capitalist state of America whose morals are bourgeois ones and based on the making of profits. Shaw's Fabianism appears when he discusses Shelley: "It is true that the revolutionist of twenty-five, who sees nothing for it but a clean sweep of all our institutions, finds himself, at forty [Shaw was thirty-nine at this time], accepting and even clinging to them on condition of a few reforms to bring them up to date." But the revolutionist does not wait until he is forty. He "demands the abolition of marriage, of the State, of the Church; he preaches the divinity of love and the heroism of the man who believes in himself and dares to do the thing he wills; he contemns the slavery to duty and discipline which has left so many soured old people with nothing but envious regrets for a virtuous youth." For his part Shaw "is not afraid of this doctrine" (315). Indeed, many of the revolutionary principles that Shaw lists will appear as themes for future plays. These passages again demonstrate Shaw's wavering between Marxist revolution and Fabianism.

Later, in discussing what type of people become artists, Shaw again brings in the Marxian analysis of capitalist society: "It is also true that under our existing industrial system machinery in industrial processes is regarded solely as a means of extracting a larger product from the unremitted toil of the actual wage-worker. And I do not think any person who is in touch with the artistic professions will deny that they are recruited largely by persons who become actors, or painters, or journalists and authors because they are incapable of steady work and regular habits" (328). The artist, then, dissatisfied with the regular workaday world will see through its structure, will become "intolerant of baseness, cruelty, injustice, and intellectual superficiality or vulgarity." As late as 1947, three years before his death, Shaw held fast to these principles for artists. In an article entitled "Art Workers and the State," he prescribed the treatment of the artist in a socialistic state "with the Marxian class war between proletarians and proprietors abolished." Such a state must make every provision for the art workers "who want to work until they drop." They must have a "holiday tour of at least six weeks and retire at forty having paid scot and lot for their education, subsistence, and pension, into a private life of leisure and experiment." [31] But at the time he wrote *The Sanity of Art* the class war had not as yet occurred in Russia, and the realist-artists of Shaw's next plays, who would see through the false idealism of capitalist society, were to become tragic heroes.

Climaxing his condemnation of Nordau, Shaw states that "though on one page he is pointing out that Socialism and all other forms of discontent with the existing social order are 'stigmata of degeneration,' on the next he is talking pure Karl Marx." Shaw condemns Nordau with Nordau's own words, listing the Marxist tenets which Nordau professes to believe in:

> Is it not the duty of intelligent philanthropy and justice, without destroying civilization, to adopt a better system of economy and transform the artisan from a factory convict, condemned to misery and ill-health, into a free producer of wealth, who enjoys the fruits of his labor himself, and works no more than is compatible with his health and his claims on life?
>
> Every gift that a man receives from some other man without work, without reciprocal service, is an alms, and as such is deeply immoral. [342]

Shaw argues that despite these Marxist convictions Nordau classes Ibsen and Wagner as degenerate—the world is too good for them—but if Max Nordau is dissatisfied, it is because Nordau is too good for the world. Nordau's followers could not and did not refute Shaw's refutation of the great nineteenth-century critic. Thus once again, as in *The Quintessence of Ibsenism* and the *Plays: Pleasant and Unpleasant,* Shaw combines Marxist-Fabian elements with the creed of the artist, who really must be the Ibsenist realist repudiating the social ideals of capitalism by making them personal so that they will "strike down the individual."

31. Shaw, "Art Workers and the State," British Museum Add. MS 50699, fol. 161.

CHAPTER FIVE

The Appearance of the Realist as Hero

Three years after the completion of *The Sanity of Art,* Shaw once again turned to the subject of the true artist in his essay *The Perfect Wagnerite* (1898). He had been interested in music since his childhood, but it was Chichester Bell, a nonpracticing physician from whom he learned Italian, physics, and pathology, who brought Wagner's work to his attention. Because he respected Bell's opinions, Shaw bought a vocal score of *Lohengrin* and, as Henderson puts it, "became, and ever afterwards remained, the 'Perfect Wagnerite.' "[1] Since he was perusing Wagner's scores while first reading *Das Kapital,* it is no wonder that he should analyze the doctrines of Marx and Wagner while he was analyzing the doctrines of Marx and Ibsen.

The Quintessence of Ibsenism concentrated on Ibsen's ideas rather than his art; similarly *The Perfect Wagnerite* imparts only "the ideas [of Wagner] which are most likely to be lacking in the conventional Englishman's equipment."[2] These ideas are the convictions of another realist, who, like Ibsen, made personal the evils of a capitalist society's ideals through the medium of his art. Shaw says that he came by Wagner's ideas "much as Wagner did, having learnt more about music than anything else in my

1. Henderson, *George Bernard Shaw,* pp. 34–35.
2. *The Works of Bernard Shaw,* 19:177 (from the preface to the first edition 1898). Further quotations from *The Perfect Wagnerite* in this chapter are from the same volume; page numbers will be given in parentheses after the quotation when necessary.

youth, and sown my political wild oats subsequently in the revolutionary school. This combination is not common in England, and as I seem, so far, to be the only publicly articulate result of it, I venture to add my commentary to what has already been written by musicians who are no revolutionists, and revolutionists who are no musicians" (177). The commentary, then, is *Das Kapital* tempered by Shaw's Fabianism and set to the tune of Wagner's cycle *The Ring of the Nibelungs*.

Shaw interprets the gold, guarded by the Rhine maidens, of the prologue to *The Ring*, as the world in all its beauty not yet tainted by the greed of commercialism. In Wagner's music drama the gold possesses a magic quality: he who gains the gold and fashions it into a ring may rule the world. Alberic, a dwarf "too stupid to see that his own welfare can only be compassed as part of the welfare of the world," steals the gold. Shaw adds, "Such dwarfs are quite common in London" (184). Alberic is Marx's capitalist, and his story is the personalized musical version of Marx's economic interpretation of history. Alberic with his newly attained power quickly begins organizing a capitalistic society: "For his gain, hordes of his fellow creatures are thenceforth condemned to slave miserably, overground and underground, lashed to their work by the invisible whip of starvation." Shaw then explains the Wagnerian symbolism in terms of contemporary society:

> They never see him [Alberic], any more than the victims of our "dangerous trades" ever see the shareholders whose power is nevertheless everywhere, driving them to destruction. The very wealth they create with their labor becomes an additional force to impoverish them; for as fast as they make it it slips from their hands into the hands of their master, and makes him mightier than ever. You can see the process for yourself in every civilized country today, where millions of people toil in want and disease to heap up more wealth for our Alberics, laying up nothing for themselves, except sometimes horrible and agonizing disease and the certainty of premature death. [185]

Having established Wagner as a Marxist, Shaw discusses the role of the true poet in contrast to the poet whom Marx described in *The Communist Manifesto* as "the paid wage laborer of the bourgeoisie" [3]: "It is only the poet, with his vision of what life might be, to whom these things are unendurable. If we were a race of poets we would make an end to them before the end of this miserable century" (185). The poet-dramatist should create characters who are such poets, realists who will teach the "moral dwarfs," comprising modern audiences, Marx's economic doctrines through plots more palatable than the technical graphs and formulas of *Das Kapital*, for "if there were no higher power in the world to work against Alberic, the end of it would be utter destruction" (185–86).

The third scene of Wagner's *The Rhinegold*, the first music drama of the cycle, takes place in Alberic's mine where slaves are piling up wealth for him under the invisible whip. Shaw explains that "this gloomy place need not be a mine: it might just as well be a match-factory, with yellow phosphorous, phossy jaw, a large dividend, and plenty of clergymen shareholders" (191). The invisible whip is veiled by the magic helmet that Mime, Alberic's brother, makes for him. This helmet "is a very common article in our streets, where it generally takes the form of a tall hat. It makes a man invisible as a shareholder, and changes him into various shapes, such as a pious Christian, a subscriber to hospitals, a benefactor of the poor, a model husband and father, a shrewd, practical, independent Englishman . . . consuming a great deal, and producing nothing" (192).

Shaw describes the Wagnerian hero, Siegfried, as a revolutionist: "a totally immoral person, a born anarchist, the ideal of Bakoonin, an anticipation of the 'overman' of Nietzsche" (212). But this is not really a criticism of Siegfried as some scholars suggest. It seems to me that Siegfried, like John Bunyan's Christian and Shaw's Dick Dudgeon, is an individualist. And in his analysis of *Little Eyolf*, Shaw had said that socialism can be achieved only through individualism.

3. Marx, *Capital, the Communist Manifesto, and Other Writings*, ed. Eastman, p. 324.

Shaw opposes Siegfried's anarchism and says that it must be replaced by a society based on the creed of the realist, echoing his views on individualism presented in *The Quintessence of Ibsenism*. Marx's synthesis, too, is a classless society and not an anarchistic one. He had written in *The Communist Manifesto:* "In place of the old bourgeois society, with its classes and class antagonisms, we shall have an association in which the free development of each is the condition for the free development of all." [4] The panacea for both Marx and Shaw is *ordered* socialism. Shaw admits that anarchism is "an inevitable condition of progressive evolution," but it must be replaced by something else. "Even the modified form of anarchy on which modern civilization is based; that is, the abandonment of industry, in the name of individual liberty to the upshot of competition for personal gain between private capitalists, is a disastrous failure, and is, by the mere necessities of the case, giving way to ordered Socialism" (235). Shaw's views of Marxism in action after his 1931 visit to Moscow indicate, as we shall see, that he firmly believed both Lenin and Stalin had finally achieved this ordered socialism.

Siegfried, the revolutionary and realist-hero, repudiates Alberic, the capitalist, and captures the magic ring, but Shaw criticizes Wagner's revolutionary measures. He regards Siegfried's destructive means of redeeming the world as the product of Wagner's inexperience in technical government: "Wagner, like Marx, was too . . . melodramatic in his hero-contra-villain conception of the class struggle, to foresee the actual process by which his generalization would work out, or the part to be played in it by the classes involved" (253). The process was, of course, the Fabian one. In following such a process, Shaw points out, Siegfried must first learn Alberic's trade because even if the proletarians all over the world united and obeyed "the call of Marx" to reduce capital to common property, they would have to become positive administrators of this property or starve in anarchy the day after the revolution (255)—Marx to the tune of Wagner but definitely tempered by Shaw's Fabianism.

4. Ibid., p. 343.

In *Caesar and Cleopatra,* completed in the same year (1898) as *The Perfect Wagnerite,* Shaw again champions the true artist, but this time through a dramatic character, the artist Apollodorus. Although Apollodorus is not fully developed, he embodies the artistic principles Shaw first promulgated in *The Sanity of Art.* He is an embryonic realist who must repudiate the social ideals of a greedy society. In a clash between him and a centurion who will not permit Cleopatra to go to Caesar's fortress, the centurion says, "I do my duty. That is enough for me." Apollodorus turns and remarks to Cleopatra, "Majesty: when a stupid man is doing something he is ashamed of, he always declares that it is his duty." [5]

But the artist-realist is not Shaw's principal concern in this drama; rather it is the Marxist economic interpretation of history. Using a historical setting to teach a contemporary audience a lesson in true heroism, he again applies Marx's indictment of nineteenth-century capitalism to a civilization chiefly concerned with making money, as he did in his analysis of Alberic in *The Perfect Wagnerite.* The ancient god Ra, in the 1912 prologue (the alternative prologue was written in 1898 at the same time as the play), clarifies this theme when he describes the growth of Rome, observing that "even as there is an old England and a new, and ye stand perplexed between the twain; so . . . was there an old Rome and a new" (357). Both old England and old Rome grew and prospered "through robbery of the poor and slaughter of the weak" (358), first in their own land and then in other lands, which they annexed to their empires. Julius Caesar, the realist-hero, knew that Roman laws and ideals were set up to make the robbery of the poor "appear seemly and honest." Ra recalls that when Pompey said, "The law is above all; and if thou break it thou shalt die"; Caesar answered, " 'I will break it: Kill me who can.' And he broke it. . . . And the gods laughed and approved" (359).

5. Shaw, *Complete Plays with Prefaces,* 3:418. Further quotations from *Caesar and Cleopatra* and the notes to the play in this chapter are from the same volume; page numbers will be given in parentheses after the quotations when necessary.

Caesar's creed is founded on the recognition that the economic situation controls all other situations, and *Caesar and Cleopatra* is a dramatic catechism in which he teaches his creed of realism to the child-queen Cleopatra. When she asks him if it was because of his love for her father that he sent Mark Anthony to help him, Caesar replies honestly that he gave his assistance merely for money. And because her father never worked and Caesar always worked, he demanded sixteen thousand talents to help him regain his throne. Caesar points out that the common people had to work long and hard for their emperor so that he could repay this debt, part of which is still due—an obvious portrayal of the Marxian exploiter.

When the tutor Theodotus laments that the library of Alexandria is burning and, finding Caesar unmoved, kneels before him saying, "Caesar: once in ten generations of men, the world gains an immortal book," Caesar replies inflexibly, "If it did not flatter mankind, the common executioner would burn it"—another reference to the Marxian belief that the poet is a paid wage laborer for the bourgeoisie. And when Theodotus asks, "Will you destroy the past?" Caesar's reply again echoes Marxist doctrine: "Ay, and build the future with its ruins" (407). Why, Shaw is asking, should a man want to preserve the records of a false society when he is willing to kill a human being out of greed for wealth—the personal attainment of wealth being one of the ideals of that society.

Caesar's catechism has a profound effect on the child-queen. "Now that Caesar has made me wise," she says to his enemy Pothinus, "it is no use my liking or disliking: I do what must be done, and have no time to attend to myself. That is not happiness; but it is greatness. If Caesar were gone, I think I could govern the Egyptians; for what Caesar is to me, I am to the fools around me" (438). But Cleopatra relapses into savagery and she has her nurse Ftatateeta kill Pothinus; in turn, Rufio, Caesar's rough-and-ready captain, kills the nurse. His explanation to Caesar illustrates Shaw's Marxian contention concerning the idealistic laws of capitalist society.

RUFIO. Why, Cleopatra had a tigress that killed men at her bidding. I thought she might bid it kill you some day. Well, had I not been Caesar's pupil, what pious things might I not have done to that tigress! I might have punished it. I might have revenged Pothinus on it. . . .

CAESAR [*energetically*] On my head be it, then; for it was well done. Rufio: had you set yourself in the seat of the judge, and with hateful ceremonies and appeals to the gods handed that woman over to some hired executioner to be slain before the people in the name of justice, never again would I have touched your hand without a shudder. But this was natural slaying: I feel no horror at it. [468]

Caesar does not propose taking the law into one's own hands. He commended Rufio for not putting himself "in the seat of the judge." Again Shaw is condemning the idealist who, having cloaked his real motives in false ideals, will exploit the poor, kill them off in factories, and then justify his actions by these same ideals.

Discussing progress since Caesar's time in the notes to the play, Shaw writes: "The descendants of feudal barons, living in squalid lodgings on a salary of fifteen shillings a week instead of in castles on princely revenues, do not congratulate the world on the change. . . . If manufacturing activity means Progress, the town must be more advanced than the country; . . . Yet the cockney proletarian is so inferior to the village laborer that it is only by steady recruiting from the country that London is kept alive" (473–74). He asks the Englishman whether he considers himself inferior to the American as a human being "because the scarcity of labor in America . . . led to a development of machinery there, and a consequent 'increase of command over Nature.'" And he wonders "whether, since a modern negro has a greater 'command over Nature' than Washington had, we are also to accept the conclusion . . . that humanity has progressed from Washington to the *fin de siècle* negro." Finally, he points out that "if life is crowned by its success and devotion in industrial organization and ingenuity, we had better worship the ant and the bee (as moralists urge us to do in our childhood), and humble ourselves before the arrogance of the birds of Aristophanes" (474–75).

Continuing with a discussion of national character, Shaw asks: "Does anyone who, in the light of a competent knowledge of his own age, has studied history from contemporary documents, believe that 67 generations of promiscuous marriage have made any appreciable difference in the human fauna of these isles? Certainly I do not" (477). Plainly Shaw intended *Caesar and Cleopatra,* set in ancient Rome, as a play for realists who see through the pecuniary basis of any society steeped in greed.

Shaw was to return to the Marxian tenet that the economic organization of the society controls its other facets six years later in *John Bull's Other Island* (completed in 1904). In this play, for the first time as a dramatist, Shaw faces the relationship between the land of his birth and the land of his adoption.

The characters, besides falling into the usual realist-idealist-philistine categories, also take on national traits. Broadbent, the idealist-capitalist, also represents the stupidity of England in her dealing with the Irish question. Larry Doyle is the Anglicized Irishman who, although he has sloughed off Irish sentimentalism to become a realist in some respects, remains primarily an idealist who sees capitalistic enterprise as the solution to Ireland's problems. Keegan, the former priest, retains some of the sentimentalism of his native Ireland, but is chiefly a realist who recognizes that capitalism is the true source of the English-Irish problem. Keegan, however, is ineffectual because he has not sloughed off enough of his Irish sentimentalism and idealism.

Although Marx's economic interpretation of history is organic to the plot and characterization of the play, Shaw's Fabian distrust of the proletariat is quite apparent throughout. During the debate over making Ireland independent, Larry Doyle lashes out at old Matt Haffigan, a representative of Irish proletarians: "I'll tell you, Matt. I always thought it was a stupid, lazy, good-for-nothing sort of thing to leave the land in the hands of the old landlords without calling them to a strict account for the use they made of it, and the condition of the people on it. . . . But I tell you plump and plain, Matt, that if anybody thinks things will be any better now that the land is handed over to a lot of little men like you, without calling you to account either, theyre mistaken." [6] In other words, if they gained control the proletariat would be as ruthless as the bourgeois class. Perhaps the proletariat must be led and checked—a theme Shaw will develop in his next play *Major Barbara* (see pp. 95 ff.).

Marx's indictment of capitalism is expounded by Keegan, who condemns a capitalistic society "as a place where the hardest toil is a welcome refuge from the horror and tedium of pleasure, and where charity and good works are done only for hire to ransom the souls of the spoiler and the sybarite . . . . Therefore, it is plain to me that this earth of ours must be hell" (585). Keegan carries this theme to its conclusion when he proves that capitalism, with its industries and efficiency, is the ruin of every nation.

Later Larry Doyle and his English friend, Broadbent, discuss the manner in which they hope to industrialize Ireland. They will take the poor soil from the Matt Haffigans and build an efficient and profitable factory on the barren rocks. Keegan asks the men what they will do with poor Haffigan. Broadbent, the English idealist, optimistically predicts that Haffigan will fare well, "He had better go to America, or into the Union, poor old chap! He's worked out, you know: you can see it." Larry Doyle, the ruthless capitalist, says much more honestly, "Haffigan doesn't matter much. He'll die presently" (604). When the shocked Broadbent tells Larry not to be unfeeling, Larry gives a realistic account of the workings of capitalism, actually a synopsis of *Das Kapital* and *The Communist Manifesto*:

> Well, our syndicate has no conscience: it has no more regard for your Haffigans and Doolans, and Dorans than it has for a gang of Chinese coolies. It will use your patriotic blatherskite and balderdash to get parliamentary powers over you as cynically as it would bait a mousetrap with toasted cheese. It will plan, and organize, and find capital while you slave like bees

6. *Complete Plays with Prefaces,* 2:560. Further quotations from *John Bull's Other Island* and its "Preface for Politicians" (1912) in this chapter are from the same volume; page numbers will be given in parentheses after the quotation when necessary.

for it and revenge yourselves by paying politicians and penny newspapers out of your small wages to write articles and report speeches against its wickedness and tyranny, and to crack up your own Irish heroism, just as Haffigan once paid a witch a penny to put a spell on Billy Byrne's cow. In the end it will grind strength and sense into you. [605]

Here, indeed, Larry Doyle is the ruthless realist who sees capitalism as it is, but his last sentence reveals the idealist who has made capitalism the rule of life. To refute the last sentence, Shaw calls upon a truer repudiator of capitalistic ideals, Keegan, who admits the efficiency of the capitalistic system but shows that its "grinding" of mankind weakens rather than strengthens him. He outlines for them how "efficiently" they will make use of Irish bullies to slave-drive their laborers in making money for them and how "efficiently" English and American shareholders will spend this money in shooting and hunting, gambling and gluttony. And then he states significantly, "For four wicked centuries the world has dreamed this foolish dream of efficiency; and the end is not yet. But the end will come" (608).

This speech of Keegan's and Larry Doyle's which occasioned it convert Marx's scientific terminology, technical graphs, and formulas into economic language that the average man can understand. Shaw is still, as enthusiastically as ever, "making personal the most mischievous of all evils, the social evils." It is no wonder, then, that in the preface to *John Bull's Other Island* Shaw rebukes the Irish statesmen for not having begun their political training by reading Karl Marx. But Shaw weaves the Irish question into a world picture. Capitalism is the root of all evil. When Broadbent replies that Keegan reminds him of Ruskin and Shelley, Keegan compares England to Ireland: "Mr. Broadbent spends his life inefficiently admiring the thoughts of great men, and efficiently serving the cupidity of base money hunters. We spend our lives efficiently sneering at him and doing nothing. Which of us has any right to reproach the other?" (608–9). To Broadbent's suggestion that the hotel he and Doyle will build will bring money from England to Ireland, Keegan replies that capitalism is to blame for the ruin of both England and Ireland: "Just as our idlers have for so many generations taken money from Ireland to England. Has that saved England from poverty and degradation more horrible than we have ever dreamed of?" (609). When Larry Doyle cynically implies that Keegan is a visionary like all Irishman, and when Broadbent asks Keegan what his version of heaven is, the former priest describes a Marxist heaven attained through a process of creative evolution, "where the state is the Church and the Church the people: three in one and one in three. It is a commonwealth in which work is play and play is life: three in one and one in three. It is a temple in which the priest is a worshipper and the worshipper the worshipped: three in one and one in three. It is a godhead in which all life is human and all humanity divine: three in one and one in three. It is, in short, the dream of a madman" (611). Keegan's last sentence reveals a cynicism that Shaw does not display one year later (1905) at the end of *Major Barbara*.

Keegan, not yet the true realist-hero, has absolutely no effect on Broadbent or Larry Doyle. Broadbent calls Keegan a "regular old Church and State Tory . . . he'll be an attraction here. Really almost equal to Ruskin and Carlyle." Doyle's reply reiterates Shaw's growing pessimism concerning the socialization of England: "Yes; and much good they did with their talk!" Broadbent proves Doyle's and Shaw's point in the final lines of the play: "Oh tut, tut, Larry! They improved my mind: they raised my tone enormously. I feel sincerely obliged to Keegan: he has made me feel a better man: distinctly better. [*With sincere elevation*] I feel now as I never did before that I am right in devoting my life to the cause of Ireland."

John Bull's Other Island demonstrates that it will take more than "talk" to penetrate the skulls of Broadbents; it will take the bullets of a munitions maker (an idea developed in *Major Barbara*) to lead human beings from what Marx and Keegan called "four wicked centuries"—centuries during which the world "has dreamed this foolish dream of efficiency."

CHAPTER SIX

Shaw's Indictment of Capitalism

Not content with generalized attacks on the capitalist system in such works as *Caesar and Cleopatra* and *John Bull's Other Island*, Shaw proceeded over a period of thirty-seven years to systematically depict in his plays "capitalist society in dissolution." In the 1930 foreword to *An Unsocial Socialist*, he said retrospectively:

> This, the last of the Novels Of My Nonage, is, according to my original design, only the first chapter of a vast work depicting capitalist society in dissolution, with its downfall as the final chapter. I found I had emptied my sack and left myself no more to say for the moment, and had better defer completion until my education was considerably more advanced. Thirtyseven years having now been devoted to this process it is too late to resume the interrupted work; for events have outrun me. The contemplated fiction is now fact. My unsocial socialist has come to life as a Bolshevist; and my catastrophe has actually occurred in Communist Russia. The opinions of the fictitious Trefusis anticipated those of the real Lenin.[1]

It is my contention that Shaw actually carried out his "original design" by indicting, one by one, the foundation stones of capitalism which Marx had pointed out in *The Communist Manifesto:*

1. *The Works of Bernard Shaw,* 5:vii.

> The bourgeoisie has stripped of its halo every occupation hitherto honored and looked up to with reverent awe. It has converted the physican, the lawyer, the priest, . . . into its paid wage laborers.
>
> The bourgeoisie has torn away from the family its sentimental veil, and has reduced the family relation to a mere money relation.[2]

Finally, he depicted the complete destruction of the entire edifice of capitalism in *Heartbreak House* (completed in 1916).

Shaw first deals with Marx's priest in *The Devil's Disciple*, completed in 1897, published in 1898, and included in *Three Plays for Puritans* in 1901. The new term *puritan,* although used in praise of John Bunyan, one of Shaw's few great heroes, must be viewed in the same light as the term *idealist.* We have seen in *The Quintessence of Ibsenism* and *Plays: Pleasant and Unpleasant* that Shaw's idealists are not what the world conceives idealists to be; similarly, his puritans are the exact opposite of what it expects puritans to be. While Mrs. Dudgeon is a puritan in the ordinary sense of the term—professing a rigorous moral code—her son Dick Dudgeon, who calls himself the Devil's Disciple, is a true puritan—a realist who knows that the bourgeoisie has converted the priest into its paid wage laborer. He sees that her religion, and her motives are based on false ideals rather than on the goodness of her nature. Mrs. Dudgeon, in fact, is one of the most despicable of all Shaw's idealists and would be considered overdrawn if *The Devil's Disciple* were not labeled a melodrama.

The time of the play is 1777; the place, New Hampshire. At the curtain rise Mrs. Dudgeon is huddled in the kitchen of her farmhouse, keeping a sleepy early morning watch, as she awaits news of the fighting between the American colonists and the British. With her is Essie, the bastard daughter of her brother-in-law Peter Dudgeon, who has been hanged as a rebel by the British. A victim of what Shaw later called Crosstianity, Mrs.

2. Marx, *Capital, the Communist Manifesto, and Other Writings,* ed. Eastman, p. 324.

Dudgeon has accepted his death as exemplifying religion which must of its very nature be unpleasant. Christy, her youngest son, enters bearing the news that his father has died of illness contracted while going to see his brother Peter hanged. Christy is closely followed by the minister Mr. Anderson, who informs Mrs. Dudgeon that just before his death her husband, Timothy, made a new will in favor of their elder son, Richard. With this news the real basis of Mrs. Dudgeon's religion is revealed. She feels that her husband has robbed her. "He had nothing of his own." she rages. "His money was the money I brought him as my marriage portion. It was for me to deal with my own money and my own son. He dare not have done it if I had been with him; and well he knew it." [3] When Mr. Anderson suggests that in her heart she is more disappointed at the will than grieved at her husband's death, she scorns him for using the word *heart*. Her heart belonged to her husband's brother Peter, but she did her duty and followed the advice of Anderson's predecessor who "warned me and strengthened me against my heart, and made me marry a Godfearing man—as he thought." She asks, "What else but that discipline has made me the woman I am?" (p. 261–62).

The scene in which the will is read develops the theme more fully because Dick is present, enabling Shaw to contrast the religion of the idealist with that of the realist. The senior uncle of the family, William, tells the much abused Essie that "we are willing to be kind to you if you are a good girl and deserve it. We are all equal before the Throne." The stage direction accompanying this magnanimous statement reads: "This republican sentiment does not please the women, who are convinced that the Throne is precisely the place where their superiority, often questioned in this world, will be recognized and rewarded" (285). The reading of the will proceeds, and when it is learned that Christy, the stupid younger son, is left fifty pounds on condition that he marry Sarah Wilkins "if she will have him," Dick asks, "How if she wont have him?" The philistine Christy

3. Shaw, *Complete Plays with Prefaces*, 3:278. Further quotations from *The Devil's Disciple* in this chapter are from the same volume; page numbers will be given in parentheses after the quotation when necessary.

answers, "She will if I have fifty pounds" (289). But the Marxian theme is most fully developed when Mrs. Dudgeon discovers that Dick has been bequeathed the homestead and she has been left only the interest on her own money. "And this is my reward!" she explains bitterly. "You know what I think, Mr Anderson: you know the word I gave to it" (290). The monetary basis of her faith having been exposed, Shaw now lets the realist talk. Recognizing the falsity of conventional religion, Dick has found truth in the opposite, the diabolistic creed. But his devil is not the real devil who appears later in *Man and Superman;* he is the Rousseauistic personification of truth based on the goodness of man's nature, or the heart, as Mrs. Dudgeon has called it. Dick's melodramatic sermon repudiates the false ideals and religions of the capitalist system. He speaks in terms that would shock even a contemporary audience unaware of the thesis behind it:

> I knew from the first that the Devil was my natural master and captain and friend. I saw that he was in the right, and that the world cringed to his conqueror only through fear. I prayed secretly to him; and he comforted me, and saved me from having my spirit broken in this house of children's tears. I promised him my soul, and swore an oath that I would stand up for him in this world and stand by him in the next. [*Solemnly*] That promise and that oath made a man of me. From this day this house is his home; and no child shall cry in it: this hearth is his altar; and no soul shall ever cower over it in the dark evenings and be afraid. [293–94]

To bring home Shaw's thesis it only remains for the Devil's Disciple to do good purely from natural human motives just as Mrs. Dudgeon did evil out of false idealistic motives. His good act occurs later in the play when the British soldiers come to arrest Mr. Anderson and take him to be hanged as an example to the rebellious colonists. Finding Dick at the Andersons' house, the soldiers mistake him for the minister and Dick allows himself to be led away.

Mr. Anderson is the embryonic realist of the play. In the beginning he clings to the ideals of conventional society which has made him its paid wage laborer. But as the action progresses he begins to perceive the cruelty of Mrs. Dudgeon and consequently the falsity of her creed, although he cannot yet condemn her conventional motives. Later the strength of his character matches even that of the Devil's Disciple. When Dick (before his arrest) comes to receive a message from the minister and is offered tea, he says cynically: "The magic of property, Pastor! Are even you civil to me now that I have succeeded to my father's estate?" (301). The minister's unruffled reply—"I think, sir, that since you have accepted my hospitality, you cannot have so bad an opinion of it"—puts Dick in his place. He looks at Anderson half quarrelsomely; "then, with a nod, acknowledges that the minister has got the better of him."

Judith, Anderson's pretty young wife, loses her respect for her husband when she suspects that he has run away leaving Dick to die on the gallows in his place. She, along with the audience, believes that Dick's natural goodness has conquered her husband's conventional creed. But when Anderson returns as the captain who defeated the British and rescues Dick from the gallows at the last moment, the audience knows that he, like the Devil's Disciple, has acted on good, natural motives, that both are realists, and that Dick Dudgeon can and will replace Anderson in the pulpit while the minister achieves his destiny as a militia captain. In other words, only when religion is divorced from ideals grounded in the commercial idea of reward will it produce truly religious persons; only when ministers and priests conduct themselves like Anderson and Dick Dudgeon will the Marxian stigma that they are paid wage laborers of the bourgeoisie be removed.

Major Barbara, completed in 1905, ten years after *The Devil's Disciple,* is also a play about conventional religion with its monetary basis, but its complex plot and characters demonstrate Shaw's remarkable growth as a playwright within this decade. In fact, its central theme—a multimillionaire who "buys" his daughter's religion to disillusion her and win her over to his own strange creed—has puzzled many critics and has often been misunderstood.

A superficial reading could suggest that Shaw has completely abandoned Marxism and even Fabianism in favor of capitalism since the play's hero Andrew Undershaft is a multimillionaire. In speaking to Stephen, his son, who in true idealist fashion, upbraids his father for sneering at the British government, Undershaft vehemently informs him that he and his partner, Lazarus, *are* the government of his country; that when they want a war the government will go to war; that when certain trade measures are needed to keep the dividends of his corporation up, the government will quickly see to it that these measures are made available; that when other people want to keep his dividends down the government will call out the police and military. He concludes viciously, "And in return you shall have the support and applause of my newspapers, and the delight in imagining that you are a great statesman. Government of your country!" [4]

And yet in the preface Shaw practically quotes verbatim Karl Marx's contention that "the bourgeoisie has left no other nexus between man and man than naked self interest"; when speaking of social reformers he says, "They even demand abstract conditions: justice, honor, a noble moral atmosphere, a mystic nexus to replace the cash nexus" (310).

Near the end of the play, Cusins, the professor of Greek, in explaining why he will become Undershaft's successor, echoes Marx: "I love the common people. I want to warn them against the lawyers, the doctors, the priests, the literary men, the professors, the artists, and the politicians who, once in authority, are more disastrous and tyrannical than all the fools, rascals, and impostors" (442). Only a closer look at the character of Andrew Undershaft will provide the solution to these paradoxical elements.

Like Dick Dudgeon, Andrew Undershaft is a diabolic realist but Shaw's strongest realist to date. Undershaft's recognition of the pecuniary basis of society is proved both by his lengthy

---

4. *Complete Plays with Prefaces,* 1:416. Further quotations from *Major Barbara* and its preface in this chapter are from the same volume; page numbers will be given in parentheses after the quotation when necessary.

speeches and by his "buying" of the Salvation Army. That Andrew Undershaft is a capitalist does not, however, mean Shaw is compromising with capitalism. In *The Devil's Disciple* Shaw created irony by inverting the meaning of the word *puritan;* in *Major Barbara* he perpetrates a far subtler irony by making his capitalist a munitions manufacturer. Undershaft tells Cusins that he is waging "war on war." Since war is an evil of capitalism but an evil that may eventually end capitalism, Andrew Undershaft, the capitalist, ironically, chose to manufacture the means for waging war because he was a realist. He invites Cusins, "Come and make explosives with me. Whatever can blow men up can blow society up. The history of the world is the history of those who had courage enough to embrace this truth" (436). Later he adds, "Dare you make war on war? Here are the means" (440). To fail to see this irony and insist that Shaw is compromising with capitalism is to misinterpret the entire play. Indeed, if Undershaft were simply a capitalist hero, why didn't Shaw make him a wheat tycoon or a wool magnate—why a munitions maker?

But Undershaft does more than this. Having proved that religion can be bought, he arms the proletariat with a new religion —a William Morris Labor Church. So long as the poor receive tea and treacle and are told that their reward will be above, they will never have the strength nor the will to fight against the well-fed bourgeoisie. But if they are well fed, strong, and educated like the workers in the Undershaft factory, they may someday realize the William Morris motto which is written "in mosaic letters ten feet high round the dome, "NO MAN IS GOOD ENOUGH TO BE ANOTHER MAN'S MASTER." I say "some day" because Undershaft is cynical of their strength at this time. He says, "It shocked the men at first, I am afraid. But now they take no more notice of it than of the ten commandments in church" (425–26).

Barbara enthusiastically explains her conversion from Salvation Armyism to the religion of her father:

My father shall never throw it in my teeth again that my converts were bribed with bread. [*She is transfigured*]. I have got rid of the bribe of bread. I have got rid of the bribe of heaven. Let God's work be done for its own sake: the work he had to create us to do because it cannot be done except by living men and women. When I die, let him be in my debt, not I in his; and let me forgive him as becomes a woman of my rank. [444–45]

But this play does more than merely dramatize Marx's priest as a paid wage laborer for the bourgeoisie. Its religious theme embraces other Marxist precepts. First of all, Undershaft is a foundling as were all the owners of his munitions works. Cusins can take his place only after Shaw concocts a melodramatic surprise: Cusins announces that he too is a foundling because his parents were married in Australia and England does not recognize a marriage in that country. It is, however, Barbara who explains to Cusins the real significance of the foundling tradition by proudly accepting her position as the daughter of a foundling: "That is why I have no class, Dolly: I come straight out of the heart of the whole people. If I were middle-class I should turn my back on my father's business; . . . Sooner than that, I would sweep out the guncotton shed, or be one of Bodger's barmaids" (444). She is, of course, championing a Marxist classless society of workers.

Even Marxian revolution is hinted at in this play. Shaw's growing disgust for the Fabian method which we already noted (see p. 70) in *Candida* is much more apparent here, in both the preface and the play itself. The preface descries the futile attempts of nineteenth-century socialists to educate the masses. Shaw writes in the tone of almost complete dejection: "I, who have preached and pamphleteered like any Encyclopedist, have to confess that my methods are no use, and would be no use if I were Voltaire, Rousseau, Bentham, Marx, Mill, Dickens, Carlyle, Ruskin, Butler, and Morris all rolled into one, with Euripides, More, Montaigne, Molière, Beaumarchais, Swift, Goethe, Ibsen, Tolstoy, Jesus and the prophets all thrown in (as indeed in some sort I actually am, standing as I do on all their shoulders)" (318–19). He calls himself and his fellow Fabians "paper apostles" who give the people only false security while they submit to oppression, and he links these paper apostles to Marx's bourgeois priests who make "a merit of such submission." His dejection, however, does not last long. There is hope in a superman (he had completed *Man and Superman* two years before [see chapter 7] and now there is hope in a strong class of workers. Shaw talks of a Salvation Army bearing "a flag with Blood and Fire on it . . . unfurled, not in murderous rancor, but because fire is beautiful and blood a vital and splendid red." After describing the nature of the new Salvation Army, he concludes, "There is danger in such activity; and where there is danger there is hope" (319–20).

In the play itself Andrew Undershaft is the general leading such an army. His flag is "blood and fire"; his followers are his well-fed workers. Unlike the Fabians, he recognizes the futility of fighting poverty with pamphlets and articles. He tells Barbara, "Poverty and slavery have stood up for centuries to your sermons and leading articles: they will not stand up to my machine guns. Dont preach at them: dont reason with them. Kill them" (435–36). A little later Undershaft again repudiates parliamentary reform when he says to Cusins, "Vote! Bah! When you vote, you only change the names of the cabinet. When you shoot, you pull down governments, inaugurate new epochs, abolish old orders and set up new. Is that historically true, Mr Learned Man, or is it not?" (436). Cusins asks, "Then the way of life lies through the factory of death?", and Barbara, now converted to Undershaft's religion, answers, "Yes, through the raising of hell to heaven and of man to God, through the unveiling of an eternal light in the Valley of the Shadow" (445).

In *The Devil's Disciple* Shaw was content to write a simple melodrama condemning bourgeois religion. Ten years later his maturing powers as a dramatist permitted him to use the same religious theme as a basis for his most complete expression of Marxism to date.

Androcles and the Lion, completed seven years after *Major Barbara* in 1912, is a deceptively simple little play, and were it not for Shaw's lengthy preface and postscript, it could prove to be even more puzzling than *Major Barbara*. Shaw himself veri-

fied the need for caution with *Androcles* in a note that he insisted
be inserted in the program for the 1915 New York production:
"The author . . . received one of the worst shocks of his life when
an American editor published its text under the heading, A
Comedy. It is not a comedy: it is precisely what the author
calls it, a Fable Play: that is, an entertainment for children on an
old story from the children's books, which nevertheless contains
matter for the most mature wisdom to ponder." [5]

In the preface Shaw stresses the communistic doctrines of
Christ and then shows how the churches professing to follow
him do not follow his teachings at all but add their power to
the ten percent who rule the capitalistic world. He puts words
into Christ's mouth that could have come out of *Das Kapital* and
The Communist Manifesto. Using the theory of religion as the
"opium of the people," Shaw writes that the well-fed bourgeoisie
"know, very sensibly, that a little religion is good for children
and serves morality, keeping the poor in goodhumor or in awe
by promising rewards in heaven or threatening torments in
hell." [6] He then claims that Christianity became a class religion:
"no longer ago than Shakespear's time it was thought quite
natural that litigants should give presents to human judges;
and the buying off of divine wrath by actual money payment
to priests, or, in the reformed churches which discountenance
this, by subscriptions to charities and church building and the
like, is still in full swing" (332).

Shaw even relates Marx's theory of revolution[7] to the teachings
of Christ: "The moment it strikes you (as it may any day) that
Christ is not the lifeless harmless image he has hitherto been
to you, but a rallying centre for revolutionary influences which

5. Quoted in Archibald Henderson, *George Bernard Shaw: Man of
the Century* (New York: Appleton-Century-Crofts, 1956), p. 594.

6. *Complete Plays with Prefaces,* 5:330–31. Further quotations from
Androcles and the Lion, its preface and postscript, in this chapter are
from the same volume; page numbers will be given in parentheses after
the quotation when necessary.

7. Marx, *Capital, the Communist Manifesto, and Other Writings,*
p. 339.

all established States and Churches fight, you must look to your-selves; for you have brought the image to life; and the mob may not be able to bear that horror" (369).

The play proper twists the condemnation of modern Christi-anity into paradoxes not too unlike those in *The Devil's Disciple* and *Major Barbara*. Early Christianity, the victim of persecution in this play, will, in a few centuries, become itself the handmaid of the persecutor because its priests will align themselves with the medieval robber barons and later the capitalist tycoons. Just as a Cauchon and an Earl of Warwick will crush a Saint Joan because she threatened their wealth and power, so today the bourgeoisie and its priests will crush anyone who threatens their power. Shaw writes in the postscript to *Androcles*, "In this play I have presented one of the Roman persecutions of the early Christians, not as the conflict of a false theology with a true, but as what all such persecutions essentially are: an attempt to sup-press a propaganda that seemed to threaten the interests involved in the established law and order, organized and maintained in the name of religion and justice by politicians who are pure opportunist Have-and-Holders" (471).

Christianity's inherent proneness to future alliance with cap-italism is apparent in the attitudes of some of the early Christians in the play. The despicable Spintho personifies the Christian who will act only to receive a reward; this is his sole reason for craving martyrdom. The strong but stupid Ferrovius, obsessed with Christ's doctrine of meekness—a doctrine that Shaw rejects or claims that the followers of Christ misinterpreted—returns to the service of the god Mars when his test of martyrdom comes. Lavinia, the realist, is the only truly religious person because, unlike Ferrovius, she never acts contrary to her nature; and unlike Spintho, she is willing to die selflessly without thought of reward. At the end of the play, therefore, Lavinia alone transcends Christianity to Undershaft's and Shaw's religion of the future; she does not align herself with a religion that is to become eventually a slave to a corrupt society. Lavinia chooses to "strive for the coming of the God who is not yet" (470).

The play's chief character Androcles is filled with a Christian doctrine that Shaw admired immensely, love for the "least of my brethren" even animals. But Androcles, too, has confused notions about his religion. He is the typical proletarian who rushes to martyrdom for the "faith of a Christian and the honor of a tailor" and tells Caesar to see how a "tailor can die" (466–67). Lacking Lavinia's realism, he needs an Undershaft to give him strength. Only when this poor yet basically good little tailor is given strength—when he dances in with the lion—will society bow to him. The emperor says, "I give this sorcerer to be a slave to the first man who lays hands on him. [*The menagerie keepers and the gladiators rush for Androcles. The lion starts up and faces them. They surge back.*]" The emperor then comments sarcastically, "You see how magnanimous we Romans are, Androcles. We suffer you to go in peace." And the play ends with Androcles's significant speech, "I thank your worship. I thank you all, ladies and gentlemen. Come, Tommy. Whilst we stand together, no cage for you: no slavery for me" (471). Arthur Nethercot sums up quite precisely the similarity between the themes of *Major Barbara* and *Androcles:*

> As Major Barbara is finally convinced by her father that physi-cal power and material well-being must come first before the religious mysticism of both of them can have any value, so the hilarious arm-in-arm waltz of Androcles with Tommy, the lion, through the Coliseum just before the curtain goes down implies that the proper combination for the future is, first, the strength and force of the lion, plus, second, the love and understanding of the Christian slave.[8]

In other words, Shaw, like Marx, believed that religion and every other "spiritual" activity can flourish only on sound eco-nomic soil. A few years later Lenin, in "The Three Sources and Three Constituent Parts of Marxism," interpreted the Marxian dialectic in these words, "Just exactly as a man's knowledge re-flects a nature existing independently of him—matter, that is, in

8. Arthur Nethercot, "The Schizophrenia of George Bernard Shaw," *American Scholar* 21 (October 1952) : 455–57.

a state of development—so also the social understanding of man (that is his various views and teachings, philosophical, religious, political, etc.) reflects the economic structure of society." [9]

Shaw's indictment of conventional religion is essentially the same wherever he finds it—the Puritanism of eighteenth-century America, the Salvation Army of twentieth-century England, or the beginning of Christianity in Roman times. But after the Russian Revolution his treatment of this theme takes on a more hopeful tone in perhaps his most powerful play, *Saint Joan* (completed in 1923).

Marx's dialectic prevails even more specifically in *Saint Joan* than in the other plays concerned with religion. According to Marx the bourgeois class had its origin in medieval times; it sprang from, or became, to use his Hegelian term, the synthesis of feudal landed aristocracy and the merchant class. In *Saint Joan* Shaw centers his attention on the landed artistocracy (Marx's thesis), and in comparing Joan to an earlier realist, Socrates, he says in the preface (written in 1924) that Socrates's accuser, "if born 2300 years later, might have been picked out of any first class carriage on a suburban railway . . . for he had really nothing to say except that he and his like could not endure being shewn up as idiots every time Socrates opened his mouth." [10] Later in speaking of Joan's chief accuser, Cauchon, bishop of Beauvais, Shaw says, "Although there is, as far as I have been able to discover, nothing against Cauchon that convicts him of bad faith or exceptional severity in his judicial relations with Joan, or of as much anti-prisoner, pro-police, class and sectarian bias as we now take for granted in our own courts, yet there is hardly more warrant for classing him as a great Catholic churchman, completely proof against the passions roused by the temporal situation" (313). Joan, the realist, like Socrates

9. From Lenin's essay in Marx, *Capital, the Communist Manifesto, and Other Writings*, p. xxiii.

10. *Complete Plays with Prefaces*, 2:266. Further quotations from *Saint Joan* and its preface in this chapter are from the same volume; page numbers will be given in parentheses after the quotation when necessary.

and others geniuses to Shaw's own day, is simply a victim of the ruling class.

In the play itself the close partnership between the Catholic church and the landed aristocracy is revealed, but Shaw gives the church a fair hearing. Cauchon is repelled by Warwick when the great English lord says,

> Well, my lord, hand over your dead branch; and I will see that the fire is ready for it. If you will answer for the Church's part, I will answer for the secular part.
> CAUCHON [*with smouldering anger*] I can answer for nothing. You great lords are too prone to treat The Church as a mere political convenience. [363]

Joan, the peasant girl, because she is a realist, recognizes the basic quest for power of both the church and the landed aristocracy. When the archbishop and King Charles and even her friend Dunois refuse to permit her to relieve the garrison in Compiègne, she shouts, "I will go out now to the common people, and let the love in their eyes comfort me for the hate in yours. You will all be glad to see me burnt; but if I go through the fire I shall go through it to their hearts for ever and ever. And so, God be with me!" (382). Later on Joan's accusation proves true: King Charles, the archbishop, and even Dunois refuse to rescue her from the stake built by English aristocrats; because she threatened the power of both church and state, she had to die. In the epilogue Shaw makes it quite clear that if she were to return in contemporary times, she would be burnt by the descendents of these ruling classes.

Although the play ends tragically with Joan's burning, and the epilogue ends pessimistically with her outcry for a world "ready to receive" God's saints, still her audiences always know that she *is* a canonized saint; they are aware that this dynamic woman did in a way triumph over man, that she is a powerful example of her sex—the sex that, according to Shaw's new religion of Creative Evolution, will give birth to a superman, Shaw's hoped for savior. (Creative Evolution first expounded in *Man and Super-*

man [1903] and developed in *Back to Methuselah* [1921] is discussed in chapter 7.)

Shaw's indictment of conventional religion included a denuciation of its link with the law or state in *Saint Joan,* but the first play in which he attacked the law in Marxist terms was *Captain Brassbound's Conversion,* completed almost twenty-five years earlier in 1899. The central theme of this play is the law's ability through its unjustness to transform a previously good man into a vicious one obsessed by revenge. The setting is contemporary Morocco, rather than England. But it is English law which Shaw denounces.

The central character is again a realist, Lady Cicely Waynflete, who, like Dick Dudgeon, recognizes the truth about her society's monetary basis. Her actions are quite vital and unconventional, Marxian sentiments permeate her words, and it is she who eventually initiates Captain Brassbound's conversion from the false ideal of revenge by repudiating it. Her brother-in-law, Sir Howard Hallam, representing the law of English society, is the idealist who blindly accepts the basic economic tenets of capitalism. The clergy is represented favorably in this play by a missionary, the Reverend Leslie Rankin, a simple sturdy Scotchman, who can say that the natives "come to me for medicine when they are ill; and they call me the Christian who is not a thief." [11]

The Marxian economic interpretation of history is an integral factor in the development of the plot. Miles Hallam, Sir Howard's brother, has obtained, from his common-law wife by underhanded means, an estate in the West Indies which he left under the management of his agent. This agent in turn appropriated the estate for himself. Sir Howard's account of how the theft was accomplished and how he retrieved the estate is comparable to Trefusis's exposition of the maneuvers of his capitalist grand-

11. *Complete Plays with Prefaces,* 1:604. Further quotations from *Captain Brassbound's Conversion* in this chapter are from the same volume; page numbers will be given in parentheses after the quotation when necessary.

fathers. The agent was able to take over the property because the law "consisted practically of the Attorney General and the Solicitor General; and these gentlemen were both retained by the agent. Consequently there was no solicitor in the island to take up the case against him." When Lady Cicely asks why a solicitor was not sent from London, Sir Howard replies that no one would take such a case unless he was paid "enough to compensate him for giving up his London practice." His explanation of how he recovered the estate equates the agent's robbery with legalized capitalist acquisition of private property. On a trip to the West Indies, Sir Howard discovered that the "dishonest agent had left the island, and placed the estate in the hands of an agent of his own, who he was foolish enough to pay very badly. I put the case before that agent; and he decided to treat the estate as my property. . . . Nobody in the island would act against me, least of all the Attorney and Solicitor General, who appreciated my influence at the Colonial Office. And so I got the estate back" (615). Thus we have a Marxian indictment of capitalism, a system in which robbery, protected by the laws of the land, plays the principal role.

Lady Cicely has no illusions concerning capitalist theft and the laws that uphold thieves. After Sir Howard's explanation, she ironically observes, "Now I suppose if I'd done such a clever thing in England, youd have sent me to prison." Sir Howard agrees, "Probably, unless you had taken care to keep outside the law of conspiracy. Whenever you wish to do anything against the law, Cicely, always consult a good solicitor first" (615).

Although Shaw is not yet the accomplished dramatist of *Major Barbara* and *Saint Joan,* his growth as an artist is revealed in this play. In *An Unsocial Socialist* Trefusis's Marxist discourse had no organic connection to the plot; in *Captain Brassbound's Conversion* Miles Hallam's property is central to the plot's development.

Having established the Marxian economic basis, Shaw personalizes the evils of social ideals. Lady Cicely, reluctantly accompanied by Sir Howard, is determined to visit the mountains in the interior of Morocco. A renegade trader, Captain Brass-bound, and his men are hired as escorts. His true identity—the son of Miles and his common-law wife—is, of course, unknown. Brassbound is an extremely powerful character, animated solely by the desire to avenge his mother's ill treatment. This desire for revenge is the principle motivation in the melodramatic action.

In contrast the cowardly Cockney, Drinkwater, one of his men, reflects the helplessness of the proletariat. Shaw's Fabian distrust of the proletariat who ape the bourgeoisie, absent in such plays as *Major Barbara, Androcles and the Lion,* and *Saint Joan,* appears in Drinkwater, "a man who is clearly no barbarian, being in fact a less agreeable product peculiar to modern commercial civilization. . . . A Londoner would recognize him at once as an extreme but hardy specimen of the abortion produced by nurture in the city slum" (601, 602).

When Lady Cicely suggests that she herself take charge of the escort, dispensing with Captain Brassbound, Drinkwater is terrified: "Yer cawnt hexpect a lot o poor honeddikited men lawk huz to ran ahrseolvs into dineger withaht naow Kepn to teoll us wot to do." Lady Cicely asks: "Do you like to be treated as he [Brassbound] treats you?" and Drinkwater's reply is that of the dominated proletarian resigned to exploitation: "Weoll, lidy: y'cawnt deenaw that e's a Paffick Genlmn. Bit hawbitrairy, preps; but hin a genlmn you looks for sich" (623).

Shaw's contention that there are class distinctions within the proletariat is humorously demonstrated in the second act when Johnson, another of Brassbound's brigands, pulls rank on Drinkwater. Drinkwater, says Johnson, "aint nobody's son: he's only a offspring o coster folk or such."

DRINKWATER [*bursting into tears*] Clawss feelin! thets wot it is; clawss feelin! Wot are yer, arter all, bat a bloomin gang o wust cowst cazhls (*casual ward paupers*)? [*Johnson is scandalized; and there is a generous thrill of indignation*]. Better ev naow fembly, an rawse aht of it, lawk me, than ev a specble one and disgrice it, lawk you. [630]

The Marxian interpretation of history looms most prominently in the action when we learn that Brassbound plans to turn Sir Howard and Lady Cicely over to Sheikh Sidi el Assif, who will pay a large bounty for the two Christians. At this point, Brassbound reveals to Sir Howard that he is Miles Hallam's son. Throughout the scene Marx's indictment of the legal profession is woven into the dialogue. Brassbound has said that he will do no more than justice, and Sir Howard exclaims, "Justice! I think you mean vengeance, disguised as justice by your passions." But Brassbound disputes this: "To many and many a poor wretch in the dock you have brought vengeance in that disguise—the vengeance of society, disguised as justice by *its* passions. Now the justice you have outraged meets you disguised as vengeance. How do you like it?" (640). Then he charges Sir Howard with refusing to secure redress for his mother, having her imprisoned, and ultimately driven from the island. She died; "you recovered the estate easily enough then, robber and rascal that you are." Lady Cicely asks, "Couldnt you have helped her, Howard?" and Sir Howard's response again emphasizes the pecuniary basis of the legal profession: "No. This man may be ignorant enough to suppose that when I was a struggling barrister I could do everything I did when I was Attorney General. You know better. There is some excuse for his mother. She was an uneducated Brazilian, knowing nothing of English society, and driven mad by injustice" (641). (Shaw's irony need not be dwelt upon.)

Sir Howard then asks Brassbound if the Sheikh Sidi el Assif, who will judge his actions, knows the power of England, and Brassbound replies contemptuously: "Who are you, that a nation should go to war for you? . . . You had better find a goldfield in the Atlas Mountains. Then all the governments of Europe will rush to your rescue. Until then, take care of yourself; for you are going to see at last the hypocrisy in the sanctimonious speech of the judge who is sentencing you, instead of the despair in the white face of the wretch you are recommending to the mercy of your God" (642). It remains for Lady Cicely to sum up Shaw's Marxian convictions. "Your uncle Howard," she tells Brassbound, "is one of the most harmless of men—much nicer than most professional people. Of course he does dreadful things as a judge; but if you take a man and pay him £5,000 a year to be wicked, and praise him for it, and have policemen and courts and laws and juries to drive him into it so that he cant help doing it, what can you expect?" (646).

The rest of the play mainly concerns Captain Brassbound's conversion from his ideal of vegeance to a realistic and thus, in Shavian terms, a healthy outlook on life. After Sir Howard and Lady Cicely are saved through the threat of action by sailors from an American cruiser, Brassbound is put on trial. Lady Cicely cleverly maneuvers his defense and his final exoneration. Before the trial she tells the Reverend Rankin, a boyhood friend of Miles, that the whole thing is a mistake: "Captain Brassbound is just like you: he thinks we have no right to judge one another; and as Sir Howard gets £5,000 a year for doing nothing else but judging people, he thinks poor Captain Brassbound a regular Anarchist. . . . You mustnt mind what Sir Howard says about him: you really mustnt" (660). Knowing the importance of clothes in a capitalistic society, she persuades Brassbound to come to the trial dressed as a gentleman, complete with a "glossy tall hat." Shaw comments in the stage directions, "To an unsophisticated eye, the change is monstrous and appalling; and its effect on himself is so unmanning that he is quite out of countenance—a shaven Samson" (670). After the trial, when Brassbound rips off the hat and invites all hands to jump on it, the proletarian respect for the gentleman appears in Drinkwater's reaction: "Naow, look eah, kepn: that ynt rawt. Dror a lawn somewhere" (679).

In the final scene, after Brassbound disposes of the last remnant of his ideal of vengeance by tearing up his mother's photograph, he complains that Lady Cicely has taken the old meaning out of his life, but has put no new meaning into it. What is he to do, he asks, where is he to go? "It's quite simple," Lady Cicely says, "Do whatever you like" (684). But that answer does not satisfy Brassbound who wants something to do, and has nothing.

He finally confesses that he needs a leader; left to himself he has become half a brigand: "I want to take service under you. And theres no way in which that can be done except marrying you. Will you let me do it?" Lady Cicely is terror stricken, "as she finds that he is unconsciously mesmerizing her." The sound of gunfire from Brassbound's ship, *Thanksgiving*, releases her from the trance, and he reacts to the call: "It is farewell. Rescue for you—safety, freedom! . . . You can do no more for me now: I have blundered somehow on the secret of command at last [*he kisses her hands*]: thanks for that, and for a man's power and purpose restored and righted" (686–87). Although at the end of the play Lady Cicely shows her philistine, mother-woman qualities, her ability to recognize the truth about the law enables her to save a man who would have spent the rest of his life attempting futilely to hide behind an ideal of vengeance against the admitted cruelty of bourgeois laws.

In his Notes to *Captain Brassbound's Conversion* Shaw states that his plot was based on a historical fact but that the character of Captain Brassbound's mother and the recovery of the estate by the next heir was his own interpolation. "It is not, however, an invention." He quickly adds, "One of the evils of the pretence that our institutions represent abstract principles of justice instead of being mere social scaffolding is that persons of certain temperament take the pretence seriously, and, when the law is on the side of injustice, will not accept the situation, and are driven mad by their vain struggle against it" (690).

Shaw's strange antipathy toward doctors has always been a puzzle to his admirers. How could a man so ahead of his age in other fields be inimical to the advancement of medical science? Shaw was not antiscientific, nor was he opposed to the medical profession as such, but to those doctors who, like priests and lawyers, catered to the bourgeois establishment with its monetary rewards. As we have seen, he had already treated this theme lightly in one of the "pleasant plays," *You Never Can Tell*. In that early play Valentine was forced by society to leave the medical profession because he "acted conscientiously" and told his patients "the brute truth instead of what they wanted to be told." The result was "ruin" and so he became "a five shilling dentist." [12] In his first tragedy, *The Doctor's Dilemma* (written in 1906 ten years after *You Never Can Tell*), Shaw presents a full indictment of one of the most respected professions of capitalist society as a rascally but realistic artist who is not a servant of the establishment is pitted against doctors who are.

The "Preface on Doctors" (published in 1911 with the play) clearly states Shaw's case. He begins by accusing capitalism of forcing physicians to become its paid wage laborers:

> That any sane nation, having observed that you could provide for the supply of bread by giving bakers a pecuniary interest in baking for you, should go on to give a surgeon a pecuniary interest in cutting off your leg, is enough to make one despair of political humanity. But that is precisely what we have done. And the more appalling the mutilation, the more the mutilator is paid. He who corrects the ingrowing toe-nail receives a few shillings: he who cuts your inside out receives hundreds of guineas, except when he does it to a poor person for practice.[13]

He admits that the doctors are helpless; most of the time their prescriptions to the poor should be "not medicine, but more leisure, better clothes, better food, and better drained and ventilated houses" (63). Thus the solution to the problems of both doctors and patients is socialism: "Until the medical profession becomes a body of men trained and paid by the country to keep the country in health it will remain what it is at present: a conspiracy to exploit popular credulity and human suffering" (67). Shaw did not change his mind about doctors through the years that followed. In the issues of the *English Review*, from December, 1917, to March, 1918 (collected in *Doctors' Delusions*, 1932),

12. Ibid., 6:622.

13. *Complete Plays with Prefaces,* 1:1. Further quotations from *The Doctor's Dilemma* and its preface in this chapter are from the same volume; page numbers will be given in parentheses after the quotation when necessary.

he said: "This leads us again, as almost every medical difficulty leads us, to the necessity for a disinterested medical service: that is, a State Medical Service continually subjected to the test of vital statistics." [14]

In the Preface to *Saint Joan* (1924) he, like Marx, draws a parallel between religion and medical science: "Today, when the doctor has succeeded to the priest, and can do practically what he likes with parliament and the press through the blind faith in him which has succeeded to the far more critical faith in the parson, legal compulsion to take the doctor's prescription, however poisonous, is carried to an extent that would have horrified the Inquisition and staggered Archbishop Laud." [15] Finally, in a 1930 postscript to the "Preface on Doctors" he says that "the need for bringing the medical profession under responsible and effective public control has become constantly more pressing as the inevitable collisions between the march of discovery in therapuetic science and the reactionary obsolescence of the General Medical Council have become more frequent and sensational" (79).

The theme, as presented in the preface, underlies the plot of *The Doctor's Dilemma,* but the play does not sacrifice art for economics. It is more than a mere indictment of the medical profession; its action and characters become almost symbolic of the whole capitalistic system, similiar to the earlier *John Bull's Other Island,* and Louis Dubedat, its hero is one of Shaw's most interesting artists.

The doctors—Ridgeon, Sir Patrick, and Walpole—all are paid wage laborers of the capitalistic system. They exhibit all of the principles of bourgeois morality, and are dutifully shocked at the prospect of Jennifer's living with Dubedat without a marriage license. Dubedat, like Dick Dudgeon in *The Devil's Disciple,* reveals their hypocrisy in contrast to his own realistic religion:

> Now I'm only an immoral artist; but if youd told me that Jennifer wasnt married, I'd have had the gentlemanly feeling

14. *The Works of Bernard Shaw,* 22:42.
15. *Complete Plays with Prefaces,* 2:301.

and artistic instinct to say that she carried her marriage cer-
tificate in her face and in her character. But you are all moral
men; and Jennifer is only an artist's wife—probably a model;
and morality consists in suspecting other people of not being
legally married. Arnt you ashamed of yourselves? Can one of
you look me in the face after it? (144)

Louis Dubedat is the true realist-artist who recognizes the
pecuniary basis of the medical profession. When Walpole decides that Louis's nuciform sac needs to be removed, Louis asks
how much Walpole will pay to be permitted to operate on him.
After Walpole registers his complete amazement, Dubedat asks,
"Well, you don't expect me to let you cut me up for nothing,
do you?" Walpole then asks whether Louis will paint his portrait
for nothing, and Louis replies, "No; but I'll give you the portrait when it's painted; and you can sell it afterwards for perhaps double the money. But I cant sell my nuciform sac when
youve cut it out" (151).

When the doctors, representatives of capitalism, have to decide
whether or not the tubercular Louis is to be saved for the world,
Ridgeon, the only competent one among them, pronounces his
death sentence by telling Jennifer, with whom Ridgeon is in love,
that the only man who can save Louis is Sir Ralph Bloomfield
Bonington. Ridgeon, of course, knows that Sir Ralph ("considered
a colossal humbug" by his contemporaries), with his ridiculous
theory of stimulating the phagocytes, will kill the artist.

Although Louis dies, *The Doctor's Dilemma* cannot be considered completely a tragedy, for Shaw's optimism again prevails.
Louis leaves his heritage of art to Jennifer, who, through her
idolatry of him, will continue to preach his artistic creed even
though she probably does not understand it. Louis himself says
that he is not a superman but adds, "Still, it's an ideal that I
strive towards just as any other man strives toward his ideal"
(149). His dying words are those of an artist free of all bourgeois
morality:

In my own real world I have never done anything wrong, never
denied my faith, never been untrue to myself. Ive been threat-

ened and blackmailed and insulted and starved. But Ive played the game. Ive fought the good fight. And now it's all over, theres an indescribable peace. [*He feebly folds his hands and utters his creed*] I believe in Michael Angelo, Velasquez, and Rembrandt; in the might of design, the mystery of color, the redemption of all things by Beauty everlasting, and the message of Art that has made these hands blessed. Amen. Amen. [*He closes his eyes and lies still*]. [172–73]

Later, at a showing of the deceased Dubedat's paintings, Ridgeon admits honestly to Jennifer that he deliberately killed her husband, "He made his widow the happiest woman in the world; but it was I who made her a widow. . . . Now you know what I did and what I thought of him. Be as angry with me as you like: at least you know me as I really am" (187). He tells her that he wanted to save her from her husband's selfishness. But Jennifer replies, "He was one of the men who know what women know: that self-sacrifice is vain and cowardly."

The physicians practicing in this capitalistic society could never understand a Louis Dubedat. Immediately after he dies Sir Patrick ironically accuses Louis of what he and all of his fellow doctors really represent: "Dont waste your time wrangling over him. A blackguard's a blackguard; an honest man's an honest man; and neither of them will ever be at a loss for a religion or a morality to prove that their ways are the right ways. It's the same with nations, the same with professions, the same all the world over and always will be" (176). Even Ridgeon, the most intelligent of them, thought he was doing Louis's wife a favor by ridding her of "the most entire and perfect scoundrel, the most miraculously mean rascal" (186). Shaw's desperation is summed up in Jennifer's outcry which is actually directed at the world rather than Ridgeon: "You are so utterly, so wildly wrong; so incapable of appreciating Louis——" (187). It is an outcry that Saint Joan echoes, only even more intensely, seventeen years later: "O God that madest this beautiful earth, when will it be ready to receive Thy saints? How long, O Lord, how long?" (2:49).

While Shaw was dramatizing how "the bourgeoisie has stripped of its halo" the priest, the lawyer, and the physician, he also advocated drastic fundamental changes in marriage laws. Marx himself had recognized the danger of such an undertaking when he exclaimed in *The Communist Manifesto:* "Abolition of the family! Even the most radical flare up at this infamous proposal of the Communists," [16] and Shaw could not go so far as to advocate abolition of the family at this time: "There is therefore no question of abolishing marriage; but there is a very pressing question of improving its conditions." [17] Later, in *Back to Methuselah,* written after the Russian Revolution, he is able to envision a society of the future that cannot even comprehend the meaning of the family (see chapter 7).

From the time he first read *Das Kapital* and wrote *An Unsocial Socialist* (1883), Shaw's gibes at the economic basis of marriage are a source of delightful comedy in practically every play. In *Getting Married* (completed in 1908), however, his indictment of this sacred foundation stone of capitalism takes on a more serious tone. There is no delightful comedy in his seventy-five page preface to this play. In it he borrows quite heavily from *The Communist Manifesto,* where Marx, reflecting his economic interpretation of history, asks, "On what foundation is the present family, the bourgeois family based?" and replies, "On Capital, on private gain. . . . . The bourgeois sees in his wife a mere instrument of production. He hears that the instruments of production are to be exploited in common, and, naturally, can come to no other conclusion, than that the lot of being common to all will likewise fall to the women" (339). Shaw too dispels any romantic illusions about marriage, pointing out its economic basis:

> If we adopt the common romantic assumption that the object of marriage is bliss, then the very strongest reason for

16. Marx, *Capital, the Communist Manifesto, and Other Writings,* p. 338. Further quotations from Marx in this chapter are from this edition; page numbers will be given in parentheses after the quotation when necessary.

17. *Complete Plays with Prefaces,* 4:319–20. Further quotations from *Getting Married* and its preface in this chapter are from the same volume; page numbers will be given in parentheses after the quotation when necessary.

dissolving a marriage is that it shall be disagreeable to one or other or both of the parties. If we accept the view that the object of marriage is to provide for the production and rearing of children, then childlessness should be a conclusive reason for dissolution. As neither of these causes entitles married persons to divorce it is at once clear that our marriage law is not founded on either assumption. What it is really founded on is the morality of the tenth commandment, which Englishwomen will one day succeed in obliterating from the walls of our churches by refusing to enter any building where they are publicly classed with a man's house, his ox, and his ass, as his purchased chattels. [320–21]

Marx's analysis suggests that the family relation reduced to a money relation exists only among the bourgeoisie, finding its "complement in the practical absence of the family among the proletarians" (339). Shaw once again interprets Marx for the layman:

In the middle classes, where the segregation of the artificially limited family in its little brick box is horribly complete, . . . all the petty vices of unsociability flourish like mushrooms in a cellar. . . . And in the very poorest class, where people have no homes, . . . sociability again appears, leaving the middle class despised and disliked for its helpless and offensive unsociability. [361]

Whereas Marx urged freeing women from their status "as mere instruments of production," stating that "it is self-evident that the abolition of the present system of production must bring with it the abolition of the community of women springing from that system, i.e., of prostitution both public and private" (339–40), Shaw does not quite go this far:

The truth is that family life will never be decent, much less ennobling, until this central horror of the dependence of women on men is done away with. At present it reduces the difference between marriage and prostitution to the difference between Trade Unionism and unorganized casual labor: a huge difference, no doubt, as to order and comfort, but not a difference in kind. [356]

In the play itself Shaw uses much the same means of "striking down the individual" with the horror of bourgeois marriage as we saw him do in the preface to *Androcles and the Lion* in regard to bourgeois religion. In the latter he made Christ the exponent of the Marxian indictment of religion. In *Getting Married* the realist Bishop is aware of the hypocrisy of bourgeois marriage even though he believes that in a capitalist society it is better to get married for legal protection. (Shaw was remembering the trouble Eleanor Marx had after her common-law husband, Dr. Aveling, left her without a penny.)

The Bishop (who is writing a book on the history of marriage) speaks for Shaw:

> Ive just come to the period when the propertied classes refused to get married and went in for marriage settlements instead. A few of the oldest families stuck to the marriage tradition so as to keep up the supply of vestal virgins, who had to be legitimate; but nobody else dreamt of getting married. It's all very interesting, because we're coming to that in England . . . .
>
> Ive told our last four Prime Ministers that if they didnt make our marriage laws reasonable there would be a strike against marriage, and that it would begin among the propertied classes, where no Government would dare to interfere with it. [421]

The close connection between property and marriage is further demonstrated when the bridegroom Sykes rebels at being legally responsbile for his future wife's tendencies toward making libelous statements. Later we discover that Sykes and Edith have been secretly married but only after they had gone to the British Family Insurance Corporation: "It insures you against poor relations," Sykes explains, "and all sorts of family contingencies" (481). Presumably Edith and Sykes live happily ever after. Yet only when a husband and wife are economically independent of each other will a successful marriage be possible.

Shaw does not acknowledge anything remotely sacred in the permanence of marriage vows. Unlike Marx who would abolish marriage and "introduce, in substitution for a hypocritically concealed, an openly legalized community of women" (340), Shaw's Fabianism comes to the fore as he urges a complete relaxation of the divorce laws: "When it comes to 'conduct rendering life burdensome,' it is clear that no marriage is any longer indissoluble; and the sensible thing to do then is to grant divorce whenever it is desired, without asking why" (392).

Misalliance, which was completed in 1910, like *Getting Married,* is a conversation piece. But Marx's bitter indictment of marriage is softened so as to be palatable to a fashionable West End audience; nevertheless his indictment is clearly the source for both the arguments in the preface and the discussions in the play itself.

In the preface Shaw considers the proper relationship between parents and children. Softening Marx's crusade to abolish "the exploitation of children by their parents" into a Fabian solution, he says, "There is a growing body of law designed to prevent parents from using their children ruthlessly to make money for the household. Such legislation has always been furiously resisted by the parents, even when the horrors of factory slavery were at their worst [when Marx wrote *The Communist Manifesto*]; and the extension of such legislation at present would be impossible if it were not that the parents affected by it cannot control a majority of votes in Parliament." [18]

Shaw compares the child to a prisoner who must endure his parents' society for his daily bread and states that only economic equality through socialism can deal efficiently with the question from the point of view of the total interest of the community. This proper relationship between parents and children stems from Marx's query in *The Communist Manifesto,* "Do you charge us with wanting to stop the exploitation of children by their parents? To this crime we plead guilty" (339).

The points introduced in the preface are dramatized by the dialogue of *Misalliance.* The realist-heroine, Lina Szczepan-

18. *Complete Plays with Prefaces,* 4:6. Further quotations from *Misalliance* and its preface in this chapter are from the same volume; page numbers will be given in parentheses after the quotation when necessary.

owska, is a most unusual character, coming from a family of entertainers noted for their feats of skill and daring. She makes her entrance in the play by literally dropping out of the sky into the estate of an underwear tycoon, John Tarleton. (She is the passenger in a plane making a forced landing.) Before her arrival the former bourgeois, but now aristocratic, group had been discussing marriage in the usual hypocritical manner. But the "new woman" cuts through their fuzzy idealism by immediately suggesting the monetary basis of the institution. When the elder John Tarleton "propositions" her, Lina calmly says, "How much will you pay?" Shaw then, like Marx, equates marriage with prostitution. Old Tarleton asks Lina what most of her offers come to, "Diamonds? Motor cars? Furs? Villa at Monte Carlo?" and she responds, "Oh yes: all that. And sometimes the devotion of a lifetime" (159–60).

Later, Shaw resumes his indictment of marriage in a scene similar to that in *Arms and the Man* in which Bluntschli lists his property to the last salad fork. Percival (the pilot of the plane) and old Tarleton bargain for the hand of Tarleton's spirited daughter Hypatia, or Patsy as she is familiarly called. Old Tarleton asks Percival whether Hypatia's marriage to him is merely a question of money with love playing no role at all. Percival coldly admits that money is the really important factor and love merely secondary. He then asks both Tarleton and Lord Summerhays as "experienced married men" if they have any more "trustworthy method of selecting a wife." When neither is able to offer one, Percival says bluntly, "Then Patsy will do as well as another, provided the money is forthcoming" (195–96). Old Tarlton does not even care what Percival's family connections are: "I dont care a tinker's curse who you are or what you are. Youre willing to take that girl off my hands for fifteen hundred a year: thats all that concerns me. Tell her who you are if you like: it's her affair, not mine" (197).

Shaw's final indictment of bourgeois marriage is delivered, as usual, by the realist—Lina to whom old Tarleton's son Johnny, has proposed marriage:

But your Johnny! Oh, your Johnny! with his marriage. He will do the straight thing by me. He will give me a home, a position. He tells me I must know that my present position is not one for a nice woman. This to me, Lina Szczepanowska! I am an honest woman: I earn my living. I am a free woman: . . . I am strong: I am skillful: I am brave: I am independent: I am unbought: I am all that a woman ought to be. . . . And this Englishman! this linendraper! he dares to ask me to come and live with him in this rrrrrrrabbit hutch, and take my bread from his hand, and ask him for pocket money, and wear soft clothes, and be his woman! his wife! Sooner than that, I would stoop to the lowest depths of my profession. . . . All this I would do sooner than take my bread from the hand of a man and make him the master of my body and soul. And so you may tell your Johnny to buy an Englishwoman: he shall not buy Lina Szczepanowska; and I will not stay in the house where such dishonor is offered me. [201–2]

The play ends on a symbolic note as Bentley, the typical wastrel aristocrat, albeit one with deep spiritual inclinations, is "saved" by the vital Lina, who intends to lift him from the stuffy hypocritical environment by whisking him off in the airplane.

Shaw's indictment of the institution of marriage defines the plot of *Misalliance,* but other elements of his socialistic beliefs are briefly touched on. His continuing opposition at this time to the ability of the Marxist revolution to restructure society and his distrust of the proletariat to do so are expressed by Gunner, a Marxologist. He enters the action under the guise of avenging his mother's virtue, violated by old John Tarleton years before. But Gunner is simply a foolish proletarian who threatens to blow up capitalism when all of the clerks in the world revolt. Lord Summerhays cynically indicates Gunner's foolhardiness by pointing out that should such a thing happen the police would merely provoke Gunner to overstep his legal rights and then imprison him until things quieted down. When Gunner questions the justice of such an action, Lord Summerhays states that when he governed a province justice had to take a second seat to law and order which in turn had to be maintained by force or fraud or both. He suggests that Gunner remember the cold fact that "anarchism is a game at which the police can beat you" (191).

Pygmalion (completed in 1912) is a much more skillful play than the two just discussed—as the success of *My Fair Lady* amply proves. Surpassing these earlier conversation pieces, Shaw successfully submerges the Marxian indictment of marriage into a hilarious comedy which is a blend of many themes and is peopled with memorable characters. The delightful Liza, for example, reflects Marx's statement that marriage among the proletarians is practically nonexistent when Mrs. Pearce, the housekeeper, upbraids Higgins for bringing the flower girl into his house:

> . . . you cant take a girl up like that as if you were picking up a pebble on the beach.
> HIGGINS. Why not?
> MRS PEARCE. Why not! But you dont know anything about her. What about her parents? She may be married.
> LIZA. Garn!
> HIGGINS. There! As the girl very properly says, Garn! Married indeed! Dont you know that a woman of that class looks a worn out drudge of fifty a year after she's married?[19]

Later when Mrs. Pearce asks Liza where her mother is, Liza replies, "I aint got no mother. Her that turned me out was my sixth stepmother. But I done without them. And I'm a good girl, I am" (217). Shaw continues his analysis of marriage among the proletarians with Liza's father, Doolittle. In *Misalliance* old Tarleton, the bourgeois underwear tycoon, is willing to pay Percival fifteen hundred a year to marry his daughter; ironically, Doolittle, a proletarian, sells his daughter—not in marriage though— to Higgins for a "fiver."

Shaw's Marxian concept of the slavery of bourgeois marriage is humorously brought out by Doolittle who, responding to Pickering's advice of marrying the "missus," exclaims,

19. *Complete Plays with Prefaces,* 1:216. Further quotations from *Pygmalion* and its preface in this chapter are from the same volume; page numbers will be given in parentheses after the quotation when necessary.

Tell her so, Governor: tell her so. I'm willing. It's me that
suffers by it. Ive no hold on her. I got to be agreeable to her. I
got to give her presents. I got to buy her clothes something
sinful. I'm a slave to that woman, Governor, just because I'm
not her lawful husband. And she knows it too. Catch her marrying me! Take my advice, Governor: marry Eliza while she's
young and dont know no better. If you dont youll be sorry
for it after. If you do, she'll be sorry for it after; but better her
than you, because youre a man, and she's only a woman and
dont know how to be happy anyhow. [231]

Later, when Doolittle announces to Liza that her stepmother "is
going to marry me," the occasion is treated like a funeral rather
than a marriage. Doolittle sadly says to Mrs. Higgins, who insists
on going to the marriage ceremony, "My poor old woman would
take it as a tremenjous compliment. She's been very low, thinking
of the happy days that are no more" (273).

The theme of bourgeois marriage as slavery and prostitution
is brought to a climax when Higgins suggests to Eliza that his
mother can find a husband for her. Her bitter reply sums up
Shaw's views:

We were above that at the corner of Tottenham Court Road.
HIGGINS [*Waking up*] What do you mean?
LIZA. I sold flowers. I didnt sell myself. Now youve made a
lady of me I'm not fit to sell anything else. I wish youd left me
where you found me. [257]

The narrative epilogue to the play shows that Eliza does eventually become a "lady" not by selling herself in marriage but by
purchasing a flower shop (with the financial aid of Pickering)
and becoming independent. Only then can she and Freddy Eyens-
ford Hill—who could never support her by his impecunious aristocracy—live happily ever after.

But Shaw's indictment of bourgeois marriage is only one thread
of *Pygmalion*'s plot. Liza Doolittle's rise from the gutter reveals
the surface difference between the classes of a capitalist society.
After learning the speech patterns of the upper classes, Liza is
accepted by them. Higgins says to his mother, "But you have no

idea how frightfully interesting it is to take a human being and change her into a quite different human being by creating a new speech for her. It's filling up the deepest gulf that separates class from class and soul from soul" (248). Clara, Freddy's bored sister who in the play hilariously takes up Eliza's "small talk" and saves her from being discovered as a member of the lower classes at Mrs. Higgins's tea, is a useless lady but a lady nonetheless by the false social standards of capitalism. Shaw provides a happy ending for her in the epilogue: inspired by the persuasive pen of H. G. Wells, she loses her boredom and goes to work in a furniture shop, thus becoming a true lady.

Toward the end of the play proper, to Eliza's complaint that he still treats her as a flower girl, Higgins replies:

My manners are exactly the same as Colonel Pickering's.
LIZA. Thats not true. He treats a flower girl as if she was a duchess.
HIGGINS. And I treat a duchess as if she was a flower girl.
LIZA. I see. [*She turns away composedly, and sits on the ottoman, facing the window*]. The same to everybody.
HIGGINS. Just so.
LIZA. Like father.
HIGGINS [*grinning, a little taken down*] Without accepting the comparison at all points, Eliza, it's quite true that your father is not a snob, and that he will be quite at home in any station of life to which his eccentric destiny may call him. [*Seriously*] The great secret, Eliza, is not having bad manners or good manners or any other particular sort of manners, but having the same manner for all human souls: in short, behaving as if you were in Heaven, where there are no third-class carriages, and one soul is as good as another. [274]

Shaw's impatience with the slow process of the Fabian method is displayed here. He wants the millenium to come; he is anxious for the day when, as Marx described it, "In place of the old bourgeois society, with its classes and class antagonisms, we shall have an association in which the free development of each is the condition for the free development of all" (343).

Four years later Shaw's impatience with Fabian gradualism has been exhausted. No longer content with indictments of the foundation stones of capitalism, he dramatizes the collapse of the edifice itself in *Heartbreak House* (completed in 1916). This play was begun, Shaw states in the 1919 preface, before a shot of World War I was fired, and its title "is not merely the name of the play . . . . It is cultured, leisured Europe before the war." [20] It is Shaw's first totally symbolic play imitative of Chekov's *The Cherry Orchard, Uncle Vanya,* and *The Seagull*—all based on a similar theme. Chekov's characters, Shaw said, "did not wish to realize Utopia for the common people: they wished to realize their favorite fictions and poems in their own lives; and when they could they lived without scruple on incomes which they did nothing to earn" (450).

Although the form is Chekovian, the contents in contrast express the final phase of capitalism which Marx had envisioned in the first volume of *Das Kapital:*

> That which is now to be expropriated is no longer the labourer working for himself, but the capitalist exploiting many labourers. This expropriation is accomplished by the immanent laws of capitalistic production itself, by the centralization of capital. One capitalist always kills many. . . . Along with the constantly diminishing number of the magnates of capital, who usurp and monopolize all advantages of this process of transformation, grows the mass of misery, oppression, slavery, degradation, exploitation; but with this too grows the revolt of the working-class . . . . Centralization of the means of production and socialization of labour at last reach a point where they become incompatible with their capitalist integument. This integument is burst asunder. The knell of capitalist private property sounds.[21]

20. *Complete Plays with Prefaces,* 1:449. Further quotations from *Heartbreak House* and its preface in this chapter are taken from the same volume; page numbers will be given in parentheses after the quotation when necessary.

21. Karl Marx, *Capital: A Critique of Political Economy,* vol. 1, *The Process of Capitalist Production,* translated from the 3rd German ed. by Samuel Moor and Edward Aveling, ed. Frederick Engels (Chicago: Charles H. Kerr & Co., 1932), pp. 836–37.

The setting is the eccentric Captain Shotover's house "built so as to resemble the after part of an old fashioned high-pooped ship with a stern gallery" (489)—obviously symbolic of the ship of state. The "magnates of capital, who usurp and monopolize," are represented by Boss Mangan, one of the many casual visitors to Captain Shotover's house. He is an agent representing "syndicates and shareholders and all sorts of lazy good-for-nothing capitalists." He tells Ellie Dunn (whose father wants her to marry him for his money) and the other visitors gathered in the garden of Shotover's house that "I get money from such people to start the factories. I find people like Miss Dunn's father to work them, and keep a tight hand so as to make them pay. Of course I make them keep me going pretty well; but it's a dog's life; and I dont own anything" (581).

His modesty soon leaves him, however, when Lady Utterword (one of Captain Shotover's daughters) scornfully says, "How sad! Why dont you go into politics, Mr Mangan?" He carefully explains to her that the powerful syndicates, recognizing how useful he would be to them in government, contributed large sums of money to the party for him. As a consequence, the prime minister asked him "to join the Government without even going through the nonsense of an election, as the dictator of a great public department" (582).

Earlier, when Mazzini Dunn tries to justify himself to Mrs. Hesione Hushabye (Captain Shotover's other daughter) for wanting his daughter Ellie to marry Mangan, he explains why the man is so powerful: "We should be sentimental about the hard cases among the work people. But Mangan keeps us in order. He is down on us about every extra half-penny. We could never do without him. You see, he will sit up all night thinking of how to save sixpence. Wont Ellie make him jump, though, when she takes his house in hand!" Mrs. Hushabye chides, "Then the creature is a fraud even as a captain of industry!" Mazzini replies, "I am afraid all the captains of industry are what you call frauds, Mrs Hushabye. Of course there are some manufacturers who really do understand their own works; but they dont make as high a rate of profit as Mangan does. I assure you Mangan is quite a good fellow in his way. He means well" (541).

This is indeed the era of centralization. Little capitalists even though they understand their own works are no match for the big monopolies who employ Mangans to make a "high rate of profit." And with this era as Marx said comes degradation. Shaw permits Ellie Dunn to describe the degradation because she has been disillusioned so many times. At the beginning of the play she tells Hesione Hushabye about a man whom she had met, Marcus Darnley; she is thrilled by this man whose life "has been one long romance." He saved the life of a tiger from one of King Edward's hunting expeditions in India: "He is a Socialist and despises rank, and has been in three revolutions fighting on the barricades" (509). Minutes later she discovers that Marcus Darnley is Hector Hushabye, Hesione's romantic husband. She is further disillusioned by Mangan who turns out to be merely a paper tiger of large syndicates. Her disillusionment overflows as she bewails the degradation and utter unreality of this era:

> There seems to be nothing real in the world except my father and Shakespear. Marcus's tigers are false; Mr Mangan's millions are false; there is nothing really strong and true about Hesione but her beautiful black hair; and Lady Utterword's too pretty to be real. The one thing that was left to me was the Captain's seventh degree of concentration; and that turns out to be——
> CAPTAIN SHOTOVER. Rum. [584]

Her outburst causes a violent reaction from Mangan. In a scene reminiscent of *King Lear,* he announces "wildly" that he is going to take off all his clothes much to the amazement and consternation of all. He wants to strip himself physically naked: "I tell you I cant bear this," he shouts, "I was brought up to be respectable. I dont mind the women dyeing their hair and the men drinking: it's human nature. But it's not human nature to tell everyone about it. Everytime one of you opens your mouth I go like this [*he cowers as if to avoid a missile*] afraid of what will come next. How are we to have self-respect if we dont keep it up that we're better than we really are?" (584). Mangan, or capitalism, cannot bear to face himself. He must hide, like all of Shaw's Ibsenesque idealists, behind the masks of bourgeois morality. When these masks are ripped off he "cowers as if to avoid a missile"—the time is ripe; the "integument is burst asunder."

Bourgeois society with all its false morality is Mangan's refuge to the end. Even when Ellie announces her spiritual marriage to Captain Shotover because there could be no blessing "on Mr Mangan's money," Mangan replies, "Dont say there was any difficulty about the blessing. I was ready to get a bishop to marry us" (587). Once again bourgeois religion is linked with capitalism.

Hector Hushabye anticipates the coming destruction of capitalism when he expresses his discomposure with all of them for merely sitting around talking, while leaving everything to Mangan "and his mutual admiration gang" whose powers of destruction baffle the imagination—"it's like giving a torpedo to a badly brought up child to play at earthquakes with." Mazzini Dunn's reply sums up all of Shaw's disillusionment with the Fabian method:

> I joined societies and made speeches and wrote pamphlets. That was all I could do. But, you know, though the people in the societies thought they knew more than Mangan, most of them wouldnt have joined if they had known as much. You see they had never had any money to handle or any men to manage. Every year I expected a revolution, or some frightful smash-up: it seemed impossible that we could blunder and muddle on any longer. But nothing happened, except, of course, the usual poverty and crime and drink that we are used to. Nothing ever does happen. It's amazing how well we get along, all things considered. [592]

The symbolism reaches its climax far less subtly than in Chekov's plays. After Mazzini's speech the conversation turns to navigation, and Captain Shotover notes that nothing happens at sea either "except something not worth mentioning"—"Nothing but the smash of the drunken skipper's ship on the rocks, the splintering of her rotten timbers, the tearing of her rusty plates, the drowning of the crew like rats in a trap" (593). Later,

Hector asks, "And this ship that we are in? This soul's prison we call England?" Captain Shotover tells him that the captain is drunk in his bunk and the crew is gambling: "She will strike and sink and split." Hector then inquires what he as an Englishman should do. Captain Shotover tells him to learn his business as an Englishman—navigation: "Learn it and live; or leave it and be damned." Mazzini replies dispiritedly, "I thought all that once, Captain; but I assure you nothing will happen." At that very moment "a dull distant explosion is heard" (594).

We learn later that the rectory was destroyed by this bomb, and Captain Shotover comments, "The Church is on the rocks, breaking up. I told him [the rector] it would unless it headed for God's open sea" (594).

It is significant that the only two occupants of the house destroyed when "a terrific explosion shakes the earth" and "they hear the falling of the shattered glass from the windows" are Mangan and Billy Dunn, the house robber—who fled to the shelter of a cave on the property. Mangan is symbolic of the heart of Heartbreak House. Billy, who had stolen Lady Utterword's diamonds earlier in the play, was identified as a former boatswain of Captain Shotover and originally a pirate who had married Nurse Guinness, caretaker of the house. Hector comments on their deaths, "the two burglars," and Lady Utterword adds, "the two practical men of business" (598).

Thus Shaw prophesies a violent end to capitalist society, and in the very last lines of the play he almost seems gleeful at the prospect of the bombers' return:

> MRS. HUSHABYE. But what a glorious experience! I hope theyll come again tomorrow night.
> ELLIE [*radiant at the prospect*] Oh, I hope so. [598]

He left no doubt in the reader's mind concerning his opinion. In the preface which he wrote two years after the Russian Revolution and which he titled "Heartbreak House and Horseback Hall," he comments, "Meanwhile the Bolshevist picks and petards are at work on the foundations of both buildings, and though the Bolshevists may be buried in the ruins, their deaths will not save the edifices" (475). True, he added that they can be rebuilt by Bunyan's "Simple, Sloth, and Presumption, by Feeble Mind and Much Afraid, and by all the jurymen of Vanity Fair," but another war will come.

And his non-Fabian acceptance of revolution is certainly apparent in the conclusion to the preface: "Revolution, lately only a sensational chapter in history or a demagogic claptrap, is now a possibility so imminent that hardly by trying to suppress it in other countries by arms and defamation, and calling the process anti-Bolshevism, can our Government stave it off at home" (484). Or as Marx had said, "The knell of capitalist private property sounds." Comparing himself with President Woodrow Wilson who "knows well that from the Peace Conference will come, in spite of his utmost, no edict on which he will be able, like Lincoln, to invoke 'the considerate judgment of mankind, and the gracious favor of Almighty God,'" Shaw concludes cynically and ominously, "In the meantime there is, for him, another history to write; for me, another comedy to stage. Perhaps, after all, that is what wars are for . . . . If men will not learn until their lessons are written in blood, why, blood they must have, their own for preference" (485). On this serious note he completes for the time being the depiction of "capitalist society in dissolution" and prophesies "its downfall as the final catastrophe." Indeed, the "opinions of the fictitious Trefusis anticipated those of the real Lenin."

CHAPTER SEVEN

Creative Evolution

"The Church is on the rocks, breaking up," Captain Shotover exclaims at the end of *Heartbreak House*. Thus, Shaw once again condemned Christianity because it had become the handmaid of capitalism. Marxism forms a strong link between Shaw's indictment of conventional religion and the formulation of his own unconventional creed, Creative Evolution, for capitalism must be broken up before Shaw's church can thrive. That Creative Evolution cannot prosper in a capitalistic society is inherent in its very nature. Based on the concepts of Lamarck, Schopenhauer, Samuel Butler, and to a certain extent Nietzsche, the essence of Shaw's creed is a Life Force constantly striving to attain perfection. Man is not its ultimate aim: it is "the Superman, then the Angel, the Archangel, and last of all an omnipotent and omnisicent God." [1]

When he completed *Man and Superman* in 1903—the first work to expound the theories of his new religion—capitalism was thriving everywhere; therefore he confined his serious treatment of Creative Evolution to embellishments of the play: the "Don Juan in Hell" scene, John Tanner's *The Revolutionist's Handbook*, and *Maxims for Revolutionists*. In the drama itself his religion plays a very indirect role, and John Tanner's revolutionary theories fall on deaf ears.

Progress is the keynote to such a religion, but progress is only an illusion in a capitalist society. In *The Revolutionist's Handbook* John Tanner or Shaw states: "A civilization in which lusty

---

1. Henderson, *George Bernard Shaw: His Life and Works*, p. 482.

pugnacity and greed have ceased to act as selective agents and
have begun to obstruct and destroy, rushes downwards and back-
wards with a suddenness that enables an observer to see with
consternation the upward steps of many centuries retraced in a
single lifetime." [2] Consequently if the aim of Shaw's creed—the
superman—is to be realized:

> he must be born of Woman by Man's intentional and well-
> considered contrivance. Conviction of this will smash every-
> thing that opposes it. Even Property and Marriage, which
> laugh at the laborer's petty complaint that he is defrauded
> of "surplus value," and at the domestic miseries of the slaves
> of the wedding ring, will themselves be laughed aside as the
> lightest of trifles if they cross this conception when it becomes
> a fully realized vital purpose of the race. [694]

Property and marriage are indeed hostile to the evolution of
the superman because they destroy equality and thus hamper
"sexual selection with irrelevant conditions." Shaw points to a
community founded at Oneida Creek in America in 1848 as the
only known modern experiment in breeding the human race;
this group "discarded both institutions" (698). Unfortunately
the experiment was a failure because its leader, when he became
senile, "guided and organized the voluntary relapse of the communists into marriage, capitalism, and customary private life,
thus admitting that the real social solution was not what a casual
superman could persuade a picked company to do for him, but
what a whole community of Supermen would do spontaneously"
(700).

In the "Don Juan in Hell" scene, the Marxist basis of Creative
Evolution is spelled out in detail. Don Juan's description of hell
is a description of capitalist society. He tells Señora Ana that hell
is the abode of honor, duty, justice, and all the other deadly

2. Shaw, *Complete Plays with Prefaces*, 3:713. Further quotations from
Man and Superman, The Revolutionist's Handbook, and *Maxims for
Revolutionists* in this chapter are taken from the same volume; page
numbers will be given in parentheses after the quotation when
necessary.

virtues in whose name the wickedness of earth is performed. In other words it is the dwelling place of the idealists, and we recall Shaw's statement in *The Quintessence of Ibsenism* that the most wicked ideals are social ideals, whose monetary basis Marx had revealed. Heaven, on the other hand, is Shaw's counterpart of the Marxian millenium: "In Heaven, as I picture it, dear lady," Don Juan continues, "you live and work instead of playing and pretending" (617). You live and work to help the Life Force in its upward struggle by removing obstacles, and the greatest obstacle is human poverty, a product of capitalist society.

The Devil enters the conversation at this point—this is not the Devil that Dick Dudgeon worshipped, but the real Devil, an arch-idealist. He scoffs at Don Juan's hopes for removing poverty and helping the Life Force evolve a superman: "I have seen his cotton factories and the like, with machinery that a greedy dog could have invented if it had wanted money instead of food. . . . There is nothing in Man's industrial machinery but his greed and sloth: his heart is in his weapons. This marvellous force of Life of which you boast is a force of Death: Man measures his strength by his destructiveness" (619). The Devil continues citing more instances to prove that man will always prefer death to life because he is essentially a coward.

Don Juan's reply envisions a Marxist solution, including a bloody revolution if necessary. He begins his rebuttal by answering the Devil's charge that man is essentially a coward: man can be made brave by putting an idea into his head. Don Juan reminds the Devil of how viciously man fought for the idea of a Catholic church and that man again will fight valiantly for another Catholic idea: "When the Spaniard learns at last that he is no better than the Saracen, and his prophet no better than Mahomet, he will rise, more Catholic than ever, and die on a barricade across the filthy slum he starves in, for universal liberty and equality." He will die to rid the world of its capitalist ghettos. When the Devil replies that man will always find excuses for killing one another, Don Juan completely exonerates such a killing: "Better ten dead men than one live slave or his master.

Men shall yet rise up, father against son and brother against brother, and kill one another for the great Catholic idea of abolishing slavery" (623). Here Shaw quotes directly from Marx who ended *The Communist Manifesto* with "the great Catholic idea of abolishing slavery": "Let the ruling classes tremble at a Communistic revolution. The proletarians have nothing to lose but their chains. They have a world to win. Working men of all countries, unite!" [3]

Only a superman, however, will be powerful enough to force the ordinary person to such bloody action. The superman will be an almost perfect intellect, a "philosophic man: he who seeks in contemplation to discover the inner will of the world, in invention to discover the means of fulfilling that will, and in action to do that will by the so-discovered means" (628). Twenty-eight years later Shaw described Lenin as "a pure intellectual type. . . . I do not know whether there will ever be a man to whom so much significance will be given as the future will give to Lenin." [4]

The ending of the "Don Juan in Hell" scene is a hopeful one. Don Juan leaves hell for heaven but Ana is doomed to stay in hell; however, just as the Devil is about to leave for his palace she asks him where she can find the superman. When she is told he has not yet been created she shouts: "Not yet created! Then my work is not yet done. [*Crossing herself devoutly*] I believe in the Life to Come. [*Crying to the universe*] A father! a father for the Superman!" She supposedly returns to earth, for the stage directions read: "She vanishes into the void" (649).

Though Shaw's optimism prevails in this scene, which is rarely produced, the play itself exudes no such optimism. John Tanner, its dynamic hero, is frustrated at every turn. When he congratulates Violet Robinson, his best friend's sister (who supposedly is to have a baby out of wedlock) for spurning the laws of bourgeois marriage, she informs him in no uncertain terms that she is indeed married and that he is insulting her more than the

3. Marx, *Capital, the Communist Manifesto, and Other Writings,* ed. Eastman, p. 355.
4. Quoted in Dana, "Shaw in Moscow," p. 349.

others. Later, Hector Malone's father, a gruff American who is suspicious of English morality, upbraids his son for paying his attentions to Violet, a married woman. Hector replies, "Thats all right. Dont you trouble yourself about that. I'll answer for the morality of what I'm doing." Jack Tanner, elated, shouts, "Well said, Malone! You also see that mere marriage laws are not morality! I agree with you; but unfortunately Violet does not." Again Jack is thwarted, for Hector announces that he is Violet's husband, so all that Tanner can do is admit defeat: "You the missing husband! Another moral impostor! [*He smites his brow, and collapses into Malone's chair*]" (665–66).

Earlier in the play, when Jack proclaims his revolutionary views to Ann Whitefield, in what Shaw calls a "sociological rage," his words are met with complete indifference. In Marxian rhetoric he tells her that marriage is nothing more than a horrible game played by avaricious mothers and adds that the only reason a son or daughter marries is to escape "these decrepit fiends who hide their selfish ambitions . . . under the mask of maternal duty and family affection" (573–74). Ann's reply, that Jack speaks so beautifully he certainly must go into politics some day, reflects Shaw's disillusionment with mere talk. Jack Tanner is a failure as a reformer.

Ann uses every trick of feminine guile to win Jack as a husband. When she is finally successful, he reluctantly admits that he is in the clutches of the Life Force. He asks her if the trap was laid for him from the beginning, and Ann replies: "From the beginning—from our childhood—for both of us—by the Life Force" (682). But Ann, unlike her alter ego Ana in the "Don Juan in Hell" scene, doesn't even know what the Life Force is. She only uses the phrase as a further lure to capture Jack.

After completing *Man and Superman* Shaw put aside his theory of Creative Evolution for eighteen years, finally returning to it in 1921. By this time capitalism had been destroyed in Russia, and Shaw was inspired to dramatize his complete bible of Creative Evolution in *Back to Methuselah*. This is Shaw's most ambitious play, a "metabiological pentateuch" comprising five full-length plays and filling 257 pages in the average edition. It also spans eons from the time of the Garden of Eden to A.D. 31,920. The only possible explanation for such a surge of optimistic ambition in 1921 is his intense enthusiam for the apparent success of Lenin's overthrow of capitalism in Russia—an enthusiasm comparable to that he displayed in writing *An Unsocial Socialist* after reading *Das Kapital.*

Shaw's reaction to the Russian Revolution contradicted that of England's arch-Marxist H. M. Hyndman, who claimed that Lenin and his revolution was a gigantic imposture. In a review of Hyndman's book, *The Evolution of Revolution* (written for the *Nation,* 1921, and collected in *Pen Portraits and Reviews,* 1932), Shaw makes it quite clear that the Russian Revolution *was* the fulfillment of Marx's dream: "If, as Mr Hyndman contends, Bolshevism is not real Marxism, but a murderous imposture, what does he think the real thing will be like? He owes us an answer to this question." Shaw had already answered him on the previous page:

> Who is to say that the historic moment has not come in Russia? Certainly not Mr Hyndman, who has so convincingly proved from history that the historic moment is as often as not a psychological moment. All that the Marxian historic moment means when analyzed is the moment when the *bourgeoisie* loses its grip on industry and on the armed forces of the Government, and lets them slip into the hands of the leaders of the proletariat when these leaders are what Marx calls class-conscious: that is, fully aware of the relations, actual, historical, and evolutionary, between the *bourgeoisie* and the proletariat, and well instructed as to the need for and nature of the transition from Capitalism to Communism which they have to operate. Surely these conditions are realized in Russia at present as nearly as they are ever likely to be anywhere.[5]

Moreover, Lenin was for Shaw an efficient midwife who gave bloody birth to the principles of Marx: "If Lenin has abolished idleness in Russia, whilst we, up to our eyes in debt, are not only tolerating it, but heaping luxury upon luxury upon it in the

5. *The Works of Bernard Shaw,* 29:143–44.

midst of starvation, then I am much more inclined to cry 'Bravo, Lenin!' and 'More fools we!' than to share Mr Hyndman's apparent horror." [6]

Surely Shaw left no doubt in anyone's mind that he considered Lenin's revolution Marxism-in-action. With that conviction he could envision a society free from the shackles of capitalism and free to aid the Life Force in its upward struggle to "as far as thought can reach."

The preface to *Back to Methuselah* begins with the assumption that it is doubtful "whether the human animal, as he exists at present, is capable of solving the social problems raised by his own aggregation, or as he calls it, his civilization." [7] Shaw's "forty years' public work as a Socialist" confirmed this doubt. Once again his disillusionment with the Fabian method is apparent and he indicates that his basic optimism needed at this time (after the slaughter of World War I) a new ideal. He follows these gloomy remarks with the usual bitter indictments of capitalist civilization which we have seen him spend years as an artist dramatizing. Then he proceeds to develop his creed of Creative Evolution, first by analyzing the evolutionist's principles of Charles Darwin in the section entitled "Darwin and Karl Marx," where he expounds on the tremendous influence the ideas of these two men had on socialist philosophy.

He eulogizes Marx for tearing off the starched shirt of capitalism and exposing the bare chest of an infamous tyrant; this made him an inspired prophet to every "generous" soul who had read *Das Kapital*. Though he accuses Marx of taking all of his facts from blue books in the British Museum and for borrowing his predecessors' opinions without breathing a whiff of "industrial air," he immediately exonerates him for making one important contribution—the elimination of the moral prestige of the bourgeoisie. Both Marx and Darwin "toppled over two closely related

6. Ibid., p. 147.
7. *Complete Plays with Prefaces,* 2:xii. Further quotations from *Back to Methuselah* and its preface in this chapter are taken from the same volume; page numbers will be given in parentheses after the quotation when necessary.

idols, and became prophets of two new creeds," but Marx had
what Darwin lacked, "a fine Jewish literary style with terrible
powers of hatred, invective, irony" (lxi–lxii). Shaw's praise of
Darwin is brief, for he attacks his doctrine of natural selection as
one so closely linked with capitalism "that Marx regarded it as
an economic product rather than a biological theory" (lxiii). This
phenomenon resulted from economists and politicians applying
Darwin's theory of the survival of the fittest to business tactics
which would inevitably eliminate the weak and thus promulgate
free trade and *laissez faire* without any government interference
except a police force and army designed to help only the strong
(lxiv). Shaw concludes that the war itself resulted from capitalist
nations carrying out Darwin's doctrine.

In contrast to Darwinism is the Lamarckian theory of purposeful selection through the human will, the real basis for Creative
Evolution. Russia was the first to apply Lamarck's doctrine to
politics through rulers like Lenin,

> who perceive that Materialist Communism is at all events
> more effective than Materialist Nihilism, and are attempting
> to move in an intelligent and ordered manner, practising a very
> strenuous Intentional Selection of workers as fitter to survive
> than idlers; whilst the Western Powers are drifting and collid-
> ing and running on the rocks [his later play, *On the Rocks*
> (1934), develops this very theme], in the hope that if they con-
> tinue to do their worst they will get Naturally Selected for
> survival without the trouble of thinking about it. [lxxii]

These two themes then, one religious, the other political and
economic, will become an undercurrent especially of the plays
whose settings are in the future. At the end of the preface to
Back to Methuselah he formally announces his new mission:

> In 1901, I took the legend of Don Juan in its Mozartian form
> and made it a dramatic parable of Creative Evolution. But
> being then at the height of my invention and comedic talent, I
> decorated it too brilliantly and lavishly. . . .
>   I now find myself inspired to make a second legend of
> Creative Evolution without distractions and embellishments.

My sands are running out; the exuberance of 1901 has aged into the garrulity of 1920; and the war has been a stern intimation that the matter is not one to be trifled with. I abandon the legend of Don Juan with its errotic associations, and go back to the legend of the Garden of Eden. I exploit the eternal interest of the philosopher's stone which enables men to live for ever. I am not, I hope, under more illusion than is humanly inevitable as to the crudity of this my beginning of a Bible for Creative Evolution. [lxxxviii–lxxxix]

The first part of the "metabiological pentateuch," *In the Beginning,* traces the urge of the Life Force, the god of Creative Evolution, in the activities of Adam and Eve. In typical Shavian irony, similar to that of *The Devil's Disciple,* the serpent becomes the symbol for good, for it is the serpent who urges Adam and Eve to create other human beings. In the second act of part one, dealing with the world a few centuries later, Marx's economic interpretation of history enters the story: Cain, whom Eve calls the "anti-man" and whom Shaw develops as a thief and a murderer, becomes the father of capitalism. The arrogant Cain voices the capitalistic plan that Marx had exposed in *Das Kapital:* "Why not tame men and women to work for us? Why not bring them up from childhood never to know any other lot, so that they may believe that we are gods, and that they are here only to make life glorious for us?" (25). Eve condemns the plan in rhetoric similar to that of *The Communist Manifesto,* saying to Adam:

I would not have such wretches in my house. Because I hate creatures with two heads, or with withered limbs, or that are distorted and perverted and unnatural. I have told Cain already that he is not a man and that Lua is not a woman: they are monsters. And now you want to make still more unnatural monsters, so that you may be utterly lazy and worthless, and that your tamed human animals may find work a blasting curse. A fine dream, truly! [25–26]

Cain's defense immediately links religion with his plan just as Marx had said the robber barons did. Adam asks Cain what the Voice said when he thought all that, and Cain piously replies,

"Why, it gave me right. It said that my deed was as a mark on me, a burnt-in mark such as Abel put on his sheep, that no man should slay me. And here I stand unslain, whilst the cowards who have never slain, the men who are content to be their brothers' keepers instead of their masters, are despised and rejected, and slain like rabbits. He who bears the brand of Cain shall rule the earth" (26).

Later Marx's analysis of capitalist wars backed by the churches with their reward of immortality—Lenin's opium of the people—is epitomized in the first capitalist's plan. Cain tells his parents that death is really the door to a future life of unending happiness. This being true, war is a glorious experience to rid the world of the unfit; only the masters (the fittest) will survive. So Cain will permit man who is nobler than the ox to become his enemy and eat his oxen and then "I will slay and eat him." Later Eve comments to Adam: "Through him and his like death is gaining on life. Already most of our grandchildren die before they have sense enough to know how to live" (33–34); thus Shaw blames Cain or capitalism for shortening the life expectancy of man.

But the first part of *Back to Methuselah* does not end on a sour note. Shaw's optimism, reinstated by Lenin's overthrow of capitalism, shines through Eve's prediction of Marx's millenium: "Man need not always live by bread alone. There is something else. We do not yet know what it is; but some day we shall find out; and then we will live on that alone; and there shall be no more digging nor spinning, nor fighting nor killing" (34).

Shaw does not forget the role of the true artist-realist in the first part of *Back to Methuselah*. For Eve, a realist, describes the true artist in her refutation of Cain's capitalistic plan. She says that some of her sons by cutting reeds of different lengths are able to produce sounds that raise her soul to untold heights and that others who make little mammoths out of clay have inspired her to will women children who actually reflect the beauty of human models these same sons create. These "artists" are the children who never want to die because there is always something to live for, some new hope and wonder: "And then you, Cain, come with your stupid fighting and destroying, and your foolish boasting; and you want me to tell you that it is all splendid, and that you are heroic, and nothing but death or the dread of death makes life worth living. Away with you, naughty boy, naughty child; and do you, Adam, go on with your work and not waste your time listening to him" (32). She at once distinguishes between the true artist and Marx's paid wage laborer of the bourgeoisie, telling Adam: "It took Enoch two hundred years to learn to interpret the will of the Voice. When he was a mere child of eighty, his babyish attempts to understand the Voice were more dangerous than the wrath of Cain. If they shorten their lives, they will dig and fight and kill and die; and their baby Enochs will tell them that it is the will of the Voice that they should dig and fight and kill and die for ever" (34).

The second part, *The Gospel of the Brothers Barnabas*, spans the centuries to Shaw's own time, "the first years after the war." In it, however, we do not find the usual Marxian condemnation of capitalistic society. True, there are references to its evils, but Shaw is much more interested in getting to the future since Lenin has already paved the way for a better society. In this second part Shaw is primarily interested in expounding his Lamarckian theory of purposeful selection for lengthening the human life span. But he also shows the close connection among biology, politics, and economics, as Marx did when he regarded Darwin's theory as an economic product rather than a biological theory. Conrad Barnabas, before revealing his theory of the "long livers," equates his biology with politics and economics. "In the character of a laborer who earned thirteen shillings a week before the war and earns thirty now, when he can get it," he asks Burge the politician, "Would you allow your son to marry my daughter, or your daughter to marry my son?" Burge replies that his question is irrelevant, that it is not "a political question." Conrad responds, "Then, as a biologist, I dont take the slightest interest in your politics; and I shall not walk across the street to vote for you or any one else at the election. Good evening" (66). Lubin, Burge's rival, quickly takes advantage of the situation and assures Conrad that his daughter "shall marry the man of her choice, whether he be lord or laborer." It is Savvy,

Barnabas's emancipated daughter, who forces her father and Uncle Franklyn to reveal their theories of Creative Evolution to the two politicians. At the end of the play Franklyn asks Haslam, a rather naïve but pleasant Anglican minister, whether he believes in the "gospel of the brothers Barnabas." His answer is a frank "no." Even Savvy, the "new woman," says, "But when you came down to tin tacks, and said that parlormaid might [be the one to live three hundred years], then I saw how absurd it was." Franklyn Barnabas thinks that the gospel should be kept secret—"We should only be laughed at . . .":

> CONRAD. I daresay. But Creative Evolution doesnt stop while people are laughing. Laughing may even lubricate its job.
> SAVVY. What does that mean?
> CONRAD. It means that the first man to live three hundred years maynt have the slightest notion that he is going to do it, and may be the loudest laugher of the lot. [88]

In the third part, *The Thing Happens,* Shaw projects into the future as far as A.D. 2170. It is significant that the first two human creatures to become "long livers" were the former parlormaid of the brothers Barnabas and Haslam, the simple Anglican pastor. In A.D. 2170 a classless society has been established. Burge-Lubin, the president, does not even know what a parlormaid is. The parlormaid, now Mrs. Lutestring, domestic minister, explains that it is an extinct species (117) and then reminisces about the good old days of capitalism; she explains how the dread of poverty constantly hovered over the proletarians who had to perform unending overwork to make à shilling equal the value of a pound. When she is asked why these people did not kill themselves or their masters, she replies that they lacked energy and conviction; "besides, how can you blame them when you would do as they do if you were in their place?" At that time the poor had not a Lenin to lead them out of their misery and all they could do was to resort to alcohol for consolation: "I had carefully arranged my little savings so that I could get drunk, as we called it, once a week; and my only pleasure was looking forward to that little debauch" (120).

Society in A.D. 2170 is still incomplete, even though, as the Archbishop, the other long liver and the former Haslam, reveals, "revolutions that followed the Four Years War" made changes effecting a classless society. But only a longer life, at least three hundred years, can give man enough time to grow up and enjoy the contemplation of Life.

The fourth part, *Tragedy of an Elderly Gentleman,* spans another eight hundred and thirty years and takes place in Ireland. Shaw amusingly transports an elderly gentleman from the British Empire, now transferred to the East, to this land of the "long livers." Even in A.D. 3000 Britain is still a capitalist world: the elderly gentleman cannot understand the purified language of a classless society, nor can they understand him. The Woman informs him that short-lived visitors are not permitted to wander around without a nurse and asks him if he doesn't know that the rules are to be kept:

THE ELDERLY GENTLEMAN. By the lower classes, no doubt. But to persons in my position there are certain courtesies which are never denied by well-bred people; and—
THE WOMAN. There are only two human classes here: the shortlived and the normal. The rules apply to the shortlived, and are for their protection. Now tell me at once who you are.
THE ELDERLY GENTLEMAN [*impressively*] Madam, I am a retired gentleman, formerly Chairman of the All-British Synthetic Egg and Vegetable Cheese Trust in Baghdad, and now President of the British Historical and Archeological Society, and a Vice-President of the Travellers' Club. [142–43]

But these archaic bourgeois boasts do not impress The Woman in the least. When she asks him why he is in her country, he again replies in typical capitalist terminology, "Is this land private property? If so, I make no claim. I proffer a shilling in satisfaction of damage (if any), and am ready to withdraw if you will be good enough to shew me the nearest way. [*He offers her a shilling*]" (143). She, "taking it and examining it without much interest" says, "I do not understand a single word of what you have just said":

THE ELDERLY GENTLEMAN. I am speaking the plainest English. Are you the landlord?

THE WOMAN [*shaking her head*] There is a tradition in this part of the country of an animal with a name like that. It used to be hunted and shot in the barbarous ages. It is quite extinct now. [143–44]

Shaw continues his contrast when later Zoo describes a Marxian community of women. One recalls Marx's epithet, "Abolition of the family! Even the most radical flare up at this infamous proposal of the Communists." Before the Russian Revolution Shaw could not advocate such a radical proposal in his indictments of bourgeois marriage (*Getting Married* and *Misalliance*); he could only recommend "divorce whenever it is desired, without asking why." Now, however, he can project into the future with complete confidence and show how marriage in a classless society has utterly disappeared. Zoo does not even know the meaning of marriage; she informs the Elderly Gentleman that she has "only four [children] as yet." He exclaims,

In Heaven's name, madam, how old are you?

ZOO. Fifty-six.

THE ELDERLY GENTLEMAN. My knees are trembling. I fear I am really ill. Not so young as I was. [151–52]

A little later Zoo reveals the complete absence of the family in her society. After the Elderly Gentleman refers to his aged mother, Zoo says,

Do you mean to say that your mother bothered about you after you were ten?

THE ELDERLY GENTLEMAN. Naturally, madam, She was my mother. What would you have had her do?

ZOO. Go on to the next, of course. After eight or nine, children become quite uninteresting, except to themselves. I shouldnt know my two eldest if I met them.

Her last revelation is too much for the old capitalist. He droops and begins babbling, "I am dying. Let me die. I wish to die" (152).

Marxian internationalism is also fundamental to this classless society. After the Elderly Gentleman gives Zoo his sentimental
account of what had happened to Ireland after England moved
its empire to the East, Zoo comments, "And what a ridiculous
thing to call people Irish because they live in Ireland! you might
as well call them Airish because they live in air. They must be
just the same as other people. Why do you shortlivers persist in
making up silly stories about the world and trying to act as if
they were true?" (156). Zoo sums up the contrast between the
old-fashioned views of the Elderly Gentleman and her own
fresh ones:

> How often must I tell you that we are made wise not by the
> recollections of our past, but by the responsibilities of our
> future. I shall be more reckless when I am a tertiary than I am
> today. If you cannot understand that, at least you must admit
> that I have learnt from tertiaries. . . . my ways did not work;
> and theirs did; and they were able to tell me why. They have
> no power over me except that power: they refuse all other
> power; and the consequence is that there are no limits to their
> power except the limits they set themselves. You are a child gov-
> erned by children, who make so many mistakes and are so
> naughty that you are in continual rebellion against them; and
> as they can never convince you that they are right: they can
> govern you only by beating you, imprisoning you, torturing
> you, killing you if you disobey them without being strong
> enough to kill or torture them. [164]

This passage prepares the audience for the final part *As Far
As Thought Can Reach* (A.D. 31,920). Here social classes are nonexistent and among the ancients the difference between the sexes
is almost negligible; furthermore the ancients are hoping to shed
their bodies soon so that they can become whirlpools of thought
unencumbered in their contemplation of Life.

At the very end of the play Shaw surveys his theme, and
through the words of Adam, Eve, Cain, and finally Lilith reveals
his optimism for the future. After Cain (the symbol of capitalism)
admits that "there is no place for me on earth any longer," Eve
can say triumphantly, "The diggers and the fighters have dug

themselves in with the worms. My clever ones have inherited the earth. All's well" (260). And Lilith, too, optimistically sums up the history of the world in symbolic terms: "I am Lilith: I brought life into the whirlpool of force, and compelled my enemy, Matter, to obey a living soul. But in enslaving Life's enemy I made him Life's master; for that is the end of all slavery" (262). Lilith had previously described the period of the world when Matter ruled supreme as an era when "cruelty and hypocrisy became so hideous that the face of the earth was pitted with the graves of little children among which living skeletons crawled in search of horrible food" (261)—the capitalist period. She says that the pangs of another birth were already upon her "when one man repented and lived three hundred years." And now:

> I shall see the slave set free and the enemy reconciled, the whirlpool become all life and no matter. And because these infants that call themselves ancients are reaching out towards that, I will have patience with them still; though I know well that when they attain it they shall become one with me and supersede me, and Lilith will be only a legend and a lay that has lost its meaning. Of Life only is there no end; and though of its million starry mansions many are empty and many still unbuilt, and though its vast domain is as yet unbearably desert, my seed shall one day fill it and master its matter to its uttermost confines. And for what may be beyond, the eyesight of Lilith is too short. It is enough that there is a beyond. [*She vanishes*]. [262]

Such was Shaw's optimism when he completed *Back to Methuselah* four years after the Russian Revolution. But his optimism was soon to wane just as it had after writing *An Unsocial Socialist,* for the newspapers were reporting Lenin's failure to completely communize Russia. Leaving A.D. 31,920, Shaw slips back to the Middle Ages for his next play, *Saint Joan,* resuming his systematic indictment of capitalistic religion and law which he had begun with *The Devil's Disciple.* A mixture of optimism and pessimism pervades *Saint Joan,* as we noted (see chapter 6). Surely its epilogue ends pessimistically with everyone deserting the saint when she threatens to return to the earth. The optimism, however, results from Shaw's Creative Evolution. After all, woman, through whom the superman will be born, forced even a bourgeois church to admit its mistake and canonize her. Perhaps Shaw the biologist's hope in women at this time caused Shaw the artist to create one of the most dynamic women characters of all times. As he read of the blunderings of Lenin in Russia during the 1920s, he attempted to abate his pessimism by turning his attention to women, hoping to thoroughly train them in socialism, so that they might continue to work for the evolution of a superman—especially if Lenin proved that he was not the hoped-for savior.

Shaw's next work, one of his most compendious nondramatic treatises, was written exclusively for women. *The Intelligent Woman's Guide to Socialism and Capitalism* (completed and published in 1928) valiantly tries to give the future creators of the superman "capitalist horror" and "socialist hope," for these are the basic means whereby Creative Evolution can be established. But it is twenty more years before the appearance of the superman, who visits the earth disguised as an archangel, in Shaw's last complete play, *Farfetched Fables*. In the interim his anxiety for the success of the first country to smash capitalism increases and the works of this period reflect his hopes and fears for Russian socialism.

CHAPTER EIGHT

From the Lands of Despair to the Land of Hope

Shaw's attitude toward Marxism in *The Intelligent Woman's Guide to Socialism and Capitalism* (1928) is one of extreme caution and nervousness, almost as if he were watching a ticker-tape report of the latest developments in the Soviet Union while writing it. Once again he is suspicious of proletarian revolution, hastily retreating from his earlier praise of Russia's uprising to espouse the Fabian or parliamentary method of reform, even though he cleverly allows enough leeway for Lenin's possible success.

That Shaw's analysis of socialism did not change substantially from what we found in his earlier *Essays in Fabian Socialism* is corroborated by the fact that he had these earlier essays reprinted in 1931. To Shaw in 1928 socialism still meant absolute equality of income. He tells his women readers at the very outset that they can read Karl Marx, Saint-Simon, Christ, or any other communist, and they will discover that "all take equality in material subsistence for granted as the first condition of establishing the Kingdom of Heaven on earth," [1] just as he himself did in the "Don Juan in Hell" scene and especially in the last three parts of *Back to Methuselah*. Moreover, he still maintains in *The Intelligent Woman's Guide* that only a national landlord can distribute income equally.

1. *The Works of Bernard Shaw*, 20:105. Further quotations from *The Intelligent Woman's Guide to Socialism and Capitalism* are taken from the same volume; page numbers will be given in parentheses after the quotation when necessary.

149

Nor is it surprising that in 1928 Shaw continues to follow
Marx's dialectic to the letter in outlining the history of capitalism. In *Saint Joan* he concentrated on the evils of the landed
aristocracy and its connection with the church; in this catechism
for women he carries the history of the middle classes up to the
period that Marx had called "centralization" when "the suprem-
acy passed from the employers to the financiers who hold it at
present." [2] But this is not a new aspect of his socialism; we have
already noted that Mangan of *Heartbreak House* was the personification of such financiers. What is new in *The Intelligent
Woman's Guide* is Shaw's concentration on the antithesis in the
Marxian dialectic, the proletariat. We will recall that in the
Essays in Fabian Socialism he made short shrift of the proletariat and immediately passed on to his own antithesis, the
state. In this work Shaw's attitude toward proletarians is far
more respectful, and he gives full credit to Karl Marx as their
savior: "Karl Marx . . . was, and still is, the most famous
champion of the Proletariat as the really organic part of civilized
society to which all the old governing and propertied classes
must finally succumb" (204). The Russian Revolution despite
its questionable aftermath, altered, quite considerably, Shaw's
opinion of a class of people that he previously had scorned
as mere apes of the bourgeoisie.

Another new trend in *The Intelligent Woman's Guide* (which
reaches its climax during the last ten years of his life) is Shaw's
willingness, even in this period of doubts and fears, to equate
the aims of the Fabians with those of Marx and Engels. He says,
for example, that because these two men "were liberally educated, and brought up to think about how things are done instead of merely drudging at the manual labor of doing them"
they, like his colleagues in the Fabian Society,

> were the first to see that Capitalism was reducing their own
> class to the condition of a proletariat, and that the only chance
> of securing anything more than a slave's share in the national

2. Marx, *Capital, the Communist Manifesto, and Other Writings,*
ed. Eastman, p. 203.

income . . . lay in a combination of all the proletarians without distinction of class or country to put an end to Capitalism by developing the communistic side of our civilization until Communism became the dominant principle in society, and mere owning, profiteering, and genteel idling were disabled and discredited. . . . Communism, being the lay form of Catholicism, and indeed meaning the same thing, has never any lack of chaplains. [207]

This is reminiscent of Don Juan's "the great Catholic idea of abolishing slavery" in *Man and Superman*.

Such views do not reflect much anxiety. However, when he begins to analyze the method of instituting socialism, the bad reports from Russia are very much in evidence. At this point he states without hesitation that nationalization of industries can be accomplished by "stable and highly organized States only, which means—and here is the political moral of it—that they cannot be done by revolutions, or by improvised dictatorship." He does concede "what a revolution can do towards nationalization is to destroy the political power of the class which opposes nationalization"—a concession which was not included in *Essays in Fabian Socialism*. He qualifies this, however, by pointing out that "such a revolution by itself cannot nationalize; and the new Government it sets up may be unable even to carry on the nationalized services it finds in existence, and be obligated to abandon them to private enterprise" (307–8). Later he uses the example of Soviet Russia to prove his point:

After the great political revolution of 1917 in that country, the Marxist Communists were so completely victorious that they were able to form a Government far more powerful than the Tsar had ever really been. But as the Tsar had not allowed Fabian Societies to be formed in Russia to reduce Socialism to a system of law, this new Russian Government did not know what to do, and, after trying all sorts of amateur experiments which came to nothing more than pretending that there was Communism where there was nothing but the wreck of Capitalism, and giving the land to the peasants, who immediately insisted on making private property of it over again, had to climb down hastily and leave the industry of the country to

private employers very much as the great ground landlords
of our cities leave the work of the shops to their tenants,
besides allowing the peasant farmers to hold their lands and
sell their produce just as French peasant proprietors or
English farmers do. [418]

But he hastens to assure his female pupils that "this does not
mean that the Russian Revolution has been a failure"; he
praises the Bolsheviks for reversing capitalism's thesis that man
was made for capital and especially commends them for teaching
their children "the Christian morality of Communism instead
of the Mammonist morality of Capitalism." He shows too how
the pleasure palaces once reserved only for the rich wasters are
now recreation centers for the workers: "Idle ladies and gentlemen are treated with salutary contempt, whilst the worker's
blouse is duly honored" (418–19).

He also observes that the Russian revolutionaries preserve the
treasures of art "which puts to shame our own lootings in China."
They even tolerate religion and did not cut off their archbishop's
head "as we cut off Archbishop Laud's"; they do not, however,
permit their children to be taught lies about the Bible and
"reverence the merely rich as their betters. That sort of doctrine
is officially and very properly disavowed as Dope" (419).

His conclusion to this "Revolutions" portion of *The Intelligent Woman's Guide* is somewhat devious. At one point he states
that a revolution may be necessary if the opponents to socialism
refuse to accept it as a parliamentary reform, but he adds that
neither a violent revolution nor parliamentary reforms can by
themselves create socialism: "We must build up Capitalism
before we can turn it into Socialism. But meanwhile we must
learn how to control it instead of letting it demoralize us,
slaughter us, and half ruin us, as we have hitherto done in our
ignorance" (421). (Later he will convert this observation into
the theme of *The Millionairess* [see p. 182].) Yet in 1928 Shaw
is certainly on the fence concerning revolution and the Fabian
method. In one sentence he states categorically that "Mr Sidney
Webb's much quoted and in some quarters much derided 'in-

evitability of gradualness' is an inexorable fact." Two sentences later he admits that "if the Capitalist leaders of the parasitic proletariat . . . declare for a blood and iron settlement instead of a settlement by votes," then such an armed struggle for political power may clear the road to socialism, "but the pavement will be torn up and the goal as far off as ever" (422). In other words, Shaw would like to have all the good things that the revolution accomplished without the bloodshed but at the same time issues a warning that should the capitalists in England force a revolution, they will be responsible for its aftermath.

Despite all this caution, however, the appendix to *The Intelligent Woman's Guide* gives glowing praise to the writings of Karl Marx (528), and Shaw adds that Sidney and Beatrice Webb's work "on the decay of Capitalism has completed Marx's work of driving Capitalism from its old pretension to be normal, inevitable, and in the long run always beneficial in modern society, to a position comparable to that of an army digging itself into its last ditch after a long series of surrenders and retreats" (524). Also, in the appendix he divides all literature into "pre-Marxian and post-Marxian" (526) and again links Marx with Ibsen:

> For women the division is made by Marx's Norwegian contemporary Ibsen rather than by Marx. Ibsen's women are all in revolt against Capitalist morality; and the clever ladies who have since filled our bookshelves with more or less autobiographical descriptions of female frustration and slavery are all post-Ibsen. The modern literature of male frustration, much less copious, is post Strindberg. In neither branch are there any happy endings. They have the Capitalist horror without the Socialist hope. [526]

Continuing to struggle against his pessimism for the success of the Russian Revolution, Shaw finally decided to visit the scene itself. Before his departure he wrote two plays which clearly reflect his state of mind at the time—*The Apple Cart* (completed in 1928 but not published until 1930) and *Too True to Be Good* (completed in 1931 but not published until 1934).

The Apple Cart offers very little hope. King Magnus, the hero, is a constitutional monarch but a realist who is aware of the monetary basis of the so-called democracy. He almost upsets the apple cart by threatening to abdicate and form a party which would seek to abolish Breakages, Limited, the capitalistic syndicate that really runs the government. The cabinet with few exceptions is a mere tool of this syndicate. Boanerges, for example, despite his "Russian blouse and peaked cap" [3] has just been taken into the cabinet as president of the board of trade—another spokesman for Breakages, Limited.

The play, which takes place in 1960, is set in Marx's "centralization" phase, the final period of capitalism which involves, as Marx predicted in *Das Kapital*, "the entanglement of all people in the net of the world market." [4] In an amusing scene, the American ambassador to England, Mr. Vanhattan, announces to King Magnus and Queen Jemima the startling news of the decision by the United States to join the British Empire. Both the king and queen argue vigorously against such a merger, but Vanhattan makes it quite clear that the two capitalist nations are already merged: "Well, we find here everything we are accustomed to: our industrial products, our books, our plays, our sports, our Christian Science churches, our osteopaths, our talkies" (298). When the queen counters with a statement that England has its own culture peculiar to that country, Mr. Vanhattan illustrates Marx's "international character of the capitalistic regime" [5] by pointing out that England sold Ely Cathedral to New Jersey, the removal of which from Cambridge was his "dear old father's first big professional job." He adds significantly, "The building which stands on its former site is a very fine one: in my opinion the best example of reinforced concrete of its period; but it was designed by an American architect, and built by the Synthetic Building Materials Trust, an international

3. Shaw, *Complete Plays with Prefaces,* 4:237. Further quotations from *The Apple Cart* in this chapter are taken from the same volume; page numbers will be given in parentheses after the quotation when necessary.
4. Marx, *Capital,* vol. 1, *The Process of Capitalist Production,* p. 836.
5. Ibid.

affair" (299). The king gives no assurance to Mr. Vanhattan and the play never pursues the point, but after the American ambassador leaves, King Magnus furiously exclaims, "Breakages, Limited, have taken it into their heads to mend the British Commonwealth" (301).

With Marx's centralization phase "grows the revolt of the working class, a class always increasing in numbers, and disciplined, organized by the very mechanism of the process of capitalist production itself." [6] King Magnus is very conscious of Marx's prediction. When Proteus, his prime minister, brags about abolishing poverty in England, he offers no comfort to the king who replies that big business, not the government, has abolished poverty in England, "By sending our capital abroad to places where poverty and hardship still exist: in other words, where labor is cheap" (256). Proteus ignores the king's objection and continues to maintain that England has the highest paid proletariat in the world. Magnus answers, "[*gravely*] I dread revolution" (257). He dreads revolution not in England but in "the countries on whose tribute we are living. That has happened before." Crassus, the colonial secretary, calls this childish, and Magnus replies: "Children in their innocence are sometimes very practical, Mr Colonial Secretary. The more I see of the sort of prosperity that comes of your leaving our vital industries to big business men as long as they keep your constituents quiet with high wages, the more I feel as if I were sitting on a volcano" (258). Lysistrata, the powermistress general, typical of the intelligent woman for whom Shaw had written his guide, agrees with the king. She too is conscious of the "international character of the capitalistic regime" and complains bitterly because Crassus gave the management of the supply of power from the tides in the north of Scotland "to the Pentland Forth Syndicate: a gang of foreign capitalists who will make billions out of it at the people's expense while we are bungling and squabbling" (258).

All of these fears are too much for the prime minister who

6. Ibid., pp. 386–87.

speaks only for Breakages, Limited. He forbids the king to make any further speeches airing such dangerous views to big business; he call it an ultimatum. Later King Magnus replies to the ultimatum by threatening to abdicate, set up his son as king, and join the House of Commons to fight Breakages, Limited. Because of Shaw's anxiety over the possible failure of the Russian Revolution at this time, he does not permit Magnus to succeed. Proteus is forced to withdraw his ultimatum, but the king does not abdicate and Breakages, Limited, continues to rule.

The play's conclusion is entirely cynical and pessimistic. Lysistrata, with tears coming into her eyes, says,

> But I am heart broken at your not coming into the House with us to keep old England in front and lead a new Party against Breakages.
>   MAGNUS [*patting her consolingly on the back*] That would have been splendid, wouldnt it? But I am too old fashioned. This is a farce that younger men must finish.

Presently Queen Jemima enters to take him to dinner. Shaw's final stage direction reads: "The King, with a grimace of hopeless tenderness, allows himself to be led away" (312–13).

In *The Intelligent Woman's Guide* Shaw's wariness of the bloody way socialism had been established in Russia was unmistakable. Even though he grudgingly admitted that through the stubbornness of capitalists' not heeding proposed Fabian reforms a revolution may occur, he predicted that such a substitute would tear up the pavements and leave "the goal as far off as ever." Perhaps his projected journey to the people who had torn up the pavement accounted for a more positive attitude two years later. For in the new (1930) preface, entitled "Fabian Essays Forty Years Later—What They Overlooked," which he included with the 1931 reprint of *Essays in Fabian Socialism,* he gives an almost complete reversal of that prediction. What the Fabians overlooked was that William Morris "the greatest socialist of that day" may have been right when he "told the workers that here was no hope for them save in revolution," because the Russian Revolution "has changed the world more in four years than

Fabian constitutional action seems likely to do in four hundred." [7] What's more, a "ruthless dictatorship" of "doctrinaire Marxians" became convinced that the establishment of socialism could not be effected except by killing anyone actively opposed to it:

> Which they accordingly proceeded to do, and be done by, with terrific energy. And, far from alienating popular sympathy, they found the country rising to this sort of leadership with such enthusiasm that the Bolsheviks, beginning in an apparently hopeless condition of military inferiority as a mob with a casual equipment of pistols opposed by disciplined troops with full munitions provided largely by British money, succeeded in raising a Red Army which achieved the impossible by completely reversing the situation and driving the reactionary White armies out of the field in irretrievable defeat. [321]

True, Shaw still prefers constitutional government to the rule of a "ruthless dictatorship" but, as he qualifies in the very last sentence of this preface, he wants only "modern constitutions and governments which really govern instead of helplessly taking orders, as ours do, from unofficial, irresponsible, and practically secret dictatorships of private industrialists and financiers" (327).

Shortly after writing this, Shaw was at last to embark for Russia. He did not publish an account of his visit to Moscow himself, but one of his companions H. W. L. Dana recorded the speeches he delivered to the Communists and accurately reported his reactions. Shaw evidently gave Dana permission to print his account which appeared in *American Mercury* under the title "Shaw in Moscow." [8] Dana was the constant companion of Shaw, his wife, Charlotte, and their millionaire friends Lord and Lady Astor, who were severely critical of communism, as this strange foursome wended their way through the working man's utopia.

7. *The Works of Bernard Shaw*, 30:319–20. Further quotations from the 1930 preface to the 1931 reprint of *Essays in Fabian Socialism* in this chapter are taken from the same volume; page numbers will be given in parentheses after the quotation when necessary.

8. Dana, "Shaw in Moscow," pp. 343–53. Page numbers of quotations from this article in this chapter will be given in parentheses after the quotation when necessary.

Dana begins his article by verifying "Mr. Shaw's conversion to Communism," remarking that Shaw dashed off *Annajanska or the Bolshevik Empress* "only a few weeks after the Bolshevik Revolution of November . . . showing already a strange half-mocking sympathy with the Soviets, making a little fun of the revolutionists, but still more of the counterrevolutionists." For additional evidence he cites Shaw's warm defense of "the Soviets in his reply to the Pope's attack on irreligion in Russia," and his hailing of·"the announcement of the Five-Year Plan with enthusiasm" (343).

Then he relates Shaw's impressions of and reaction to the people and things that he encountered in his grand tour of the first capital of communism. On meeting an Irish youth who had traveled to Moscow and who told the famous author that he had decided to remain in Russia for ten years, Shaw replied, "If I were your age I would do the same!" Dana adds, "And we felt he really meant it" (344).

Shaw's visit to Lenin's tomb and his subsequent comments on the leader of the revolution reaffirm his earlier expressed profound respect for this revolutionary. Dana remarks that "perhaps no foreigner ever lingered so long" at Lenin's tomb, and suggests that one of the reasons for Shaw's great admiration for Lenin was the fact that he, like Marx, Engels, and Shaw himself, was a "pure intellectual type." Shaw "pointed out that [Lenin] had evidently never worked with his hands . . . 'his ancestors evidently never worked with their hands for six hundred years.' " But Lady Astor insisted, " 'He is not a proletarian: he is an aristocrat.' Shaw retorted, 'You mean an intellectual, not an aristocrat' " (344). Lenin's success had affirmed Shaw's opinion that intellectuals must lead the workers in their fight against capitalism.

Perhaps the greatest tribute Shaw paid to Lenin was in a talking film he made during the visit: " 'I do not know whether there will ever be a man to whom so much significance will be given as the future will given to Lenin. If the experiment which Lenin started succeeds, it will be the opening of a new era. If the experiment fails, then I shall have to take leave of you when

I die with something of melancholy; but if the future is the future as Lenin saw it, then we may smile and look forward to the future without fear' " (349).

Early in this brief visit a significant shift in Shaw's attitude toward the Russian Revolution was evidenced, as his optimism returned. Dana records both his amusing and serious reactions. When Shaw was shown thirteenth-century Russian churches with their crosses intact he said, " 'You Russians are not thorough-going revolutionists at all. . . . We English [referring to Henry VIII's destroying of monasteries] are really the thorough-going revolutionists. You in Russia are only half-way revolutionists!' " (345). In a serious vein, however, Shaw declared in a speech to the House of Trade Unions that according to the theories of Karl Marx the revolution ought to have begun in an industrial country like England: " 'English workers ought to be ashamed that they did not lead the way instead of the Russians. . . . When the Five-Year Plan is brought to a triumphant success, we in the West must follow in your footsteps, whether we will or no.' " Dana observes that when Shaw ended this speech to the Russian workers he "beamed . . . and said, 'I look around and see all these faces with a quite new look on them, a look you cannot see yet in the capitalist West, but which I hope to see everywhere some day' " (349). Earlier Shaw had compared capitalist workers to the group of workers in an electric plant he was addressing: " 'If our workers produce more, that merely enables some share-holder to stay longer on the Riviera . . . . Your work is building up Socialism' " (347). During a speech on his seventy-fifth birthday, Shaw excused Lord and Lady Astor for being big capitalists: " 'It is the fault of the British proletariat, and indeed the proletariat of the whole world, who alone can rescue them from that position' " (349).

Shaw also found, to his delight, that a Russian People's Court was a people's school " 'not so much for the punishment as for the education of the criminal' " (346). He had been advocating such treatment for the criminal all his life.

Shaw's debates with Lady Astor were some of the most amusing incidents of the trip. She, of course, had been trying vainly to convert every Russian she met to capitalism and democracy. In their conversation with some Russian authors, she had attempted to convince them that they were not as free as they would be in a democracy, when Shaw retorted: " 'At least, Lady Astor, they are free from the illusion of democracy' " (348). Later in this same conversation, Dana records Shaw as saying, " 'Mr. H .G. Wells and I are listened to now, because we've got money.' Lady Astor blurted out, 'Nonsense, G. B. S., you know that's nonsense!' Shaw turned to her, 'Well you know, Lady Astor, you would never have asked me to your country house if I had been a pauper' " (348).

Shaw's comic sense was also in evidence during his dinner with the Russian publishers and authors. He had remarked, " 'Of course, Rudyard Kipling is an Imperialist, but Wells hates the *bourgeois*.' Radek [a Russian Communist newspaperman] interrupted, 'That's not so!' Shaw tried to explain, 'Well, that's because Wells is *bourgeois* himself. . . . Mr. Wells and Mr. Chesterton, like Ruskin before them, are always contradicting themselves.' Radek burst in again, 'That *is* so' " (348). At the same dinner Shaw told the Russians, " 'I reserve the right to criticize every people—including the Russians.' " But, Dana notes, "He cast over the assembled group a benign smile that, in spite of what he had been saying, was completely friendly."

After his meeting with Stalin, Shaw observed, " 'I expected to see a Russian working man, and I found a Georgian gentleman. He was not only at ease with himself, but he had the art of setting us at our ease. He was charmingly good humored. There was no malice in him, but also no credulity' " (350)—Shaw had failed to persuade Stalin that Churchill was " 'hopelessly pre-Marx in his historical equipment' " (351).

On the eve of his departure from Russia Shaw remarked, " 'I am leaving the land of hope, and returning to the lands of despair' " (351). In Warsaw, he told a reporter, " 'It is a torture to get back to capitalism. Capitalism is tottering. When you have seen Bolshevism on the spot, there can be no doubt that Capitalism is doomed' " (351). And when he arrived back in England, "Shaw told the English people: 'Russia is all right, and we are all wrong. We had better follow Russia's example as soon as possible' " (352). Certainly Shaw of all people would not have given Dana permission to publish these remarks if he had not made them, and they cannot be ignored. For these attitudes became an integral part of his work throughout the remainder of his long career.

Too True to Be Good, as we have noted, was completed a month before Shaw left for Russia in 1931, and its preface was written two years after his return in 1933. The contrast of the play with its preface mirrors the relationship between his before-and-after feelings.

As the curtain rises, the fetid odor of a sickroom greets the audience. The Patient, as she is expressionistically referred to, is immediately recognized as the personification of the idle rich with nothing to do but languish in her room bereft even of natural light and air, taking the medicines of a capitalist doctor (similar to those in *The Doctor's Dilemma*) who like The Elderly Lady, her mother, caters to and encourages her every neurosis. Although Shaw livens the atmosphere with the presence of a fascinating talking microbe called The Monster, who complains bitterly that The Patient has given him her illnesses, the scene is grim, and Shaw's contempt for the final period of capitalism becomes even more marked as the first act develops. As soon as the mother and doctor leave the room, a night nurse signals to her burglar-accomplice, who enters. Actually not a nurse but a former chambermaid known as Sweetie, she has planned with Popsy, the burglar, to rob The Patient of a valuable pearl necklace. When The Patient discovers that her necklace is to be stolen, all of her weakness suddenly disappears and she almost kills Popsy by kicking him in the "solar plexus." Her surprising strength inspires Popsy (who reveals that he was ordained a priest at Oxford) to persuade The Patient to leave the sickroom and be voluntarily kidnapped by Sweetie and him. The ransom money would enable the three of them to have a glorious adventure in a sun-drenched land. The Patient eagerly agrees—to Shaw even a life with two criminals would be far healthier than near death in the confines of a capitalist sickroom. The Monster at the end of the first act announces: "The play is now virtually over, but the characters will discuss it at great length for two acts more. The exit doors are all in order. Goodnight." [9]

Discuss it they do on a beautiful beach in a mountainous country, and in the course of these discussions Shaw bitterly denounces the church, the League of Nations, marriage, war—all the evils that will soon disappear in "the land of hope." The Patient, disguised as a native girl, is now vigorously healthy; "her muscles are hard and glistening with unguent" (663). Sweetie, disguised as a countess, is carrying on a love affair with Colonel Tallboys and a sergeant. Popsy, now known as Aubrey, has resumed his clerical role and preaches to anyone who will listen. All three are living on the money received from the sale of The Patient's necklace, while anxiously awaiting the ransom money from her mother. Though The Patient is physically healthy in this earthly paradise, she is dissatisfied. True, she discovered in this land of sunshine that she had been "devoured by parasites: by tourist agencies, steamboat companies [etc.] . . . all trying to get my money by selling me things I dont really want." She also learned that "they preyed on me to keep themselves alive: they pretended they were making me happy when it was only by drinking and drugging—cocktails and cocaine— that I could endure my life" (704). But this new awareness had not made her happy. The Countess becomes bored by her promiscuous life; and Aubrey, Shaw's spokesman, begins to recognize the worthlessness of their existence. Even Colonel Tallboys envies Private Meek's proletarian privileges. For the colonel is burdened with the responsibilities, unable to "do anything but give orders and look significant," whereas the private is free to pursue his interest, to do "everything natural to a complete man" (709–10).

When The Patient's mother arrives in search of her kidnapped daughter, her upper-class notions disappear after the exasperated Colonel Tallboys whacks her on the head with his umbrella. She

9. *Complete Plays with Prefaces,* 4:656. Further quotations from *Too True to Be Good* in this chapter are taken from the same volume; page numbers will be given in parentheses after the quotation when necessary.

then becomes aware of that the bourgeois family is not a sacred institution. Even failing to recognize her own daughter, she admits that she had hated her and wants to forget "that there are such miserable things in the world as mother and daughters" (715).

Shaw offers some hope for these two females emancipated from the sickroom of capitalism: The Patient will found a sisterhood "to clean up this filthy world and keep it clean" (705), and she will take her mother along as a companion "on trial."

Toward the end of the play Shaw's eagerness to visit Russia is clearly revealed. When The Patient asks Private Meek for her passport, he empties a heap of passports on the beach and explains that everyone wants to go to "The Union of Federated Sensible Societies." Unfortunately, they will not permit anymore English because "their lunatic asylums are too full already." They did, however, offer one visa for Colonel Tallboys. Colonel Tallboys had explained earlier in the play that he took up watercolor painting to keep from going insane. Private Meek tells him that they have seen some of the Colonel's work and will "make him head of their centres of respose and culture if he'll settle there." The Colonel cannot believe this offer because it "indicates a degree of intelligence of which no Government is capable" (716), but he must refuse it because his wife would never live there.

This brief glimpse of the "Union of Federated Sensible Societies" is quickly over, and the play ends with a lengthy, gloomy speech delivered by Aubrey the burglar-preacher. It is perhaps the most pessimistic ending that Shaw had as yet written. Aubrey drones on and on about how the capitalist minds are "stripped naked," how they have "outgrown" their religion, "outgrown" their political system. He says that a preacher must preach the way of life but their way is "the way of death." He cries out for a way of life but has none; yet he must "preach and preach and preach no matter how late the hour and how short the day." At that moment a fog completely envelops him, but Shaw says that even though we do not hear it the

incorrigible preacher will not be denied his peroration, which
could we only hear it distinctly, would probably run—
—or whether in some pentecostal flame of revelation the Spirit
will descend on me and inspire me with a message the sound
whereof shall go out unto all lands and realize for us at last
the Kingdom and the Power and the Glory for ever and ever.
Amen. [720]

In the final stage directions of the play Shaw's disgust with the
Fabian way is summed up when he admits: "The author, though
himself a professional talk maker, does not believe that the world
can be saved by talk alone." He has only one hope left and that
is "the woman of action" who believes "lost dogs always find
their way home." But he even qualifies this hope in the last
sentence: "So they will, perhaps, if the women go out and look
for them" (720).

Though it was a "torture to get back to Capitalism" and he
had already been back for two years when he wrote the preface
to *Too True to Be Good,* at least his anxiety for the success of
the Russian experiment had been dispelled by his visit, and he
could offer solutions to the seemingly impossible problems posed
by the characters in the play.

In a discussion of the low morale of soldiers fighting for capitalist governments, he says, "It must be admitted that a private
soldier outside that surprising centre of culture, the Red Army
of Russia, has so little to be happy about when sober that his
case is hardly a fair one. But it serves to illustrate the moral of
my play, which is that our capitalistic system, with its golden
exceptions of idle richery and its leaden rule of anxious poverty,
is as desperate a failure from the point of view of the rich as of
the poor" (611).

He then begins his analysis of the plight of The Patient
languishing in her sickbed at the beginning of the play. Her
illness is a direct result of the final stage of capitalism: "When
joint stock companies were formed to run big industrial concerns
with money raised on the . . . terms that the money is never
repaid, the system became so extensive that the idle upstart rich
became a definitely mischievous and miserable class quite differ-

ent in character from the old feudal rich" (618). The Patient was temporarily cured of her misery by the two criminals who took her to a beautiful country where they lived sumptuously. But the result was that they got "nothing for their money but a multitude of worries and a maddening dissatisfaction" (609). Money and leisure are not the answer as The Patient discovered. Shaw found the answer in Russia where the rank and file of the Communist party do an ordinary day's work and "sacrifice" all their leisure time to politics which requires "a comparatively ascetic discipline and virtually no pecuniary gain" (632). The Patient went off to found a sisterhood to "clean this filthy world" but she was vague about the nature of her sisterhood, "Since I came here I have been wanting to join the army, like Joan of Arc. It's a brotherhood, of a sort" (706). Such a combined sisterhood and brotherhood Shaw found already existing in "the rank and file of the Communist Party" (632).

The Patient's mother discovered the falsity of the sanctity of marriage, and Shaw in the preface says that if Saint Vincent de Paul were alive today he "would probably propose a clean sweep of all our difficulties about marriage and divorce by forbidding people to marry for longer than a year, and make them renew their vows every twelve months" (629–30).

All of the disillusionment with religion that appears during the discussions and is climaxed at the end of the play when Aubrey, who wants to preach, finds he has "no Bible, no creed" and can only babble as the fog envelops him, is cleared up by Shaw in the preface. He found in Russia a new church modeled after the old Catholic church but "purged of supernatural pretension, assumption of final perfection, and the poison of private property." He adds that "Mr Stalin . . . would be strikingly like a Pope, claiming for form's sake an apostolic succession from Marx, were it not for his frank method of Trial and Error, his entirely human footing, and his liability to removal at a moment's notice if his eminence should upset his mental balance" (631–32). The members of the Communist party in Russia cannot dedicate themselves eternally: they can drop out into the laity when they please, and if they do not please and nevertheless have become slack in their ministry, they are pushed out" (629–30).

These solutions force his readers to contrast a model society he had seen with the sick world of the play written on the eve of his departure. The preface ends with an ominous warning to "the lands of despair" then in the throes of the great economic depression: "If anyone can suggest a better practically tested plan, now is the time to do it; for it is all up, with the old Anarchist-Liberal parliamentary systems in the face of thirty millons of unemployed, and World Idiotic Conferences at which each nation implores all the others to absorb its unemployed by a revival of international trade" (632).

In the plays of the thirties Shaw is a man wholly absorbed with the "torture" of having to live in lands that still refused to heed his warning. But before we examine these plays, let us turn to some nondramatic work he composed immediately after his trip to Russia, two years before he wrote the preface to *Too True to Be Good*. On October 11, 1931, he turned his attention to England's capitalist American cousins in a radio broadcast entitled "A Little Talk on America." He opens by addressing the Americans as "dear old boobs who have been telling one another for a month past that I have gone dotty about Russia," and then proceeds to explain why he has gone "dotty," exhibiting all of the elation he felt while visiting the Soviet Union.

First of all, he points out that both England and America are financially bankrupt:

> Our budget shows a deficit of 850 million dollars; yours shows a deficit of 4,500 million . . . Russia, on the other hand, flaunts her budget surplus of 750 millions. Not only that, but Russia's people are employed to the last man and woman; her scientific agriculture is doubling and trebling her harvests; her roaring and multiplying factories, her efficient rulers, her atmosphere of . . . hope and security for the poorest . . . has never been seen in a civilized country on earth.[10]

10. Shaw, "A Little Talk on America," British Museum Add. MS 50705, fols. 1–2. Folio numbers of further quotations from this manuscript in this chapter will be given in parentheses after the quotation when necessary.

He notes that Russia has nothing but contempt for capitalist incompetence but offers some consolation to Americans by recalling that it was an American, Henry George, who years ago led him to Karl Marx "who opened my eyes still wider, leaving it quite plain to me that our Capitalist system, though we could foozle along with it for a time at the cost of frightful unhappiness and degrading poverty for nine tenths of the population was bound to end in the bankruptcy of civilization" (fol. 2).

After this consideration for his American radio audience, he launches into a typical Shavian argument in which he will bind together Fabianism and Marxism and will even take credit for a great deal of what happened in Russia—an idea he expresses again in his *What I Really Wrote about the War* (published this same year).[11] In his broadcast he makes it clear that fourteen years *after* he was exposed to Karl Marx, "a Russian named Oulianoff, better known to you as Lenin, followed my example and read Marx" (fol. 3).

Irony after irony follows: He praises World War I because it transformed the only European power bigger than the United States into a federation of Communist republics and asks, "That was not quite what you expected, was it? Your boys were not sent to the slaughter cheering for Karl Marx and echoing his slogan, 'Proletarians of all lands, unite'? However, this is what happened" (fol. 3). But America did not bear all the responsibility for establishing communism in Russia: "You share it with me—*me* now speaking to you, Bernard Shaw." After all, it was he in 1914 (much to the fury of the Allies) who advised all the soldiers to go home and stop the senseless slaughter, and the Russian soldiers did just that.[12] "That was the opportunity for Lenin and his friends who had followed my example and educated themselves politically by reading Karl Marx" (fol. 4). He then appeals to American patriotism by equating what Lenin and his friends in Russia did with what Washington, Jefferson,

---

11. *The Works of Bernard Shaw*, 21:281.

12. Ibid.; see his statement in *Common Sense about the War* (written in 1914 as a supplement to the *New Statesman*) where he first takes credit for the revolution's occurrence.

Hamilton, Franklin, and Tom Paine had established in the United States 141 years earlier. Suggesting a little game, he challenges his listeners to black out the conditions in America and Russia and guarantees that if they do so they will discover "when the right answer is America, they will guess Russia; when the right name is Washington, they will cry Trotsky. They will declare that the puzzles are too easy to be worth solving, that Jefferson is Lenin, that Franklin is Litvinoff, that Paine is Lunacharsky." And climaxing this equation, he adds: "Today there is a statue of Washington in London; and tomorrow there will no doubt be a statue of Lenin in New York with the inscription, 'Blessed are ye when men shall revile you and say all manner of evil against you' " (fol. 5).

In the peroration to the broadcast, Shaw offers some traveling tips to Americans who should want to rush there and see for themselves "whether it is all real." He says that proletarians of all lands are welcome if they are skilled laborers and are of good character—"they are very particular about character in Russia" (fol. 6). He predicts that the Russian feeling for American visitors will be a mixture of pity for refugees from the horrors of American capitalism and an enormous (it is interesting that he strikes out the word *enormous* from the typed manuscript and substitutes in his own handwriting the word *colossal*) intellectual contempt for American imbecility in not having established communism "in your own country"; he advises them to be careful because the Russian conscience is different "so that the achievements which are an American's pride and glory seem to the Russians infamous crimes" (fol. 8).

He adds ominously that if an American tries to pull off any capitalist tricks in Russia he will simply "have ceased to exist and . . . relatives will be politely informed that they need have no anxiety about you as you are not coming home any more" (fol. 9)—a theme he will develop fully in his preface to *On the Rocks*.

Shaw congratulates himself as the first person to instill the idea of liquidation in the Russians. Years before he had advocated each person's justifying his existence in a civilized society, and that if he could not do so he should be summarily and painlessly terminated: "A great part of the secret of the success of Russian Communism is that every Russian knows that unless he makes his life a paying proposition for his country he will probably lose it" (fols. 9–10). In *What I Really Wrote about the War,* he develops this idea further as he approves the action of the leaders of the revolution in ruthlessly exterminating all opposition and lauds them for their mercifully swift assassinations of the Czar and his family rather than yielding to the mockery of a trial replete with a public execution to delight the masses. The leaders first erred in merely taking the land from the landlords and handing it over to the husbandmen, for then they had to take the land themselves as public work to realize the full potential of modern possibilities. But he condones their hanging the uncooperative landlords, drunken workmen, and corrupt overseers. He praises the revolutionists for placing the prosperity of the entire country above the prosperity of the individual by dividing equally the profits of the successful farmers, and he concludes by praising the revolutionists as the "sole hope and promise of civilization." [13]

Although he ends the broadcast by admitting that Russia is not a paradise, he quickly excuses its mistakes on the grounds that it is very difficult to undo the evils of czarism in fourteen years and optimistically declares that these evils, nevertheless, are retreating before the spread of communism as steadily as they are advancing upon us before the last desperate struggle of our bankruptcy. In *What I Really Wrote about the War,* he insists that from the proletarian point of view the new civilization of Russia is "doing those things that we ought to have done and leaving undone those things that we ought not to have done" [14]

Finally he reminds Americans that its own ship is sinking "and the Russian ship is the only big one that is not rolling and tapping out SOS on its wireless" (fol. 11), and he flatters American youth by urging them to "not let themselves be outrun in the

13. Ibid., pp. 281–83.
14. Ibid.

great race of civilization by any Russian that ever set foot to the ground."

These two works reflect the feelings he had when he sat down to write his next play. On the faces of the Russian workers he had seen "a new look . . . a look you cannot see yet in the Capitalist West." As he observed the bread lines of the Great Depression, he probably despaired of ever seeing this "look . . . everywhere some day" even on the faces of American youths he had challenged.

On the Rocks (completed in 1933), the first major play written after his return from Moscow, is almost completely bereft of humor, even the irony found in *The Apple Cart* and *Too True to be Good* is missing. In the preface Shaw is willing to condone even the bloodiest aspects of the Russian Revolution's aftermath. His defense of Stalin's bloodbath is starkly humorless, and he approaches this delicate subject by means of a historical argument—as usual, his history comes right out of *Das Kapital*. Shaw argues that the peasants were driven off the land to give way to sheep and shepherds, who in turn were exterminated to give way to deer and gamekeepers; factories replaced the deer and the proletarians were hired to work them, but eventually machines replaced the proletarians who then sold themselves "as soldiers, servants, prostitutes, police officers, scavengers, and operators of the immense machinery of amusements and protection for the idle rich classes created by the private property system." [15] They even organized themselves into trade unions hoping that by strikes and riots they would reduce the state of their extermination, but the proprietors eventually engaged themselves in suicidal wars which caused the rate of extermination to rise again. Consequently, capitalist governments have killed off the real cream of society, the workers. Hence "the power to exterminate is too grave to be left in any hands but those of a thoroughly Communist Government responsible to the whole community"

15. *Complete Plays with Prefaces,* 5:485. Further quotations from *On the Rocks* and its preface in this chapter are taken from the same volume; page numbers will be given in parentheses after the quotation when necessary.

(486). In Russia the Cheka liquidates only those who are not publicly useful. Capitalist nations find this novel method terrifying because they are accustomed to a "limited liability in morals," which permits making a corner in wheat or copper, causing prices to rise so as to generate enormous private fortunes, or making mischief between nations to stimulate the private trade in armaments. Shaw concludes: "Such limited liability no longer exists in Russia, and is not likely to exist in the future, in any highly civilized state" (495). Russia is purging its nation for the common good while capitalist nations exterminate for private gain. We have already seen how, in his broadcast to America, Shaw himself took credit for teaching Russia this concept of justice.

The play itself is a cynical exposition of the hopelessness of capitalistic England in the depths of the Great Depression. Shaw paints a grim picture. His disillusionment over the Fabian method of instituting socialism in England is clearly brought out by Chief of Police Basham's report to Sir Arthur Chavender, the prime minister. He tells Sir Arthur that the only way to quell the angry unemployed is to pacify them with speeches:

> And the fellows who make the speeches can be depended on never to do anything else. In the first place, they dont know how. In the second, they are afraid. I am instructing my agents to press all the talking societies, the Ethical Societies, the Socialist societies, the Communists, the Fascists, the Anarchists, the Syndicalists, the official Labor Party, the Independent Labor Party, the Salvation Army, the Church Army, and the Atheists, to send their best tub-thumpers into the streets to seize the opportunity.
> SIR ARTHUR. What opportunity?
> BASHAM. They dont know. Neither do I. It's only a phrase that means nothing: just what they are sure to rise at. [529]

Sir Arthur Chavender as prime minister is an idealist and a wind bag like the Reverend Morell in *Candida*, but at least Chavender is not convinced of his ideals. Early in the play, as he prepares a speech to be delivered to the Anglo-Catholics who are reported to be veering toward Christian communism, his lack of faith in his own ideals is brought out. In the speech Sir Arthur is supposed to stem the tide towards communism among the Anglo-Catholics by telling them that socialism will ruin the family. His dictation of the speech to Hilda, his secretary, is filled with humorous tangents and obvious examples of his lack of conviction. After Hilda reminds him of the theme of his speech, he blurts out,

> Who says Socialism will break up the family? Dont be a fool.
>   HILDA. The Archbishop wants you to say it. At the Church House.
>   SIR ARTHUR. Decidedly. I am going mad. [534]

Immediately afterwards Sir Arthur's own family bursts into the room bickering. This demonstration of their basic incompatibility proves conclusively that the family is *not* a sacred "foundation."

Later Sir Arthur does become a convinced realist and loses all his hesitations and lack of convictions. At the Lady Doctor's retreat house he reads Karl Marx, Lenin, Trotsky, and Stalin, and begins to recognize the pecuniary basis of his society. As usual Shaw effects Chavender's conversion to socialism through the advice of a woman. Woman will lead the way.

When Sir Arthur, now a realist, returns from the Lady Doctor's retreat, he announces his startling socialist program of nationalization. The reactions of the various characters to this program illustrate Shaw's complete cynicism toward England's salvation. At first each cabinet member agrees to the program because he sees profit to himself and his contingents at the expense of others. Only Sir Dexter Rightside, the die-hard conservative, sees the whole program as a serious threat to capitalism and fights it from beginning to end.

Shaw's scorn for organized labor in England is again revealed when the Isle of Cats Deputation representing organized labor opposes Sir Arthur's program and joins Sir Dexter's opposition. Shaw had told the Russian workers during his visit that English workers ought to be ashamed of themselves for not having led the revolution of the proletariat since, according to Marx, England, being an industrialized nation, was far riper for the revolution than Russia was. In *On the Rocks* Shaw shows that not only will organized labor in England refuse to lead a revolution, it will even oppose a bloodless, parliamentary method of instituting socialism.

Hipney ("old and tried friend of the working class") sums up Shaw's attitude in these matters in a long speech which traces the starry-eyed enthusiasm of the young Fabians to the present futile results of their labors. He admits that in the beginning their efforts frightened the "stoutest of the tyrants and the bosses and the police." But, he adds wrathfully, as soon as the working man was given the vote he became a docile tool of these imperialist bosses who after mistreating the colonies (Egypt, Ireland, and India) beyond belief were reelected by the working class constituencies in overwhelming majorities. These working classes could be stampeded by merely telling them "the Russians were coming," or easily rallied by promising them "to hang the Kaiser, or lord knows what silliness that shouldnt have imposed on a child of four." Old Hipney admits that this was the end of democracy for him and adds wistfully, "Though there was no man alive that had hoped as much from it, nor spoke deeper from his heart about all the good things that would happen when the people came to their own and had votes like the gentry. . . . My God! It delivered us into the hands of our spoilers . . . . It took the heart out of old Hipney." The speech ends in a burst of rage reflecting Shaw's willingness to accept "any Napoleon or Mussolini or Lenin or Chavender that has the stuff in him to take both the people and the spoilers and oppressors by the scuffs of their silly necks and just sling them into the way they should go with as many kicks as may be needful to make a thorough job of it" (604–5). Glenmorion (Liberal member of Parliament and president of the Board of Trade, who favors parliamentary reform) speaks for Shaw when he suggests that Fabian reform "is not a matter of today or tomorrow. I calculate that at the very least it will take fifty years to get it through [Parliament]" (598).

As far as England is concerned, Shaw rejects class war and even the Fabian evolutionary method. What is left? In *On the Rocks* practically nothing. Since Russia and her program are praised throughout, perhaps he still had hopes for a superman type of dictator like Lenin to force Marxism into action, but Sir Arthur Chavender, like King Magnus in *The Apple Cart,* refuses to take the lead. Although Shaw had made him a realist in regard to his society—Sir Arthur says to his wife concerning the corrupt haves and have-nots, "I know better now: I know that it can be helped, and how it can be helped. And rather than go back to the old whitewashing job, I'd seize you tight around the waist and make a hole in the river with you" (618)—still Sir Arthur retires from politics. When his wife asks why he doesn't lead his country out of the mess, he says, "Why dont I lead the revolt against it all? Because I'm not the man for the job, darling . . . . And I shall hate the man who will carry it through for his cruelty and the desolation he will bring on us and our like" (619).

At the very end of the play, Shaw's growing distrust of democracy and gradualism is especially evident as he describes the mob's ineffectual milling about and its final break-up by the police. One note of optimism is injected: Sir Arthur, who hears the mob singing "England Arise" and watches Hilda rush out to join them, comments, "Suppose England really did arise!" (620). But such optimism is nullified by his prefatory remark, "She'll be back for tea" and by Shaw's final comments on Sir Arthur's curtain speech, "Unemployed England, however, can do nothing but continue to sing, as best it can to a percussion accompaniment of baton thwacks, Edward Carpenter's verses":

> England, arise! the long, long night is over,
> Faint in the East behold the dawn appear;
> Out of your evil dream of toil and sorrow—
> Arise, O England, for the day is here;
> From your fields and hills,
> Hark! the answer swells—
> Arise, O England, for the day is here!" [620]

The hopeful verses add an ironic poignancy: Shaw had seen Marxism-in-action in Russia but could see no hope for it in his own land. Such desperation explains why, at this time, he lost his famous sense of humor, his aversion to violence, and condoned even the blood purges and mass extermination policies of so ruthless a dictator as Stalin. In *On the Rocks* he gave his last trumpet warning to the capitalist West; in his next play an avenging angel actually does blow his trumpet to usher in Judgment Day.

A nondramatic work *The Rationalization of Russia*[16] (written in 1932–33 but not published until 1964) helps clarify the rather enigmatic theme of this next play *The Simpleton of the Unexpected Isles*. Much of the substance of *The Rationalization* we have seen in his famous broadcast to America, but it does contain two correlated ideas previously treated indeterminately by Shaw: (1) an almost wholehearted espousal of revolution, and (2) an almost complete castigation of the Fabian method of parliamentary reform.

His development of the first begins:

> As a convinced Communist I strive to rescue the rich from their riches with much more tenderness than to rescue the poor from their poverty . . . I should be sorry to take a pistol in my hand and blow off the back of poor old Soames' pate [Soames is capitalism personified] just as Soames himself would be sorry to operate similarly on Stalin; but I cannot conceal from myself that the thing has to be done if our civilization is not to go the way of all the previous civilizations which have been forsythed [a play on Galsworthy's family in *The Forsyte Saga*] into bankruptcy . . . . From the Communist point of view there is no arguing with that sort of thing. There is nothing for it but Bang. [fols. 48, 49, 53, 54]

Two phrases here are new to his writing: "As a convinced Communist" and "Bang." There is no ambiguity here, and what follows is the most complete disavowal of the Fabian method of instituting socialism that we have encountered thus far. He asks,

16. Shaw, "The Rationalization of Russia," British Museum Add. MS 50676 (published by the University of Indiana Press in 1964). Folio numbers of quotations from this manuscript in this chapter will be given in parentheses after the quotation when necessary.

"How is it then that the leaders of the Russian revolution have been able to do what I cannot do: that is, set up an effective inquisition to enforce to the death the dogma that forsythism—parasitism is the sin against the Holy Ghost . . . ?" In answer he accuses Parliament of taking thirty years to do thirty minutes of work. He accuses the Labor party in office in the House of Commons of dropping the subject of socialism completely, of reviling the Russian Communists, in other words of helping capitalism in every way. And he adds sarcastically, "But something worse happened; the Home Rule for Ireland after thirty years was passed, but the die hards wouldn't accept it and Sinn Fein revolted and won . . . and, having demonstrated the futility and inefficiency of Parliamentary methods was ironically rewarded by a Parliament of its own as bad as England's" (fols. 64, 68).

All of these things convinced Shaw and those who had read Marx that "the bourgeoisie is rotten. The Army is rotten. The monarchies are rotten. And what has rotted them all to the core is Capital in private hands in pursuit of private profit" (fol. 71).

His optimism returns momentarily as he reflects that two great men, the Communist German Jew and the Tory British gentleman (John Ruskin) shouted at the top of their voices (like Captain Shotover in *Heartbreak House*) that Europe was on the quicksands and that their shouts finally penetrated the ears of the Russian revolutionaries who swiftly "exterminated" the capitalists from that great nation.

But this optimism is momentary, for *The Rationalization of Russia* ends with a repetition of Shaw's regrets for his completely ineffectual work as a Fabian reformer: "When I think of all the time and work I have wasted on Parliamentary elections, for instance: the crowds that have come to hear me calling on them to vote for Tweedledum against Tweedledee and practising all the arts of the platform on them until they rose and sang 'For he's a jolly good fellow' in a transport of delusion in which they seemed to themselves to be doing something of political importance!" (fol. 89).

Although *The Simpleton of the Unexpected Isles* (completed

in 1934) is actually a sequel to *On the Rocks,* its tone and form, as the strange title suggests, are quite different. As a sequel to *On the Rocks,* it brings his apology for Stalin's blood purge (confined to the preface of the earlier play) into the action of the plot itself. In form, however, it resembles *Back to Methuselah,* permitting him to break the strictures of the dramatic realism and gaze into the distant future, where he again is free to call upon the optimistic theories of Creative Evolution and thus effect a hopeful tone as the final curtain falls. Despite this optimistic ending, the bitter tone of *On the Rocks* pervades the greater part of *The Simpleton.* Shaw purposefully chose the nonrealistic form of *Back to Methuselah* so that he could preach his hopeful theories of biology, such is not his motive in *The Simpleton.* In *Back to Methuselah* he quickly passes over the revolutions that had effected classless societies and concentrates on a utopian world where such societies had existed for centuries. In contrast *The Simpleton* dwells on the painful but necessary processes of effecting a society conducive to the working out of Creative Evolution's utopian theories. As in Russia, capitalistic countries must first be purged of the causes of despair before they can prosper.

In the preface (written in 1935, a year after the play), Shaw very painstakingly and cleverly analyzes the purgation or Day of Judgment theme. He begins by reaffirming his "business in the world." In a typical Marxian indictment of the institutions of capitalism, he singles out the university as a "paid wage laborer of the bourgeoisie," which turns out playwrights who compose inoffensive entertainments, not real drama: "If author and journalist are both placid Panglossians, convinced that their civilization is the best of all civilizations and their countrymen the greatest race on earth: in short, if they have had a university education, there is no trouble: the press notices are laudatory if the play is entertaining." [17] He, of course, is no such bourgeois

---

17. *Complete Plays with Prefaces,* 6:525. Further quotations from *The Simpleton of the Unexpected Isles* and its preface in this chapter are taken from the same volume; page numbers will be given in parentheses after the quotation when necessary.

artist nor could such a "Panglossian" condition exist in Russian education where the children are safeguarded from the myth of a life after death not only by secular schools, but by positive instruction that no individual has to suffer after death for sins committed before it. With such freedom, however, comes responsibility, and Shaw, the arch opponent of censorship, now defends "the list of activities blacklisted by the Russian State as felonious." He argues that since the Russians have turned their economic morals downside up by rejecting the capitalistic utopia and following the prophets, Marx and Engels, they are really carrying out not only the invectives of the Old Testament, but the communist teachings "of Jesus, Peter, and Paul" (530).

His next logical step is the delicate job of defending Stalin's Cheka. He reminds his Christian readers of other Judeo-Christian precedents, among them, the Catholic Inquisition and Protestant Committees. What follows is the usual Marxian joining of Christianity and capitalism: "I can assure the Foreign Office that the landed gentry in the person of my grandfather, the tramway companies, and the capitalist planters, made the question of whether individual dogs and men are worth their salt familiar to me a whole generation before the Tcheka existed" (535). Then he explains the play's theme:

> In it I still retain the ancient fancy that the race will be brought to judgment by a supernatural being, coming literally out of the blue; but his inquiry is not whether you believe in Tweedledum or Tweedledee but whether you are a social asset or a social nuisance. And the penalty is liquidation. He has appeared on the stage before in the person of Ibsen's button moulder. And as history always follows the stage, the button moulder came to life as Djerjinsky. My Angel comes a day after the fair; but time enough for our people, who know nothing of the button moulder and have been assured by our gentleman-ladylike newspapers that Djerjinsky was a Thug. [538]

The prologue to *The Simpleton* is a dramatization of the biblical theme, "Unless ye are born again of water and the Holy Ghost ye shall not be saved": the only way in which the Emigration Officer and the Young Woman can wash the stains of capitalism from their souls is by a death-defying plunge into the sea. Wilks, a subordinate to the Emigration Officer, refuses to leave capitalism or the Emigration Office and blows his brains out after realizing that he was no Cecil Rhodes; that he did not find diamonds in his back yard; that the rule of capitalism is the "golden rule of exceptions" which makes a man rich and the "leaden rule of poverty for the millions"—he was one of the millions. And yet he dies still singing the praises of capitalist England, "Let the whole earth be England; and let Englishmen rule it. [*Singing*] Rule Britannia: Britannia rules the wa——" (548). Here we have the same bitterness that pervades the ending of *On the Rocks*. Wilks ably demonstrates the reason why English proletarians would never rebel. But this is only the prologue to *The Simpleton*.

The play proper begins twenty years later. The Priest and Priestess who had effected the purifying plunge for the Young Woman and Emigration Officer now greet Iddy, a stupid clergyman who wandered to the Unexpected Isles. Iddy explains that he was kidnapped by pirates who used him for a respectable front; he is the symbol of Christianity used for centuries, as Marx had said, by pirates or capitalists as their respectable front.

On the isles everything is turned "downside up" as Shaw said the Russians had to do when they instituted socialism, but the Unexpected Isles are by no means the utopia found in the last part of *Back to Methuselah*. In Russia, at this time, the Communists were still in the process of achieving Marx's millennium, and its process included ruthless extermination of the unfit. The same transitional period exists on the Unexpected Isles. Although the marriage experiment—attempted by Pra and Prola, Mr. and Mrs. Hyering (the Emigration Officer and the Young Woman of the Prologue), Sir Charles and Lady Farwaters (she was a religious fanatic in the prologue)—corresponds somewhat to a Marxian community of women; since the six parents are a blend of the East and West, it is a failure. Their four "super children" —Janga, Kanchin, Vashti, and Maya—are symbols of love, pride, heroism, and empire, but they are failures and hence are

liquidated by the avenging angel. Their failures, as Lady Farwaters explains, resulted from their having been taught "everything except how to work for their daily bread instead of pray-
ing for it" (603). In other words, they lack the economic skills,
the *sine qua non* of Marx's millennium.

The real theme of the play—the dramatic apology for Stalin's
blood purge—begins when the avenging angel announces Judgment Day. The scene preceding it prepares the audience:

> IDDY. . . . We must believe that to establish that beautiful
> and good world on earth is the best thing we can do, and the
> only sort of religion and politics that is worth bothering about.
> PROLA. What about people who have no original ideas, Iddy?
> PRA. The great majority of mankind?
> IDDY. Theyll be only too glad to do what you tell them,
> Prola, if you can make them feel that it's right.
> PROLA. And if they are incapable of feeling it?
> JANGA. Kill.
> KANCHIN. Kill.
> VASHTI. Kill.
> MAYA. Kill. [591]

And who are killed, or rather (in deference to Shaw's "aversion
to violence") who disappear from the face of the earth? The
nonproductive: Janga, Kanchin, Vashti, and Maya, ironically;
members of the medical profession; in fact, all of the "important
people"—the same people who were disappearing in Russia while
Shaw was writing the play. Prola defends the process of cleansing:
"If the angels fail us we shall set up tribunals of our own from
which worthless people will not come out alive. When men no
longer fear the judgment of God, they must learn to judge themselves" (606).

And who will be spared? Hyering offers the answer, summing
up all of the Marxian principles which Stalin was putting into
effect at that time: "I have an uneasy feeling that we'd better get
back to our work. I feel pretty sure that we shant disappear as
long as we're doing something useful; but if we only sit here
talking, either we shall disappear or the people who are listening to us will" (607). A return of Shaw's comic sense preludes

The Simpleton's relatively hopeful ending, for in its final scene he again combines his religion of optimism—Creative Evolution—with Marxist-Stalinist economics: once the worthless have been liquidated, then mankind must strive to produce a super race. Pra exclaims, "Then I, Pra, must continue to strive for more knowledge and more power, though the new knowledge always contradicts the old, and the new power is the destruction of the fools who misuse it." Prola adds,

> We shall plan common wealths when our empires have brought us to the brink of destruction; but our plans will still lead us to the Unexpected Isles. We shall make wars because only under the strain of war are we capable of changing the world; but the changes our wars will make will never be the changes we intended them to make. We shall clamor for security . . . and the future is to those who prefer surprise and wonder to security. I, Prola, shall live and grow because surprise and wonder are the very breath of my being, and routine is death to me. Let every day be a day of wonder for me and I shall not fear the Day of Judgment. [*She is interrupted by a roll of thunder*]. Be silent: you cannot frighten Prola with stage thunder. The fountain of life is within me.
>
> PRA. But you have given the key of it to me, the Man.
> PROLA. Yes: I need you and you need me. Life needs us both.
> PRA. All hail, then, the life to come!
> PROLA. All Hail. Let it come.
> *They pat hands, eastern fashion.* [611]

Such is Shaw's frame of mind in 1934. The despair, doubt, and cynicism of *On the Rocks* is dispelled at the end; and the job of man and woman begun by Adam and Eve in *Back to Methuselah* can and will be successful, as Lilith had predicted at the end of that play. But when will this take place? Only after a ruthless extermination of the unfit—only in a classless society of producers. Shaw had warned his fellow Englishmen, "Russia is all right, and we are all wrong. We had better follow Russia's example as soon as possible." *The Simpleton of the Unexpected Isles* dramatized the warning just as *On the Rocks* dramatized his feeling of "torture" at being back in the "capitalist West."

To the casual reader of Shaw, both the title of *The Million-airess* (completed in 1935) and the dynamic quality of the heroine of the play could suggest a complete aboutface of its quixotic author. Not only does he return from the future to the present, from "unexpected isles" to the island of Britain, from mysterious almost mythical people like Pra and Prola to a vibrant flesh and blood woman like Epifania, but he seems content to accept the capitalist system and create a charming heroine from its highest ranks. The cynicism and unreality of the two preceding plays is missing; the typical practicality and vitality of the now seventy-nine-year old playwright has returned. The basis of his practicality and vitality is once again a combination of Marxian economics and Creative Evolution.

In its "Preface on Bosses," Shaw blames capitalism for spoiling the good work of dominating personalities by channeling their vitality into money-making:

> What is to be done with that section of the possessors of specific talents whose talent is for moneymaking? History and daily experience teach us that if the world does not devise some plan of ruling them, they will rule the world. Now it is not desirable that they should rule the world; for the secret of moneymaking is to care for nothing else and to work at nothing else; and as the world's welfare depends on operations by which no individual can make money, whilst its ruin by war and drink and disease and drugs and debauchery is enormously profitable to moneymakers, the supremacy of the money-maker is the destruction of the State. A society which depends on the incentive of private profit is doomed.[18]

Such an indictment leads logically to a condemnation of modern liberal democracy based on capitalist economics, for this kind of democracy leads logically to tyranny since it espouses the rule by heredity and class, in other words, the rule of money: "It is in fact, not democracy at all, but unabashed plutocracy" (178).

18. *Complete Plays with Prefaces,* 6:176. Further quotations from *The Millionairess* and its preface in this chapter are taken from the same volume; page numbers will be given in parentheses after the quotation when necessary.

Out of this indictment comes Shaw's strange but short-lived fascination for Mussolini. He begins his praise of the Italian dictator by giving a historical account of the failure of the franchise, democracy, and parliament:

> An epochmaking revolution in Russia . . . poohpoohed as a transient outburst of hooliganism fomented by a few bloodthirsty scoundrels, exactly as the American revolution and the French revolution had been poohpoohed when they, too, were contemporary.
>
> Here was clearly a big opportunity for a man psychologist enough to grasp the situation and bold enough to act on it. Such a man was Mussolini. [186]

Parliaments are supposed to feel the pulse of the people but they do not, and hence, he concludes that Mussolini, who *did* know what the Italians wanted, "was responding to the real democratic urge whilst the cold tea leaves of the nineteenth century were making them sick" (188).

After praising Mussolini, Shaw turns to the other dictator, Adolph Hitler. He condemns this boss for his anti-Semitism (especially for having exiled Einstein), condemns the whole Hitlerian doctrine of race superiority and suggests the danger of bosses: "Morris's simple and profound saying that 'no man is good enough to be another man's master' holds good unless both master and man regard themselves as equally the fellow servants of God in States where God still reigns, or, in States where God is dead, as the subjects and agents of a political constitution applying humane principles which neither of them may violate" (194).

Russia is that kind of state because its political constitution exalts the working man in contrast to the democracy where only the financier and soldier are the "cocks of the walk" and "their parasites and worshippers carry all before them" (194). Since Karl Marx and Engels brought to light the terrible conditions of the working classes which form the basis for the "pursepride and snobbery of the upper middle classes and the prestige of the landed gentry and peerage there has been no substantial excuse for believing in the alleged harmony of interests" (195).

Shaw then returns to the main thesis of the preface and the theme of the play itself—how society can best benefit from the vitality of dominating personalities. Society must not liquidate them, for they are far too valuable; instead it must produce more of their type so that it will have a wider choice. This can be accomplished by communism which will give a social conscience to bosses and make them servants of all the people, but only Creative Evolution can free their souls. Epifania, the protaganist of *The Millionairess,* with all her vitality does not have a chance in a feudal and capitalist society; only the most complete communism and democracy will give her that chance, just as it unloosed the power of a Jesus or a Lenin, a Saint Thomas More or a William Morris. "And this, I take it, is one of the highest claims of Communism and Democracy . . . . I say cheerfully to the dominators 'By all means dominate: it is up to us to so order our institutions that you shall not oppress us, nor bequeath any of your precedence to your commonplace children' " (202).

The first two acts of the play are an amusing revelation of Epifania's dominating nature. Through her antics we learn how this volatile woman has channeled her genius into the art of making money. But, she tells Adrian, her "Sunday husband," that within a fortnight she has tired of all that money can buy. When he asks her why she wants it then, her answer paraphrases what Shaw had said in the preface: "Because money is power. Money is security. Money is freedom. . . . And there is the continual pleasure of making more of it, which is quite easy if you have plenty to start with. I can turn a million into two million much more easily than a poor woman can turn five pounds into ten, even if she could get the five pounds to begin with. It turns itself, in fact" (235–36).

The first two acts are climaxed by the hilarious jujitsu exhibition on the part of Epifania, who resenting Adrian's remark about her father (Adrian could not understand how her father "contrived to get a legal claim on so much of what other people made"), literally kicks him out of the restaurant where they are meeting. After this scene, however, the tone of the play shifts. Immediately following the brawl with Adrian, Epifania, groaning from exhaustion, screams and attracts the attention of an Egyptian—a mysterious gentleman from the Far East. The gentleman is a doctor, but certainly not a "paid wage laborer of the bourgeoisie":

> EPIFANIA. . . . I am on the point of death. I need a doctor. I am a rich woman.
> THE DOCTOR. In that case you will have no difficulty in finding an English doctor. [238]

And here Shaw begins to inject his serious theme and with it his Marxism into this seeming farce. Epifania argues with the Egyptian about English society:

> EPIFANIA. . . . We are the only real aristocracy in the world: the aristocracy of money.
> THE DOCTOR. The plutocracy, in fact.
> EPIFANIA. If you like. I am a plutocrat of the plutocrats.
> THE DOCTOR. Well, that is a disease for which I do not prescribe. The only known cure is revolution; but the mortality rate is high; and sometimes, if it is the wrong sort of revolution, it intensifies the disease. I can do nothing for you. I must go back to my work. Good morning. [240]

At the end of the scene the Doctor informs Epifania, who wishes to marry him, that his mother made him swear if any woman ever wanted to marry him, that woman had to prove herself worthy by going out in the world with "two hundred piastres" and for six months earning her own living. By pure or poor coincidence Epifania's father had made her force similar conditions on her sisters; in fact, as the first act unravelled, that is how Alastair, her husband, had won her hand in marriage; therefore, Epifania agrees to pass his mother's test if he agrees to pass her father's—that he increase one hundred and fifty pounds to fifty thousand in six months' time.

Epifania's dominating personality is further revealed as she carries out her part of the wager. In the third act Shaw takes us to "Commercial Road" with its sweatshops of modern capitalism; he shows the helplessness of the proletarians through the actions of The Man and The Woman who are utterly incapable of raising their station in life. Epifania appears and shows them how to improve their lot by using the capitalist's own methods of eliminating the middle man. Telling them that she can manage their little clothes factory in a half a day a week, she takes work as a scullery maid at a hotel to fill up her time. After she leaves, The Man is completely bewildered, but The Woman tells him to do what Epifania told them: "We're like children—— [*She begins crying again softly*]." Shaw adds: "There is nothing more to be said" (255).

At the beginning of the last act, Alastair and his "girl friend" Patricia whom he will marry when Epifania divorces him are lounging in the former Pig and Whistle, the scene of Epifania's fight with Adrian and the place where the bet with the Doctor was made. But now completely redecorated, the inn has become a fashionable riverside hotel called The Cardinal's Hat. The manager informs Alastair and Patricia that a woman who had received a job as a scullery maid completely took over and transformed the old inn. He speaks of her wonderful managerial abilities, but when he is asked what happened to his parents, the former owners, who were forced into retirement, he says that the change was too much for them at their age: "My father had a stroke and wont last long, I'm afraid. And my mother has gone a bit silly. Still it was best for them; and they have all the comforts they care for" (260). Thus Shaw shows how utterly ruthless a dynamic boss could become.

If, however, Epifania had a social conscience, she could be, with her tremendous energy and capability, a savior of a nation, lifting it from a sweatshop or a Pig and Whistle state to "an association in which the free development of each is the condition for the free development of all." But Epifania does not have a social conscience. She displays her remarkable abilities for a selfish purpose, to win the bet with the Egyptian doctor, crushing whoever gets in her way.

And now the Doctor's side of the wager is presented. Instead of turning the one hundred and fifty pounds into fifty thousand, he uses it to help the widow of his old teacher. He agrees that the wages Epifania pays to the employees of her enterprises would be a fortune to a laborer on the Nile. But what of the old people whose natural home this place had become? the old man with his paralytic stroke? the old woman gone mad? the cast out creatures in the workhouse? Was not this preying on the poverty of the poor? Shall I, the servant of Allah, live on such gains? Shall I, the healer, the helper, the guardian of life and the counsellor of health unite with the exploiter of misery?

EPIFANIA. I have to take the world as I find it.

THE DOCTOR. The wrath of Allah shall overtake those who leave the world no better than they found it.

EPIFANIA. I think Allah loves those who make money.

SAGAMORE [Epifania's lawyer]. All the evidence is that way, certainly.

THE DOCTOR. I do not see it so. I say that riches are a curse; poverty is a curse; only in the service of Allah is there justice, righteousness, and happiness. [273–74]

The Doctor explains why he gave his one hundred and fifty pounds to the widow: she was no ordinary widow; her husband was a brilliant and socially useful scientist who never "took out a patent" on his important discovery because "he believed that knowledge is no man's property" (275). Not only did the Doctor fail to make fifty thousand pounds but he owes Epifania for being in arrears at her hotel. Now, however, Shaw introduces Creative Evolution into the plot. Epifania unconsciously feels the urge of the Life Force to *join* or *unite* her business brains with the Doctor's social conscience. She demonstrates this impulse in a businesslike way. After Alastair says to the Doctor, "Well, old man, you may not have done a lot for yourself; but you have done damned well for the widow. And you have escaped Eppy. She wont marry you with your pockets empty." Epifania replies, "Pray why? Fifty thousand pounds must have been made out of that discovery ten times over. The doctor, in putting my money into the widow's necessary expenses, may be said to have made a retrospective investment in the discovery" (276).

Following Epifania's speech of rather strained reasoning, Adrian accuses her of unfaithfulness and Epifania responds with Shaw's usual description of marriage. Then she makes a last effort to capture the Doctor, telling him to face it as he would a dangerous operation. The Doctor still refuses, whereupon Epifania, flinging out her writs to him cries, "Can you feel my pulse every day as an old bachelor?" This last attempt of Eppy does the trick. The Doctor says, "Ah! I had forgotten the pulse. One, two, three: it is irresistable: it is a pulse in a hundred thousand. I love it: I cannot give it up" (277–78).

Certainly the Doctor's fascination for Eppy's pulse is comic, but it has its serious aspects too. The Doctor confirmed, when he returned to Eppy after his failure to win the wager and after her amazing success, that her pulse "beats still, slow, strong" —"the life! the pulse! is the heartbeat of Allah save in Whom there is no majesty and no might" (273). The pulse, therefore, symbolizes the vibrance and vitality of an almost superwoman, but one who, because of the capitalist system, has channeled her worth into selfish pursuits. The Doctor with his social conscience is attracted to that pulse.

That Shaw was attempting to reconcile the role of the vibrant individualist in a communistic state such as Russia was already apparent as early as 1932 in a broadcast, entitled "Rungs of the Ladder," he had made one year after his return from the Soviet Union. In this address he warns that "if you have a genius for making money there is no limit to the atrocities you may commit and the number of people you may ruin and slaughter provided you keep technically within the law." This is what Epifania did, of course, in taking over the Pig and Whistle. But he also envisions the possibility of a genius who could make poor people rich or rich people poor in the light of genuine religious truth or who could substitute the good of the community for the maintenance of vested interests as the object of government. At the time of the broadcast, however, his cynicism prevails, for he adds that such a person would be very lucky if he "escaped martyrdom." [19]

Three years later in the optimistic *Millionairess,* he joins a genius for making money with a social conscience, and avoids

19. Shaw, "Rungs of the Ladder," British Museum Add. MS 50705, fols. 3, 4.

martyrdom. But the return of Shaw's optimism did not last long. Shortly after writing this play, his sensitive and perceptive ear detected the faint but distinct rumblings of another world war, and so the last play of the thirties[20] reflects the same cynicism and despair of *Too True to Be Good* and *On the Rocks*, and its ending contains a Judgment Day scene similar to that of *The Simpleton of the Unexpected Isles* but without its suggestion of eventual salvation.

When Shaw sat down to write *Geneva* (completed in 1938, but not published until 1946), he undoubtedly foresaw that the entire world would soon be plunged into a conflagration far more devastating than the skirmish of 1914. Sadly he witnessed the futile attempts of the World Court in Geneva to stave off the onrush of so horrible a catastrophe, and in his professed role of the artist who must "make personal" the social evils of the world, he wrote a fable caricaturizing the foibles of leaders from every major nation of the world. His theme was to make "personal" the international social evil of nationalism found in every nation, even Russia, though it was the most advanced of all. Yet even in such a sweeping castigation, he completely excludes the Russian dictator from his farcical trial of idiotic dictators, and creates in the person of Stalin's representative the least foolish of the non-English delegates.

The play opens in the shabby offices of the International Committee for Intellectual Co-operation, and the very shabbiness of these offices suggests, of course, what the nations of the world think of intellectual cooperation. The audience is introduced to the various national representatives, among them an English Bishop and a Russian commissar (whom Shaw describes as "a very smart Russian gentleman"). The scene involving these two men is hilarious, and the Bishop is made a complete fool. When, for instance, he learns that the Commissar is a Bolshevik who had befriended him the night before, the prejudiced English prelate faints. Later, as the discussion continues and the Com-

20. He completed *Cymbeline Refinished* in 1938 and *In Good King Charles's Golden Days* in 1939. Neither of these plays is pertinent to this study.

missar informs him that the Comintern "is the State Church in Russia exactly as the Church of England is the State Church in Britain," the poor Bishop again faints. After he recovers, he is informed that the Commissar has just told him the Russian Comintern is analogous to the Church of England:

> Bishop. . . . I still have life enough in me to deny it. Karl Marx—Antichrist—said that the sweet and ennobling consolations of our faith are opium given to the poor to enable them to endure the hardships of that state of life to which it has pleased God to call them. Does your Komintern preach that blasphemy or does it not?
> Commissar. Impossible. There are no poor in Russia.
> Bishop. Oh! [*he drops dead*].[21]

To a bourgeois clergyman the absence of poverty is too startling. Commissar Posky adds cynically, "Was he ever alive? To me he was incredible."

In the second act, Begonia Brown, the typist of the International Committee for Intellectual Co-operation, is wryly told by the disillusioned secretary of the League of Nations that she is responsible for an international situation of gigantic importance. It seems as though the flightybrained typist arranged for a hearing of the great powers at the International Court. Warrants have been issued for the arrest of the great Fascist dictators, and consternation reigns supreme. The remainder of act 2 and all of act 3 prepare the audience for the great trial.

Throughout these two acts of conversation, the Russian commissar proves again to be a most sensible man as he enlightens various people on the procedures of his government. In one scene a "pistol-packin'" widow from the Republic of the Earthly Paradise (a satirical symbol of democratic utopias) argues her bizarre prejudices with the Jew. After the Widow is introduced to Commissar Posky she exclaims, "He is a Bolshevist. All Bol-

21. *Complete Plays with Prefaces*, 5:671. Further quotations from *Geneva* and its preface in this chapter are taken from the same volume; page numbers will be given in parentheses after the quotation when necessary.

shevists are Jews. Do you realize that if I lived under the horrible tyranny of the Soviet I should be shot?" and the Jew replies, "I take that to be a very striking proof of the superior civilization of Russia." But Commissar Posky differs with her: "We do not shoot Jews as such: We civilize them. You see, a Communist State is only possible for highly civilized people, trained to Communism from their childhood. The people we shoot are gangsters and speculators and exploiters and scoundrels of all sorts who are encouraged in other countries in the name of liberty and democracy" (695). In act 3 Shaw, through his *raisonneur,* the Judge (of the International Court), gives his full views on Russia. All of the characters in this act are "mongrels" (an attack on Hitler's Arianism); yet all are class conscious and nation conscious. The secretary of the League, who is also a realist and hence another *raisonneur,* starts the discussion: "When I came here I was a patriot, a Nationalist, regarding my appointment as a win for my own country in the diplomatic game. But the atmosphere of Geneva changed me. I am now an Internationalist. I am the ruthless enemy of every nation, my own included. Let me be frank. I hate the lot of you" (700). He then condemns the nationalism of each representative of the League. To the Commissar he says, "This Russian here: I hate him because his Government has declared for Socialism in a single country" (701). In 1938, then, Shaw was, in a way, a Trotskyite—a "pure" Marxist whose battle cry was, "Workers of the world, unite." But the Commissar, replies, "Only because infinite space is too much for us to manage. Be reasonable" (701). Evidently Shaw did not judge Russia's insularism too harshly.

The Judge continues to elaborate on and amplify the Secretary's accusations. He says that each national representative is not stupid; each has ability, in fact, yet all lack knowledge. He lumps Dame Begonia's opinion about "drawing the line at Communism" with the Commissar's nationalism. Each character protests, whereupon the Judge says, "Never mind your opinions: I am dealing with facts. It is evident that the lady is wrong as to the facts, because the inhabitants of a country conducted as she supposes Russia to be conducted would all be dead in a fortnight"

(706). The Judge, however, goes on to say that human nature should be on a higher plane than a nationalist one. The British diplomat, Sir Orpheus Midlander, sighs, "Too true: oh, too true. But we must take the world as we find it." The Judge condemns this typical do-nothing attitude of England, and once more Shaw praises Russia as the most advanced nation in the world at this time:

> THE JUDGE. Wait a bit. How do you find the world? You find it sophisticated to the verge of suicidal insanity. This makes trouble for you as Foreign Secretary. Why not cut out the sophistication? Why not bring your economics, your religion, your history, your political philosophy up to date? Russia has made a gigantic effort to do this; and now her politicians are only about fifty years behind her philosophers and saints whilst the rest of the civilized world is from five hundred to five thousand behind it. In the west the vested interests in ignorance and superstition are so overwhelming that no teacher can tell his young pupils the truth without finding himself starving in the street. The result is that here we despair of human nature whereas Russia has hopes that have carried her through the most appalling sufferings to the forefront of civilization. Then why despair of human nature when it costs so much trouble to corrupt it? Why not stop telling lies? Are we not as capable of that heroic feat as the Russians? [706–7]

Yet, to Shaw, Russia's heroic feat is not heroic enough. In *The Communist Manifesto* Marx had said, "In the national struggles of the proletarians of the different countries, they [the Communists] point out and bring to the front the common interests of the entire proletariat, independently of all nationality." [22] The Commissar does not espouse internationalism but contends that only on Russian soil could progress be made. Shaw ironically attacks such a nationalistic view through the equally nationalistic words of Sir Orpheus who reminds the Commissar: "Moscow took all its ideas from England . . . John Ruskin's gospel compared

22. Marx, *Capital, the Communist Manifesto, and Other Writings,* ed. Eastman, p. 334.

with Karl Marx's was like boiling brandy compared with milk and water" (707). The Jew furthers the irony by reminding both the Commissar and Sir Orpheus that only through the Jews (Karl Marx was a Jew) could a Soviet Russia be produced. A race squabble ensues, but ends when the Jew, through flattery, succeeds in taking to dinner the Widow, his Jew-baiting enemy. Shaw completes the irony when Begonia Brown explains the Widow's acceptance: "Geneva is like that. You find yourself dining with all sorts" (710).

Despite Russia's refusal to follow Marx's internationalism, she still is leagues ahead of the other nations. Earlier in the act the Judge says of the Russian Commissar, "I come to our Russian friend. He must be a man of ability, or he could not be a Commissar in a country where nothing but ability counts. He has no fears for the future, whereas we are distracted by the continual dread of war, of bankruptcy, of poverty" (705).

Act 4 becomes the high point of *Geneva,* for in it Shaw examines the three Fascist dictators—Bombardone (Mussolini), Battler (Hitler), and Flanco (Franco). Flanco pleads his case by saying, "I stand simply for government by gentlemen against government by cads. I stand for the religion of gentlemen against the irreligion of cads. For me there are only two classes, gentlemen and cads: only two faiths: Catholics and heretics. . . . I maintain that all spare money should be devoted to the breeding of gentlemen" (744–45). Bombardone is more sensible than Battler, but is, nevertheless, a conceited ass and a nationalist (a shift from Shaw's praise of him in the preface to *The Millionairess*). Battler is painted to be a fool with the Jew "bee in his bonnet" who weeps bitterly (when the news concerning the earth turning to ice is heard) because his little dog, Blonda, will be frozen to death. It is significant, as we noted, that Shaw does not bring Stalin himself to trial. It is as though he would not degrade this dictator.

During the trial scene, when the dictators are foolishly expounding nationalism, the Commissar, after the Judge asks him if he has anything to say, replies,

Nothing. These gentlement talk of their countries. But they do not own their countries. Their people do not own the land they starve in. Their countries are owned by a handful of landlords and capitalists who allow them to live in it on condition that they work like bees and keep barely enough of the honey to keep themselves miserably alive. Russia belongs to the Russians.We shall look on whilst you eat each other up. When you have done that, Russia—Holy Russia—will save the soul of the world by teaching it to feed its people instead of robbing them.

Flanco interjects, "Your country is full of conspiracies to get the old order back again. You have to shoot the conspirators by the dozen every month." But Shaw gives the Commissar the last word: "That is not many out of two hundred million people, General. Think of all the rascals you ought to shoot!" (748).

Geneva concludes with another Judgment Day scene. This time Shaw studies the reactions of the nations of the world to the announcement that it is freezing to death; he wants to prove that nationalism would prevail even on that awesome day. Bombardone reacts stoically; he will make his people stop the rush to the equator. Battler, after the initial outburst of tears for his little "doggie," says, "We shall work to the last, and set an example to the new race of iceproof men who will follow us" (758). Flanco must await the decision of the Catholic church, and the Commissar "must consult Moscow" since the "Marxian dialectic does not include the quantum theory" (757). Sir Orpheus Midlander, or England, in true capitalist fashion, wants the news of the end of the world to be hushed so that the Jews cannot profit on the stock market. The Deaconess, who personifies the Christian religion (the opium of the people), breaks down completely and whimpers, "But in heaven I shall lose my Jesus. There He will be a king; and there will be no more troubles and sorrows and sins to bring to Him. . . . He made heaven for me on earth; and now that is all over. I cannot bear it" (755).

Of course, at the very end of the play the Secretary informs the Judge that the end-of-the-world business is all a hoax, but that people would believe anything if they thought it was the "voice of Science" speaking; at least it broke up the farce of the trial.

In the preface, written seven years later in 1945, the year Germany surrendered, Shaw continues to chide Stalin for abandoning Marx's international aim because nationalism results in mutual suspicion. Conservatives believe that the Russian rulers are bloody despots who enslave their people. Russians believe that "Western plutocracies" seek nothing but what Marx called surplus value. These people are extremely dangerous "because on the strength of their irrelevant schooling they believe themselves politically educated, and are accepted as authorities on political subjects accordingly" (636). And yet he qualifies the condemnation and again questions the Fabian method: "From Pisistratus to Porfirio, Ataturk, and Stalin, able despots have made good by doing things better and more promptly than parliaments. They have kept their heads and known their limitations" (643).

At the end of the preface, in the section entitled "Great Men," he lists Karl Marx, along with Descartes, Kant, Swift, Schopenhauer, Butler, Bergson, Wagner, Blake, Shelley, Ruskin, and Morris as leaders who "mark not human attainment but human possibility and hope" (646). This suggests an attitude quite different from the cynical one reflected in the ending of the play itself, written seven years earlier, and is typical of the optimism exuded during the forties, the last ten years of Shaw's artistic career.

CHAPTER NINE

Fabianism and Marxism Reconciled

With the opening of a new decade Bernard Shaw was witnessing another world war. Practically everything he had predicted in *Geneva* was coming true: the League of Nations had failed to achieve "peace in our times"; each nation, including Soviet Russia, was beating her nationalist drums; and the farcical trial of the dictators became a bloody reality. Even the bizarre "quantum theory" that caused such hilarious confusion in the last act of *Geneva* was to become an ironic reality in the formula that produced a bomb capable of melting rather than freezing the world to death. The nations of Shaw's world were again acting out Darwin's theory of survival of the fittest rather than Lamarck's theory of constructive or creative evolution. Shaw had every reason, then, to spend his last ten years in dejection and to comfort himself by injecting a note of "I told you so!" into his final efforts as a playwright. Instead, he renewed his attempts to convince the world that its salvation could be obtained only if its governing bodies adopted his principles, the Webb's principles, and now, more than ever, Stalin's principles.

In 1942 Sidney and Beatrice Webb published *The Truth about Soviet Russia*. It is a summary of their conclusions concerning the internal organization of the Soviet Union from 1941 to 1942 and was reprinted with modifications and additions from the introduction to the reissue (1941) of their work, *Soviet Communism: A New Civilisation*. In it they wholeheartedly espouse the government of a nation that had come into being not as a

197

result of gradual parliamentary reform—the Fabian way—but by Lenin's direct application of Marx's theory of bloody proletarian revolution. Their postscript which describes the 1936 constitution of the U.S.S.R. contains the following praise, typical of the entire volume:

> It explains why the defeated, starving, illiterate inhabitants of Tsarist Russia became in the course of twenty years the relatively comfortable and cultured, healthy and skilled, courageous and adventurous Soviet people of 1941–42; who alone among the inhabitants of the European Continent have been able to resist and beat back the mighty military machine of Hitler Germany, intent on the conquest and enslavement of the world.[1]

Shaw, who had helped so much to make the Fabian Society famous but whose periodic impatience with its doctrine of slow, parliamentary reform we saw reflected in many of his works, could now write unqualified endorsement to his fellow Fabians' and lifelong friends' acceptance of Russian communism. The essay, entitled "The Webbs," is included as an introduction to *The Truth about Soviet Russia*.

He begins by crediting the success of Lenin's revolution to its Marxist basis. True, he criticizes Marx for being "a foreigner without administrative experience, who gathered his facts in the Reading Room of the British Museum, and generalized the human race under the two heads of *bourgeoisie* and proletariat apparently without having ever come into business contact with a living human being" (5). But he also balances such a typical Shavian scorn for the scholar with a renewed eulogy to the doctrine we saw inherent in his artistry from the time he wrote *An Unsocial Socialist*—Marx's economic interpretation of history, the *sine qua non* to the Soviet system: "When he published the

---

1. Webb and Webb, *The Truth about Soviet Russia,* pp. 127–28. Further quotations in this chapter are taken from the 1944 edition; page numbers will be given in parentheses after the quotation when necessary.

facts as to the condition to which Capitalism had reduced the masses, it was like lifting the lid off hell. Capitalism has not yet recovered from the shock of that revelation, and never will" (6). Only after a reassertion of the importance of the father of modern socialism does he show how the Webbs took up where Marx left off and improved as they complemented his pioneering efforts.

Then he attempts to reconcile the once diametrically opposed systems of socialism. He praises the Webbs for making "organized labor in England class conscious for the first time" and adds significantly that their work "was translated by Lenin" (12). But the true test of the "depth and genuineness of our [Fabian] Socialism" was the Russian Revolution. Shaw complains bitterly of how the capitalist press created doubts concerning the success of Lenin's revolution—doubts that he himself entertained during what we called the anxious period before his visit to Moscow. He admits that there were initial mistakes made by the postrevolutionaries but the Webbs were sensible enough to wait until the communist state was "fairly launched" and then in their "last two volumes they gave us the first really scientific analysis of the Soviet State." They discovered how the Russians utilized "developments of our political and social experiments and institutions, including trade unionism and cooperation, which we thought they had abolished"; therefore, the Webbs (and Shaw) "unhesitantly gave the Soviet system their support, and announced it definitely as a New Civilization" (13).

Hope for the "New Civilization" never diminished. In 1948 Eleanor O'Connell, a very close friend of Shaw's, reported to Hesketh Pearson that in the course of a conversation she reminded him that had he lived in Russia instead of England during the greater part of his life he would have been shot. He replied, "Stalin is a good Fabian, and that's the best that can be said about anyone." [2] A year later, in the preface to his last major play, *Farfetched Fables*, he said, "For nomenclatory purpose I may be called a Fabian Communist and Creative Evolu-

2. Quoted in Hesketh Pearson, *Bernard Shaw: His Life and Personality* (London: Methuen & Co., 1961), p. 458.

tionist if I must have a label of some sort." [3] Stalin was now a
Fabian, and Shaw, a Communist.

In 1944 he completed his final and amazingly complete treatise
on economics and politics, *Everybody's Political What's What?*
On its first page he not only praises Marx for demanding a new
way of life but champions the surplus value theory as well:

> He proved up to the hilt that capital in its pursuit of what he
> called Mehrwerth, which we translate as Surplus Value (it in-
> cludes rent, interest, and commercial profit), is ruthless, and
> will stop at nothing, not even at mutilation and massacre,
> white and black slavery, drugging and drinking, if they prom-
> ise a shilling per cent more than the dividends of philanthropy.
> . . . He thereby created that demand for "a new world" which
> not only inspires modern Communism and Socialism but in
> 1941 became the platform catchword of zealous Conservatives
> and Churchmen.[4]

Toward the end of the work he even goes so far as to call the
surplus value theory "an indispensable specific practical factor
in the Socialist plan in spite of its rejection as an abstract theory,
making the product much cheaper to the consumers, and dis-
tributing among them the rent of the more productive mines and
lands" (315). Undoubtedly, Lenin's and Stalin's utilization of
Marx's *mehrwerth* in Russia finally converted Shaw who as a
young Fabian had nothing but scorn for this particular tenet.

In 1944 he also wants to make it quite clear that the triumph
of the proletariat occurred only in Russia. He refers to a movement which "grew up to steal the thunder of the Socialists and
substitute State Capitalism for private Capitalism whilst main-
taining private property with all its privileges intact, and buy-

---

3. Shaw, *Complete Plays with Prefaces*, 6:478. Further quotations from
Farfetched Fables and its preface in this chapter are taken from the
same volume; page numbers will be given in parentheses after the
quotation when necessary.

4. Shaw, *Everybody's Political What's What?* (New York: Dodd, Mead
& Co., 1944), pp. 1–2. Further quotations from this work in this chapter
will be followed by the relevant page number given in parentheses when
necessary.

ing off the proletariat with doles and higher wages" (12). This movement took many forms: nazism in Germany; fascism in Italy; the New Deal and the New Order in America and England. Only Russian communism, inspired by Marx, inaugurated by Lenin, and made successful by both Lenin's and Stalin's application of Fabian principles, is the friend of the proletariat; only this combination resulted in a true classless society. And his confidence in the "new world" is unbounded: "If, as is not impossible, the Western Powers were to declare war on the U.S.S.R., which would mean a war of State Capitalism against Democratic Communism, the number of conscientious objectors might run up to millions and make such a war impossible" (305).

A change of attitude toward the English proletariat is also apparent in *Everybody's Political What's What?* We noted a completely friendly and respectful attitude toward Russian workers in Shaw's remarks during his journey to Moscow, but *On the Rocks*, written two years later, dramatized his utter lack of faith in the English proletariat. Now, eleven years later, though he observes that the English agricultural proletarians are still ignorantly convinced of the holiness of private property, they really mean well: "Bring them up as collective farmers paying rent to the State for the common good as they now pay taxes to it, and precisely the same ethical impulses that now make them bigoted Conservatives will make Bolshevists of them. Russia has proved it" (7–8).

Later, however, he again portrays his earlier distrust of the English industrial proletariat. Capitalism has deprived the proletariat of leisure, pocket money, or the sort of clothes that can be worn without shame, and yet the poor must have their pleasures. The only pleasures they know, however, are those that "produce anaesthesia": drinking, tobacco, betting on horses or dogs to maintain a continual hope of unearned riches, and, above all, sexual intercourse which they have been taught to hide as original sin. These pleasures are always identified with vice and sin; and art, because it is enjoyable, with wickedness: "Inevitably the poor proletarian educates his child as he trains his dog, by the whip, and punishes aestheticism as corruption, thereby making aesthetic education impossible" (184). Leisure and money are the remedy for these social ills, and only socialism can make the people demand freedom of enterprise and freedom of thought in their leisure. In England socialism will at first wage a losing fight under the dictatorship of the proletariat. He recalls what happened after Sidney Webb made the trade unions class conscious and even effected the election of a Labour party with its prime minister: the Labour party was only nominally socialist; "Its front benches denounced the Russian Communist Revolution as virulently as any Die Hard" (262). And yet there is hope. In Russia entire generations of aristocrats have "to pretend that their fathers 'worked on their lands with their hands'" and "conditions of humanity are promiscuously inter-marriageable," causing that civilization to make "strides that leave the rest of Europe gasping miles behind" (249). To achieve such a transformation of the English proletariat, it must be at first rigidly controlled as in Russia, "where Socialism and De-mocracy at last achieved real power by making the little fingers of its police thicker than the Tsar's loins, proving the wisdom of Ruskin's 'old Tory' prevision that social salvation must in-volve, not less government and more liberty, but just the re-verse" (263). Gone, then, is the Shavian scorn for the English proletarian characterized by the Lickcheeses and Drinkwaters of earlier plays and the ineffectual mobs milling around at the end of *On the Rocks*.

Comparing the English system of government with Russia's he urges the establishment of new parliaments, "regional councils, vocational councils, industrial councils, co-operative consumers' councils, financial councils, educational councils, planning and co-ordinating councils, councils for supernational affairs" because such efficient councils came into being "in ultra-democratic Rus-sia under the inexorable necessities of human nature and cir-cumstances" (35). He suggests that a change from the British system to the Russian system could be accomplished by panels of competent persons who if they proved to be slackers should be " 'liquidated' (the word covers shooting in grave cases) .... What the Russians can do we can do" (36).

His views concerning revolution in *Everybody's Political What's What?* are still cautious and at times contradictory. In the beginning he says, "For the State or the municipality to seize my land and throw me into the street would need a Bolshevik revolution to legalize it," indicating that he recognized the power of revolution to achieve quick results. But he qualifies, "and a new public department for the management of all the estates in the country ready in full working order to take over from me" (17)—a criticism of the initial postrevolution failure in Russia. Again he recognizes revolution when he says,

> The legislators can cure the relative poverty of their constituents only by ruining themselves unless they possess the industrial genius needed to increase the productivity of labor sufficiently to feather both nests at one stroke. When the possibilities in this direction have been exhausted there is nothing for the proletariat but slavery mitigated only by doles to keep alive the goose that lays the golden eggs or a complete political capsize establishing the Dictatorship of the Proletariat. [39–40]

Nevertheless, he still favors a less violent means of instituting socialism:

> But if the government should conclude at any future time that it can make a better use of the city for the national welfare than I and my fellow shareholders are making of it for our private profit, it can easily buy it from us and obtain the money by a tax on the incomes of all the landlords in the country. Here again the transaction has only to be repeated often enough to effect the complete nationalization of the land without departing from the usual routine of business, without revolutionary legislation, and without mention of the word Nationalization, or the word Compensation, which is abhorrent to the doctrinaire nationalizers. [18]

And yet he adds ominously, "The revolutionary alternative is to declare the land public property and . . . shoot the few who actively object, and leave the rest to shift for themselves as best they can with their incomes cut off and their houses taken from them, as in Russia in 1917" (18). His conclusion is practical if ambiguous: after all, despite the lack of postrevolutionary planning, Russia *was* communized.

Finally he discusses leadership. The important question he would ask political candidates is whether they are "pre-Marx or post-Marx, Capitalist or Fascist or Communist" (351). To qualify for office, they would have to be "post-Marx" and "Communist," for he had said previously, "Marxism is not an infallible gospel for all future ages; but it has turned up trumps in Russia, and is quite sound enough to go on with for the present" (156). Moreover, the only two leaders singled out for special praise in *Everybody's Political What's What?* are Lenin and Stalin, whom he called "exceptionally clever, politically well read, and heroically public spirited Bolshevik statesmen . . . now recognized as beyond question the ablest rulers our age has produced" (90).

On the last page of this lengthy study, he once more implies the link between Marxism and Fabianism by stressing the need for modern statesmen to be well versed in the history of revolutions including "the Russian Revolution of 1917 under Lenin." They should also know "Macaulay's history of England and the Communist Manifesto of Marx and Engels," for if they go into any public office ignorant of these works they are eligible "only as porters and housemaids" (366).

Shaw was eighty-eight when he completed *Everybody's Political What's What?* but he was to write four more plays: *Buoyant Billions* (completed in 1947); *Farfetched Fables* (completed in 1948); *Shakes versus Shav* (1949); and the incomplete *Why She Would Not* begun in July, 1950. Three months later he died. *Shakes versus Shav* has no pertinence to this study, and few valid conclusions can be drawn from *Why She Would Not*. *Buoyant Billions,* does not fit into any particular pattern. In the "prefacette," as he calls it, he uncharacteristically adopts an apologetic attitude. "Forgive it," he says, it "is all I can write by way of preface to a trivial comedy which is the best I can do in my dotage." At least it will not "rub into you" the carnage of the recent wars "nor even of the next one." He muses, "how many people really prefer bogus war news and police news to smiling comedy with some hope in it! I do not. When they begin I switch off the wireless." [5]

For the moment, it seems that the old vitality is gone, and, except for the first act, *Buoyant Billions* is indeed "a trivial comedy" which rambles on without much continuity. Act 1 is entitled "The World Betterer," and the spirit of Marx pervades practically every page. A young son is trying to persuade his wealthy father to permit him to travel about bettering the world. We soon learn that Karl Marx's philosophy is the motivation for the World Betterer's dream, but he is a combination realist-idealist and hence somewhat of a fool. Although many of the speeches of the Son reveal the opinions Shaw had held throughout his lifetime, many romantic utterances of the youth are certainly un-Shavian, and since the character is not fully developed throughout the rest of the play, it is difficult to tell whether Shaw is commending or blaming Marx as an inspirer of youth.

And yet when the Father tells the Son that the prophets and poets are not practical men, that we need practical men, and that any change in the law will still come through parliament, the Son reveals Shaw's complete disillusionment concerning the parliamentary or the Fabian method of instituting changes:

Too slow. Class war is rushing on us with tiger springs. The tiger has sprung in Russia, in Persia, in Mexico, in Turkey, in Italy, Spain, Germany, Austria, everywhere if you count national strikes as acts of civil war. We are trying to charm the tiger away by mumbling old spells about liberty, peace, democracy, sanctions, open doors, and closed minds, when it is scientific political reconstruction that is called for. So I propose to become a political reconstructionist. Are you in favor of reconstruction? [754–55]

In answer to this question, the Father persists in his theory of constitutional change, but the Son begins a discussion of revolu-

5. *Complete Plays with Prefaces*, 1:752. Further quotations from *Buoyant Billions* and its preface in this chapter are taken from the same volume; page numbers will be given in parentheses after the quotation when necessary.

tion which reveals that the ninety-two-year-old Shaw continues to accept reluctantly this Marxist doctrine:

> Voting instead of fighting. No use. The defeated party always fights if it has a dog's chance when the point is worth fighting for and it can find a leader. The defeated dictator always fights unless his successor takes the precaution of murdering him.
>
> FATHER. Not in England. Such things happen only on the Continent. We don't do them here.
>
> SON. We do. We did it in Ireland. We did it in India. It has always been so. We resist changes until the changes break us. [755–56]

A little later the Son, after giving a history of revolutions ending with the Russian Revolution of 1917, concludes that revolution is always dirty work and asks his father why this is the case. The Father thinks that he has clinched the argument by stating that revolution is unconstitutional. But the Son's answer completely upsets the Father's logic: "The object of a revolution is to change the constitution; and to change the constitution is unconstitutonal" (756). Shaw seems to say grudgingly that revolution is the only way to better the world because parliamentary reform is caught in a vicious circle.

When the Father suggests that all changes could be effected without bloodshed by picking righteous leaders and that there are many such leaders in England, the Son replies, "Yes; and when they find them why do they run after them? Only to crucify them" (757). The Father observes that these persecutions took place long ago in barbarous times. The Son contradicts him with a typical Shavian-Marxian indictment of modern society, ending with flowing praise for the much persecuted Karl Marx:

> My dear father: within the last thirty years we have had more horrible persecutions and massacres, more diabolical tortures and crucifixions, more slaughter and destruction than Attila and Genghis Khan and all the other scourges of God ever ventured on. I tell you, if people only knew the history of their own times they would die of horror at their own wickedness.

Karl Marx changed the mind of the world by simply telling the purseproud nineteenth century its own villainous history. He ruined himself; his infant son died of poverty; and two of his children committed suicide. But he did the trick. [757]

This praise of Marx leads to an ambiguous praise of Marxism-in-action in Russia, when the Father says, "The Russian madness will not last. Indeed it has collapsed already. I now invest all my savings in Russian Government Stock. My stockbroker refuses to buy it for me; but my banker assures me that it is the only perfectly safe foreign investment. The Russians pay in their own gold." The Son replies, "And the gold goes to rot in American banks, though whole nations are barely keeping half alive for lack of it" (757).

The discussion leads next to a consideration of labor parties and proletarians, and Shaw's condemnation of the English Labour party as unrepresentative of the workers, an opinion that he manifested earlier in *Everybody's Political What's What?* After the Father observes that the trade unions, in their war against capitalism, blew up plants in Manchester and Birmingham, the Son cynically replies, "They soon dropped it. They did not even destroy the slums they lived in: they only blew up a few of their own people for not joining the unions" (759).

Thus far in the play Shaw is the old Shaw carrying on a serious indictment of society, "making personal," as the artist, the social evils that Marx had revealed by graphs and formulas in *Das Kapital;* but then his mood shifts. He avoids an ominous analysis of a future war when the Son raises the subject of the atom bomb; instead he injects a note of hope for the world:

No: mankind has not the nerve to go through to the end with murder and suicide. Hiroshima and Nagasaki are already rebuilt; and Japan is all the better for the change. When atom splitting makes it easy for us to support ourselves as well by two hours work as now by two years, we shall move mountains and straighten rivers in a hand's turn. The the problem of what to do in our spare time will make life enormously more interesting. No more doubt as to whether life is worth living. Then the world betterers will come to their own. [759]

This note of hope and optimism continues to the end of the first act, as the Father concludes the discussion by scolding his son: "Oh, you are incorrigible. I tell you again you are too clever: you know too much: I can do nothing with you. I wonder how many fathers are saying the same to their sons today." The Son replies, "Lots of them. In your time the young were post-Marxists and their fathers pre-Marxists. Today we are all post-Atomists." The Father explodes, "Damn the atomic bomb!" The Son retorts, "Bless it say I. It will make the world bettering possible. It will begin by ridding the world of the anopheles mosquito, the tsetse fly, the white ant, and the locust. I want to go round the world to investigate that, especially through the Panama Canal. Will you pay my fare?" (760). The Father finally agrees, and the World Betterer sets out on his mission.

The remaining three acts deal with marriage and other subjects in a manner that Shaw himself admitted in the "prefacette" was frivolous in contrast to his handling of these themes in earlier plays. The World Betterer is almost a completely different person reduced to a sort of half-baked college man out for a lark. It would seem safe to conjecture that Shaw turned on the wireless after writing the relatively serious first act, heard some "bogus war news" and decided to complete a "smiling comedy with some hope in it."

In the opening paragraph of the preface to *Buoyant Billions,* Shaw asks his readers, "Is it not a serious sign of dotage to talk about oneself, which is precisely what I am now doing? Should it not warn me that my bolt is shot, and my place silent in the chimney corner?" (749). The very next play clearly proves that indeed his bolt was not shot, for *Farfetched Fables,* his last complete artistic gift to the world, is a vigorous farewell from the ninety-three-year-old "Fabian Communist." Both the preface and the six fables are an incredibly full summary of his lifelong principles, and there is a final treatment of the Creative Evolution theme begun over forty-five years earlier in *Man and Superman.*

In the First Fable Shaw depicts how the end of capitalist society will come about. It does not end with an atomic bomb since all nations had agreed to abolish it and consequently have again made war possible; rather, as a young woman tells a young chemist, somebody will discover a poison gas lighter than air: "It may kill the inhabitants of a city; but it will leave the city standing and in working order" (493). The young chemist— "a paid wage laborer of the bourgeoisie"—immediately dreams of making such a gas.

In the Second Fable the greedy young chemist has succeeded in producing the gas, and, because England stupidly refuses to buy his formula, he has sold it to a "South African negro Hitler, Ketchewayo the Second" (495), who now is holding the world at his mercy by dropping bombs on the "Isle of Wight because it's a safe distance from his own people, just as we selected Hiroshima in 1945." The fable ends with the gas filtering into the War Office in London, killing Lord Oldhand of the Foreign Office and the commander in chief who had narrated the story. Just before the bomb falls a salvo of shots is heard. When the commander in chief inquires about these shots, Lord Oldhand says, "We have ordered a salute of five guns to celebrate the hundred and first birthday of the President of the Board of Trade." Shouts of "Gas! Gas!" follow; Oldhand staggers, and *"[with a vacant grin which develops into a smile of radiant happiness, sings]* 'It's a long way to Tipperary——' " Shaw adds, "He falls dead" (498). Capitalist England succumbs while its representative patriotically sings a British war song.

The symbolism is complete, for before the gas enters the room, we learn that the "middleclass" chemist who invented it was also killed by it: bourgeois science makes an end to bourgoeis society. Only after class society is exterminated, does Shaw begin his final treatment of Creative Evolution.

The Third Fable dramatizes how each member of a future society is tested in relationship to his ability. The Gentleman tells the visiting tramp who does not want to be tested, "If you refuse you may be classed as irresponsible. That means that youll be enlisted in the military police or kept under tutelage in a Labor Brigade. Or you may be classed as dangerous and incorrigible, in which case youll be liquidated" (502). Shaw's society of the future is run in much the same way as Stalin's Russia.

The next three fables carry us further into the future. In the Fourth Fable Shaw's comic sense is evident as he prepares the audience for the future bodiless supermen. He tells us, through a Diet Commissioner who is reading a report, that Vegetarianism, instituted in Britain "by a prophet whose name has come down to us in various forms as Shelley, Shakespear, and Shavius" (504), had replaced meat eating and begun the transition to the present mode of living on air which was invented by a woman—a woman from Russia, of course. The fable ends as the commissioner states that what he has just read was the tenth edition of his primer for infant schools in the rudimentary biology series.

The Fifth Fable shows that man has already progressed to the point of reproduction without physical contact. The characters, Shamrock, Rose, Thistle, and a Hermaphrodite, rumaging through history books of the nineteenth century, are shocked at the crude methods used by people who could not even "change their working hours by the sun oftener than twice a year; and it took one of the worst of killing matches they called wars to make them go even that far" (508). But these characters are hoping for the day when they can lose their bodies and spend all of their time in meditation. Rose optimistically ends the fable: "The pursuit of knowledge and power will never end" (511).

The sixth and final fable hails the arrival of Shaw's long awaited superman. Before he appears, however, Shaw makes it quite clear to his audience that this world of the future is by no means perfect and the road to perfection will be a bumpy one. The setting is a sixth form school in which five students are questioning the teacher. In the discussion the teacher informs them that "Disembodied Races still exist as Thought Vortexes, and are penetrating our thick skulls in their continual pursuit of knowledge and power, since they need our hands and brains as tools in that pursuit." One of the students observes that many of their thoughts are "damnably mischievous," such as destroying cities and slaughtering one another, and concludes that surely such thoughts do not pursue knowledge and power. The teacher answers, "Yes; for the pursuit of knowledge and power involves the destruction of everything that opposes it." She also adds, "We are ourselves a throw-back to the twentieth century, and may be killed as idiots and savages if we meet a later and higher civilization" (517–18). The students argue that their civilization is the highest yet evolved and the story about disembodied thoughts is merely a fairy tale.

"A youth, clothed in feathers like a bird, appears suddenly" (519). He tells the children to call him Raphael. They ask him whether he likes having a body. He answers, "I do not like or dislike. I experience." One of the students informs him that he cannot experience bodied life unless he has a girl and inquires if he brought one with him. "No," he replies. "I stop short of your eating and drinking and so forth, and of your reproductive methods. They revolt me." The same student queries, "No passions then?"

> RAPHAEL. On the contrary: intellectual passion, mathematical passion, passion for discovery and exploration: the mightiest of all the passions.
> THE TEACHER. But none of our passions?
> RAPHAEL. Yes. Your passion for teaching.
> YOUTH 2. Then you have come to teach us?
> RAPHAEL. No. I am here to learn, not to teach. I pass on.

[He vanishes]. [520]
The students are disappointed at his brief visit and his refusal to answer their questions, but the Teacher tells them to read an old poem called the Book of Job where they will find that the "old god" crushed Job "by shewing that he could put ten times as many unanswerable questions to Job as Job could put to him" (521).

Perhaps Shaw's audiences are also disappointed by the extremely brief visit of his superman. I do not think they should be. Such an ending is a most appropriate culmination of Shaw's aims as a playwright; in fact, the entire play could be called a microcosm of his writing career. After he read *Das Kapital* he wrote an entire series of plays castigating the foundation stones of capitalism, finally destroying the entire edifice in *Heartbreak*

House. In *Farfetched Fables* he accomplishes the same purpose in the first two fables.

Only after the possibility of a real classless society became a fact with Lenin's destruction of capitalism in Russia could he peer into the future and write his bible of Creative Evolution, *Back to Methuselah.* Yet doubts and fears for the permanence of the Russian experiment caused him much anxiety until he visited that land in 1931. He returned to indict with renewed vigor the evils of capitalism while pointing to "the land of hope" as a model civilization. When finally the Webbs convinced him that Stalin was employing Fabian methods in what they called "The New Civilization," his romance with Marx ended with the reconciliation of Fabianism and Marxism. After capitalism is destroyed at the end of the second fable in his final play, he could again peer into the future for the next four fables. Doubts and fears, however, still are present because England stubbornly refused to follow the example of "the ablest rulers our age has produced." The Teacher, when asked how old the world is, replies, "We do not know. We lost count in the dark ages that followed the twentieth century" (518).

And yet a superman does appear filled with "intellectual passion . . . the mightiest of all the passions." [6] Shaw once described Lenin as "pure intellect," but the capitalist nations were ignoring his Fabian communism and if they continued to do so dark ages might well follow the twentieth century. Surely, then, the ending of his last play is a most appropriate culmination of his aims as a playwright. He tried to teach the world what he thought was a system to alleviate its troubles, but now like Raphael he is through teaching and his audience must simply "learn."

The preface (completed a year later than the play) is an even more detailed review of his entire life's work than the play and, though diffuse, overshadows the fables as a summary of his philosophy. He begins by redefining his position as an artist, and the new definition differs very little from those found in *The Quintessence of Ibsenism* and *The Sanity of Art.* The artist is to make personal the "social evils" of the world, or, as

6. Henderson, *Shaw: Man of the Century,* p. 576.

he says now, "events . . . must be arranged in some comprehensible order as stories. Without this there can be no history, no morality, no social conscience" (457). He also wants all playwrights to know that had he not suspended his artistic endeavors "to write political treatises and work on political committees long enough to have written twenty plays, the Shavian idiosyncrasy which fascinates some of them (or used to) and disgusts the Art For Art's Sake faction, would have missed half of its value, such as it is" (463).

He then launches into an analysis of Creative Evolution and immediately cites the need for a classless society as basic to its success. For the Life Force to be aided properly in producing a better world, every home must be a cultural one; therefore, every bread winner must have an income sufficient to maintain this culture. In a capitalist society with its "combination of class culture and general savagery" only class war results, threatening the final destruction of civilization (459).

What follows is a typical indictment of bourgeois religion and its partnership with capitalism reminiscent of *Androcles and the Lion*. He argues that "the apostles were Communists so Red that St Peter actually struck a man and his wife dead for keeping back money from the common stock." Humorously he condemns the bourgeois translators of the New Testament who "could not pretend that St Peter was a disciple of the unborn Adam Smith rather than of Jesus; so they let the narrative stand, but taught that Ananias and Sapphira were executed for telling a lie and not for any economic misdemeanor" (462).

And yet Shaw firmly believes that some kind of religion is essential, that "every grade of human intelligence can be civilized by providing it with a frame of reference peculiar to its mental capacity." Even the Russians realized this and hence founded the Cominform:

> Having ceased to believe in the beneficiently interfering and overruling God of Adam Smith and Voltaire, no less than in the vicarage of the Pope and his infallibility in council with the College of Cardinals, Cominform makes Karl Marx its

Deity and the Kremlin his Vatican. It worships his apostles at its conventicles and in its chapels, with Das Kapital as its Bible and gospel, just as Cobdenist Plutocracy used to make a Bible of Adam Smith's Wealth of Nations with its gospel of The Economic Harmonies and its policy of Free Trade. [469]

At first glance such a description may seem derisive, but the prefatory phrase "peculiar to its mental capacity" and Shaw's continuing admiration for Marxism certainly raise this type of religion to a higher level than all the other organized faiths linked with "Cobdenist Plutocracy."

In fact, he jumps directly from this discussion to a section entitled "Should I Be Shot in Russia?" and begins to develop the union of Fabianism with Marxism. First of all he ridicules those who say that in Russia one cannot criticize the government: "As a matter of fact the Russian newspapers are full of complaints and grievances. There is a Government Department whose function it is to receive and deal with such complaints" (470). We will recall that in *Everybody's Political What's What?* he had advocated a series of similar councils or government departments which exist only in "ultra-democratic Russia." He says that as a playwright in England he was stymied by censorship and adds, "No such misfortune has happened to me in Russia" (471). He complains that the Webbs's articles could never get into British newspapers, but in Russia "when Fabians were despised there as bourgeois Deviators, the Webbs were translated by Lenin" (470).

The build up to Fabian Marxism is continued in the section called "Sham Democracy." After blaming the revolutionists for nearly bringing their country to the brink of disaster by insisting on communizing everything at once, he states that facts forced them "to make room in Bolshevism for more private enterprise than there is in England." As soon as this happened "the basic difference between British and Russian economic policy vanished or criss-crossed. Lenin and Stalin had to cry *Laisser-faire* to all the enterprises not yet ripe for nationalization." The Labour party in England sponsored by the Fabians "nationalized as many industries as it could manage . . . whilst jealously restricting official salaries more grudgingly with a view to equality of income than the Kremlin." Despite this obvious similarity between the economic policies of the two countries "Stalin's Russo-Fabian slogan, Socialism in a Single Country, is countered by Churchill's manifestos of Plutocratic Capitalism Everywhere and Down with Communism, which is more than Trotsky claimed for international Marxism" (475-76). Shaw simply cannot comprehend why his countrymen who know that England could not exist for a week without "omnipresent Communism" shout "their abhorrence of Communism as if their Parties were cannibal tribes fighting and eating one another instead of civilized men driven by sheer pressure of facts into sane co-operation" (476).

He then argues that the worst feature of "sham-democratic misgovernment" is the fact that the British parliamentary system is far too slow for modern organization of society. He uses as one of his examples the fate of the Factory Acts: after they were finally passed it took fifty years for Parliament to enforce them. He contrasts such sluggishness to the swiftness of the Soviet system and ends with a glowing eulogy to the standard bearer of the "Russo-Fabian slogan, Socialism in a Single Country." Shaw states categorically that the efficiency and democracy of Soviet Russia "gives Stalin the best right of any living statesman to the vacant Nobel peace prize, and our diplomats the worse. This will shock our ignoramuses as a stupendous heresy and a mad paradox. Let us see" (476).

On the second to the last page he formally announces the joining of Fabianism with Marxism:

> When the Russian Bolsheviks went ruinously wrong by ignoring "the inevitability of gradualness" and attempting a catastrophic transfer of industry and agriculture from private to public ownership, it was the Englishman Sidney Webb and his Fabians who corrected them and devised the new economic policy Lenin had to announce, and Stalin to put in practice. Thus Englishmen can claim to have been pioneers in the revolutionary development of political organization since Cobdenism conquered us. [489]

And on the last page, Karl Marx appears as the last man to whom Shaw gives a respectful farewell: "The nineteenth century, which believed itself to be the climax of civilization, of Liberty, Equality, and Fraternity, was convicted by Karl Marx of being the worst and wickedest on record" (490). He complements Marx's indictment of the nineteenth century with his own indictment of the twentieth which "not yet half through, has been ravaged by two so-called world wars culminating in the atrocity of the atomic bomb."

Thus, both the final play and its preface reflect optimism and pessimism—optimism because in one country, at least, Fabian principles are bolstering a successful communist state; pessimism because his own country still refuses to follow these principles. Such stubbornness not only retards the Life Force in its attempt to create a better world, but could cause "dark ages" to follow "the twentieth century."

An obvious conclusion may be drawn from this study: Bernard Shaw's sole aim in life was to make the world a better dwelling place for his fellow human beings. From *Widowers' Houses* to *Farfetched Fables* a genuine desire for the eventual perfection of the human race transcends all of his bitterness and devastating criticism of institutions which, to his way of thinking, were deterring mankind from achieving so lofty a goal. Even his last unfinished play, *Why She Would Not,* written three months before he died, shows evidence of his lifelong purpose. Although it is far too fragmentary to suggest a clear-cut theme, there is a suggestion that the harnessing of atomic energy and rapid advances in American technical improvements may eventually offer man the needed leisure to cooperate fully with the Life Force in evolving a perfect state. Perhaps, had he lived, this method would have replaced his always reluctant acceptance of revolution as the most efficient means of achieving a society wherein such leisure could be realized.

Be that as it may, it is hoped that this study will help to perpetuate an image of one of the greatest humanists of all time and that its readers will regard his Marxian romance successfully culminated in the reconciliation of Fabianism with Marxism, as further evidence of Shaw's intense search for a better world. Perhaps it was inevitable that the graphs and formulas of one of the most influential economic and political theorists of the nineteenth century should help to unleash and direct the comic genius of one of the most influential English dramatists whose life bridged the nineteenth and twentieth centuries.

Selected Bibliography

WORKS BY GEORGE BERNARD SHAW

Complete Plays with Prefaces. 6 vols. New York: Dodd, Mead & Company, 1963.

Everybody's Political What's What? New York: Dodd, Mead & Company, 1944.

The Matter with Ireland. New York: Hill & Wang, Inc., 1960.

Platform and Pulpit. Edited by Dan H. Laurence. New York: Hill & Wang, Inc., 1960.

The Works of Bernard Shaw. 33 vols. London: Constable & Co., 1930–38.

London. British Museum. Bernard Shaw, Additional Manuscripts:

MS 50523, 1943
MS 50524, 1944–45
MS 50525, 1946
MS 50526, 1946–50
MS 50538, 1921–50. 1939–58
MS 50553, 1883–1932
MS 50557, 1884–1944
MS 50616, 1905
MS 50665, 1936, 1937
MS 50667, (no date)
MS 50676, 1932
MS 50688, 1917–1933
MS 50689, 1888–1948
MS 50693, 1879–1901
MS 50694, 1902–7.
MS 50695, 1908–15
MS 50696, 1916–19
MS 50697, 1920–32
MS 50698, 1933–43
MS 50699, 1944–50
MS 50700, 1884–88
MS 50705, 1931

WORKS BY KARL MARX

Capital, the Communist Manifesto, and Other Writings. Edited with an introduction by Max Eastman. With an essay on Marxism by V. I. Lenin. New York: Random House, The Modern Library, 1932.

Capital: A Critique of Political Economy. Translated from the 3rd German edition by Samuel Moore and Edward Aveling. Edited by Frederick Engels. Vol. 1, *The Process of Capitalist Production.* Chicago: Charles H. Kerr & Co., 1932.

Historical and Critical Studies

Beer, M. *History of British Socialism.* Vol. 2. London: G. Bell & Sons., 1920.

Berlin, Isaiah. *Karl Marx: His Life and Environment.* London, New York, Toronto: Oxford University Press, 1948.

Broad, C. Lewis, and Violet M. *Dictionary to the Plays and Novels of Bernard Shaw.* London: A. C. Black, 1946.

Burns, E. *Russia's Productive System.* New York: E. P. Dutton & Co., 1930.

Coker, F. W. *Recent Political Thought.* New York, London: D. Appleton Century Co., 1934.

Dana, H. W. L. "Shaw in Moscow." *American Mercury,* 25 (1932): 343–53.

Ellis, R. W., ed. *Bernard Shaw and Karl Marx: A Symposium 1884–1889.* New York: Random House, 1930.

Engels, F. *Socialism, Utopian and Scientific, The Mark.* New York: International Publishers, 1935.

Fabian Essays. 5th ed., London: Fabian Society, 1931.

Fabian Tracts Numbers 1–106. London: Fabian Society, 1884–1901.

Henderson, Archibald. *George Bernard Shaw: His Life and Works.* Cincinnati: Stewart & Kidd Co., 1911.

———. *George Bernard Shaw: Man of the Century.* New York: Appleton-Century-Crofts, 1956.

Hoover, C. B. *Economic Life of Soviet Russia.* New York: Macmillan Co., 1931.

Irvine, William. *The Universe of G.B.S.* New York: Whittlesey House, 1949.

Irving, St. John. *Bernard Shaw: His Life, Work, and Friends.* London: Constable & Co., 1956.

Kautsky, K. *The Economic Doctrines of Karl Marx.* Translated by H. J. Stinning. New York: Macmillan Co., 1936.

Knowlton, Thomas Anson. *The Economic Theory of George Bernard Shaw.* University of Maine Studies, 2nd ser., no. 39. Orono, Maine: The University Press, 1936.

Kronenberger, Louis, ed. *George Bernard Shaw: A Critical Survey.* Cleveland and New York: World Publishing Co., 1953.

Laurence, Dan H., ed. *Collected Letters, 1874–1897.* London: M. Reinhardt, 1965; New York: Dodd, Mead, 1965.

Lee, Algernon. *The Essentials of Marx.* New York: Vanguard Press, 1926.

Lenin, V. I. *Collected Works of V. I. Lenin.* New York: International Publishers, 1927.

Loucks, W. N., and Hoot, J. W. *Comparative Economic Systems.* New York: Harper & Bros., 1938.

McGovern, William H. *From Luther to Hitler.* New York: Houghton Mifflin Co., 1941.

Nethercot, Arthur. *The First Five Lives of Annie Besant.* Chicago: University of Chicago Press, 1960.

———. *Men and Supermen.* Cambridge: Harvard University Press, 1954.

———. "The Quintessence of Idealism." *PMLA* 62 (1947): 844–59.

———. "The Schizophrenia of George Bernard Shaw." *American Scholar* 21 (1952): 455–57.

———. "The Truth About Candida." *PMLA* 64 (1949): 639–47.

Pearson, Hesketh. *G.B.S.: A Full-Length Portrait.* Garden City, N.Y.: Garden City Publishing Co., 1942.

Pease, E. R. *The History of the Fabian Society.* New York: E. P. Dutton & Co., 1916.

Pettet, Edwin B. "Shavian Socialism and the Shavian Life Force." Ph.D. dissertation, New York University, 1951.

Rattray, R. F. *Bernard Shaw: A Chronicle.* Luton: The Leagrave Press, 1951.

———. *Bernard Shaw: A Chronicle and an Introduction.* London: Duckworth, 1934.

Ruhle, Otto. *Karl Marx: His Life and Work.* New York: The New Home Library, 1943.

Sabine, George H. *A History of Political Theory.* New York: Henry Holt & Co., 1949.

Spargo, John. *Karl Marx: His Life and Works.* New York: B. W. Heubsch, 1910.

Ward, A. C. *Bernard Shaw*. Men and Books Series. New York: Longmans, Green & Co., 1951.

Webb, Sidney, and Beatrice. *The Truth about Soviet Russia*. With an Essay on the Webbs by George Bernard Shaw. New York: Longmans, Green & Co., 1944.

West, Alick. *A Good Man Fallen Among Fabians*. London: Lawrence Wishart, 1950.

Acknowledgments

The author wishes to thank The Society of Authors, on behalf of the Bernard Shaw Estate, for permission to use previously unpublished extracts from Shaw texts in the British Museum; the staff of the Scholars' Room at the British Museum for their generous assistance; and Loyola University for a research grant to pursue studies at the British Museum.

He extends particular thanks to Arthur L. Nethercot, Professor Emeritus, Northwestern University, who inspired and directed the doctoral dissertation from which this study derives. He is grateful also to Ronald W. Gast for timely and invaluable aid, and to Karen Ksycki, Arthur L. Moore, Terrence Topolski, Michael Schramm, Scott Harris, and Russell Lawrence Beaudreau for assistance and encouragement. Finally, he is grateful to his students at Loyola University, Chicago, for their inspiration and encouragement during the years he was researching this work.

Index

American Mercury, 157
Archer, William, 14, 41
Astor, Lord and Lady, 157-60
Austin, John, 38

Bauer, Bruno, 3, 4
Baxter, Beverly, 70
Bell, Chichester, 79
Bentham, Jeremy, 38
Berlin, Isaiah, 3
Bloody Sunday, 51
Butler, Samuel, 46, 131

Carpenter, Edward, 174
Chekov, Anton, 124, 127
Cherry Orchard, The (Chekov), 124
Communist Manifesto, The (Marx), 8, 9, 44-48, 55, 59, 60, 63-66, 81-82, 87, 100, 115, 118, 134, 139, 192, 204, passim
Creative Evolution, 104, 131-47, 177, 181, 182, 187, 197, 208-9, 212, 213

Dana, H. W. L., 157-61
Darwin, Charles, 13, 137-38, 141, 197
Degeneration (Entartung) (Max Nordau), 75
Deutsche Jahrbucher (Arnold Ruge), 4
Doll's House, A (Ibsen), 42, 70
Dream of John Ball, A (Morris), 67

"Election Manifesto of 1892" (Fabian Society), 61
Ellis, Richard W., 27
Emperor and Galilean (Ibsen), 46
Enemy of the People, An (Ibsen), 41-42
Engels, Friedrich, 4, 15, 158, 183, 204, passim
English Review, 111
English Ricardians, 4

"Essay on Liberty" (Mill), 68
Essays in Fabian Socialism, 32-37, 54, 67, 149-50, 156
Evening Standard (London), 70
Evolution of Revolution, The (Hyndman), 136

Fabian Society, 23, 28-29, 42, 50, 61, 67, 150, 198
Feuerbach, Ludwig, 4, 14-15
Fichte, Johann, 14
Foote, G. W., 68
Fortnightly Review, 61
Fourier, François Marie Charles, 4-5
Free Thinker, 68

George, Henry, 13
Gurly, Thomas, 60

Hammersmith Society, 61
Hampstead Historical Society, 30
Hedda Gabler (Ibsen), 46-47
Hegel, Georg Wilhelm Friedrich, 4, 5, 14, 38, 50
Henderson, Archibald, 5, 12, 79
History of the Fabian Society, The (Edward R. Pease), 39-40
Hitler, Adolph, 183
Hobbes, Thomas, 38
Hornet, 5
Huxley, T. H., 13
Hyndman, Henry M., 32, 61, 136

Ibsen, Henrik, 41, 48-50, 77, 153
Ingersoll, Charles, 13
Irvine, William, 6, 16

Jevons, William Stanley, 29, 33, 34, 36
John Gabriel Borkman (Ibsen), 49-50
Justice, 27

Kant, Immanuel, 14
Kapital, Das (Marx), 12, 16, 17, 18, 22, 24, 27, 28, 29, 30, 31, 42, 47, 57, 66, 80, 81, 87, 100, 115, 124, 136–37, 139, 154, 170, 207, 211
Kritik der evangelischen Geschichte der Synoptiker (Bruno Bauer), 4

Lamarck, Jean Baptiste Pierre Antoine de Monet de, 131, 138, 197
Larking, G. B. S. (Shaw), 27–29
Lassalle, Ferdinand, 53
Lenin, Nikolai, 16, 134, 136, 140, 149, 158, 168, 198, 199, 200, 204, 212, 214, passim
Liberty, 75
Life Force, 131, 213, 216
Little Eyolf (Ibsen), 47–49, 81
Lohengrin (Wagner), 79

Malthus, Thomas, 13
Marx, Karl, 23, 25, 29, 30, 31, 33, 35–36, 40, 66, 77, 102, 116, 129, 137–38, 140, 153, 158–59, 183, 192–93, 198, 200, 204, 205, 206, 213, passim; early life and influences, 1–6; his dialectic, 38; his surplus value theory, 18–19
Marx-Aveling, Eleanor, 41–42, 117
Mill, John Stuart, 5, 13, 49
Modern Painters (Ruskin), 31
Morris, Mae, 40
Morris, William, 40, 61, 97, 156
Mussolini, Benito, 183

Nation, 136
National Reformer, 30
National Secularist Society, 68
Nethercot, Arthur, 102
Nietzsche, Friedrich Wilhelm, 81, 131
Nordau, Max, 75–77

O'Connell, Eleanor, 199
Olivier, Sidney, 28
Owens, Robert, 5

Pall Mall Gazette, 75
Pearson, Hesketh, 199
Pease, Edward R., 28, 39–40
Pillars of Society (Ibsen), 41
Progress and Poverty (Henry George), 13, 67

Proudhon, Pierre Joseph, 4

Rattray, R. F., 41
Rhenische Zeitung (Marx), 4
Rhinegold, The (Wagner), 81
Ricardo, 33
Ring of the Nibelungs, The (Wagner), 80–82
Ruge, Arnold, 4
Ruskin, John, 31, 192
Russian Revolution, 7, 40, 128, 146, 150–59, 199, 204, 206

Saint-Simon, Claude Henri de Rouvroy de, 4, 5
Saturday Review, 75
Schopenhauer, Arthur, 131
Sea Gull, The (Chekov), 124
Shaw, Bernard, his dialectic, 38; early life and influences, 1–5; in Russia, 157–66
—Works: *Androcles and the Lion,* 99–102, 107, 117, 213; *Annajanska or the Bolshevik Empress,* 158; *Apple Cart, The,* 153–57, 170, 174; *Arms and the Man,* 66, 70–73, 119; "Art Workers and the State," 76; *As Far as Thought Can Reach (Back to Methuselah),* 145–46; *Back to Methuselah,* 115, 135–47, 149, 177, 179, 181, 212; "Basis of Socialism, The," 33; *Buoyant Billions,* 204–9; *Caesar and Cleopatra,* 83–86, 91; *Candida,* 66–70, 171; *Captain Brassbound's Conversion,* 105–10; *Cashel Byron's Profession,* 11; *Common Sense about the War,* 167 n. 12; "Degenerate's View of Nordau, A," 75; *Devil's Disciple, The,* 92–95, 97, 99, 101, 112, 139, 146; *Doctor's Delusions,* 111; *Doctor's Dilemma, The,* 111–15, 161; "Don Juan in Hell," 131–35, 149; "Driving Capital Out of the Country," 37; *Essays in Fabian Socialism,* 32–37, 54, 67, 149–50, 156; *Everybody's Political What's What,* 200–4, 214, 217; "Fabian Essays Forty Years Later—What They Overlooked," 156; "The Fabian Society —What It Has Done and How It Has Done It," 53; "Fabian Suc-

cesses and Failures," 68; *Geneva*, 189–95, 197; *Getting Married*, 115–18, 144; *Gospel of the Brothers Barnabus (Back to Methuselah)*, 141–42; *Farfetched Fables*, 147, 199, 204, 208–16; *Heartbreak House*, 92, 124–29, 131, 150, 176, 211; *Immaturity*, 1–2, 6–7, 20; "Impossibilities of Anarchism, The," 51–52; *Intelligent Woman's Guide to Socialism and Capitalism, The*, 147, 149–53, 156; *In the Beginning (Back to Methuselah)*, 139–41; *Irrational Knot, The*, 8–10, 11, 21; *John Bull's Other Island*, 66, 86–89, 91, 112; "Lectures: 1917–1933: 'What indeed,'" 53; "Little Talk on America, A," 166–68; *Love Among the Artists*, 11; *Major Barbara*, 36, 87, 89, 95–99, 101, 102, 106, 107; *Man and Superman*, 17, 94, 99, 131, 151, 208; *Man of Destiny, The*, 70–73; *Maxims for Revolutionists*, 131; *Millionairess, The*, 152, 182–89, 193; *Misalliance*, 118–21, 144; "Mr. G. B. Shaw's Offer to Carlow," 60–61; *Mrs. Warren's Profession*, 36, 62–66; *On the Rocks*, 168–75, 177, 179, 181, 189, 201, 202; *Pen Portraits and Reviews*, 136; *Perfect Wagnerite, The*, 79, 81–82, 83; *Philanderer, The*, 61–62, 67; *Plays: Pleasant and Unpleasant*, 62, 67, 73, 77, 92; *Pleasant Plays*, 66, 67, 70, 73, 75; "Points Disputed Among Socialists," 37; *Pygmalion*, 71, 121–23; *Quintessence of Ibsenism, The*, 42–46, 77, 92, 133, 212; *Rationalization of Russia, The*, 175–76; *Revolutionist's Handbook, The*, 131; *Saint Joan*, 103–07, 112, 146, 150; *Sanity of Art, The*, 75, 77, 79, 83, 212; *Shakes versus Shaw*, 204; *Simpleton of the Unexpected Isles, The*, 175–81, 189; "Socialism Equipped with All the Culture of the Age," 53; *Thing Happens, The (Back to Methuselah)*, 142–43; *Three Plays for Puritans*, 92; *Too True to Be Good*, 153, 161–66, 170,

189; "To Your Tents, O Israel" (Shaw and S. Webb), 61; *Tragedy of an Elderly Gentleman (Back to Methuselah)*, 143–45; *Unpleasant Plays*, 54, 61, 65, 67; *Unsocial Socialist, An*, 1, 13, 16–25, 27, 54, 57, 63, 65, 106, 115, 136, 146, 198; "Webbs, The," 198–99; *What I Really Wrote about the War*, 167–69; "What Socialism Is," 53; *Why She Would Not*, 204, 216; *Widower's Houses*, 36, 50, 54–66, 71, 216; *You Never Can Tell*, 73–75, 110

Shaw, Charlotte, 157
"Shaw in Moscow" (Dana), 157
Shelley, Percy Bysshe, 76
Smith, Adam, 33, 68
Social Democratic Federation, 32, 53, 61
Soviet Communism: A New Civilisation (Webbs), 197
Spencer, Herbert, 13
Stalin, Joseph, 160, 165, 200, 204, 214

Terry, Ellen, 70
"Three Sources and Three Constituent Parts of Marxism, The" (Lenin), 102
To-Day, 27, 29, 30
"To Your Tents, O Israel" (Shaw and S. Webb), 61
Tristan and Isolde (Wagner), 14, 42
Truth about Soviet Russia, The, (Webbs), 197–98
Tucker, Benjamin, 75–76

Uncle Vanya (Chekov), 124

Wagner, Richard, 41, 77–79
Wallas, Graham, 28
Webb, Sidney, 23, 28, 61, 152, 202; and Beatrice Webb, 153, 197, 190, 212, 214
Wells, H. G., 123
Why Are the Many Poor? (Fabian tract), 28
Wicksteed, Rev. Philip H., 29–30, 34

Zetetical Society, 13, 28

Bernard Shaw's
Marxian Romance

By Paul A. Hummert

Although no one name appears so frequently throughout Shaw's work as does that of Karl Marx, this study is the first to examine in depth the influence of Marxian philosophy on Shaw's thought and art. The author points out the importance of Marxist elements wherever they occur in the Shaw canon, and discusses events in Shaw's life that led him to criticize certain aspects of *Das Kapital* and yet adhere to its basic philosophy. The study's main concern, however, is to analyze the role played by Marx in shaping Shaw's art as a dramatist: to show how his influence contributed to the type of themes, symbols, characters, plots, and dialogue that develop from *Widowers' Houses* to *Why She Would Not*. Shaw's five novels and relevant nondramatic works also are considered.

In chapters 1 through 4 Mr. Hummert examines Shaw's earliest major works. His predisposition to Marxism is seen in the four novels written between 1879 and 1882; and *An Unsocial Socialist*, completed after he had read *Das Kapital*, reveals his acceptance of most of Marx's theories. Subsequent changes in his attitude, particularly after he joined the Fabian Society in 1884, are shown in *Essays in Fabian Socialism, The Quintessence of Ibsenism,* and his first six plays, written between 1892 and 1896.

Chapters 5 through 7 focus on the years from 1897 through the 1920s when Shaw was maturing as a dramatist. Although his realist-hero appears in *Caesar and Cleopatra* and *John Bull's Other Island*, the character was not fully realized until Shaw began his systematic indictment of the